Successful Expert Testimony
Fifth Edition

Successful Expert Testimony
Fifth Edition

Max M. Houck
Christine Funk
Harold A. Feder

CRC Press
Taylor & Francis Group
Boca Raton London New York

CRC Press is an imprint of the
Taylor & Francis Group, an **informa** business

Copyright by Harlan Feder

CRC Press
Taylor & Francis Group
6000 Broken Sound Parkway NW, Suite 300
Boca Raton, FL 33487-2742

© 2018 by Taylor & Francis Group, LLC
CRC Press is an imprint of Taylor & Francis Group, an Informa business

No claim to original U.S. Government works

Printed on acid-free paper

International Standard Book Number-13: 978-1-138-03358-0 (Hardback)

Library of Congress Cataloging-in-Publication Data

Names: Houck, Max M., author. | Funk, Christine, author. | Feder, Harold A., author.
Title: Successful expert testimony / by Max M. Houck, Ph.D., FRSC, Christine Funk, Esq., and Harold A. Feder.
Description: Fifth edition. | Boca Raton, FL : CRC Press, [2018] | Includes bibliographical references and index.
Identifiers: LCCN 2018002861| ISBN 9781138033580 (hardback : alk. paper) | ISBN 9781315305714 (ebook)
Subjects: LCSH: Evidence, Expert--United States. | Witnesses--United States.
Classification: LCC KF8961 .H69 2018 | DDC 347.73/67--dc23
LC record available at https://lccn.loc.gov/2018002861

Visit the Taylor & Francis Web site at
http://www.taylorandfrancis.com

and the CRC Press Web site at
http://www.crcpress.com

I'm dedicating this book to my parents for being so supportive of my education. I owe what I have attained to them. I am also dedicating this book to Jay Siegel, my teacher, my mentor, my friend. His advice was invaluable over my career and I miss him more than he would know.

This book is also dedicated to the narrow-minded, short-sighted, ignorant nitwits who irritate me, much as sand does oysters, to the point of productivity. I hope this is a pearl.

M.M.H.

To Jef, who believed in me from the beginning. For Madeleine, whose skepticism and inquiring mind give me hope for the next generation. And, finally, much gratitude to my co-editor, Max, whose willingness to include me on madcap adventures brings me great joy, expands my horizons, and generally makes me a better person for it.

C. F.

Contents

Foreword   xiii
Authors   xxi

1   **Expert Witnesses: An Overview**   1

    Key Terms   1
    Introduction   1
    History of Experts in Trials   4
    Civil and Criminal Cases   7
    The Criminal Justice Process   7
    Discovery and Deposition   9
    Preparation for Trial   11
    At Trial   11
    Conclusion   12
    Review Questions   13
    Discussion Questions   13

2   **Methods, Testing, and Science**   15

    Key Terms   15
    Introduction   15
    Accreditation, Certification, and Standardization   16
    What Is Science?   17
    Formulating a Working Hypothesis   19
    Use of a Standard Protocol   20
    Published Method   20
    Toward Admissibility   21
    Conclusion   22
    Review Questions   22
    Discussion Questions   23

3   **The Players**   25

    Key Terms   25
    Introduction   25
    The Attorney's Role   26

The Courts   28
The Judge's Role   30
The Jury's Role   31
Expert's Role   32
Example of the Role of Scientist   33
Expert's Role in Court   37
Thorough Analysis   37
Ability to Teach   37
Competence   38
Believability   38
Ability to Persuade   38
Enthusiasm   39
Conclusion   39
Review Questions   39
Discussion Questions   40

4   The Legal Context   41

Key Terms   41
Introduction   41
Discovery   41
The Discovery Components   44
The Expert and the Discovery Process   46
    Criminal Case   46
    Civil Case   47
Preparing for Deposition or Trial Testimony   49
Federal Rules of Evidence   56
    General Rules Regarding Witness Testimony   57
    Rules Regarding Expert Testimony and Opinion Testimony   58
Federal Rules of Evidence 702 and 703   59
    Rule 702   59
    Rule 703   60
Review Questions   60
Discussion Questions   61

5   Testimony   63

Key Terms   63
Introduction   63
Your Report   64
Preparation for Testimony and Communicating with Attorneys   66
Preparation for Testimony without Communicating   70
Demeanor, Dress, and Deportment   71
At Trial   73

Review Questions 75
Discussion Questions 76

6   Direct Examination of Experts   77

Key Terms 77
Introduction 77
Direct Examination and Strong Narratives 79
    Important Points to Remember 81
    Redirect Examination 88
    Elements That Enhance Direct Examination 88
    Be a Teacher 89
    Creating Instructional Materials: A Global Approach 89
Creating Instructional Materials: A Concrete Approach 91
    Presenting Complex Data 91
Review Questions 92
Discussion Questions 93

7   The Visual Display of Information   95

Key terms 95
Introduction 95
    Visually Displaying Quantitative Information 96
    Data-Ink 99
    Chartjunk 99
    Graphs, Graphics, and Comparisons in Court 101
    Demonstrations: If the Glove Doesn't Fit, You Must Acquit 105
Conclusion 107
Review Questions 107
Discussion Questions 107

8   Cross-Examination   109

Key Terms 109
Introduction 109
Cross-Examination: Friend or Foe? 110
Know the Attorney's Goals 112
    Laying Foundation 112
    Cross-Examination Techniques 112
    Making the Expert Their Witness 113
    Attacking the Expert's Field of Expertise 114
    Attacking the Expert's Qualifications 115
    Attacking the Factual Basis for the Expert's Conclusions 115
    The Use of Hypotheticals 116

Using a Learned Treatise   117
An Attack on the Expert's Conclusions   118
Testing the Entire Field   118
Reducing Vulnerability to Cross-Examination   119
Understand What Happens Next   121
Conclusion   122
Review Questions   122
Discussion Questions   123

9 Ethics   125

Key Terms   125
Introduction   125
What Is Unethical Conduct?   125
Examples of Scientist Misconduct   127
Examples of Attorney Misconduct   128
Interprofessional Relationships   129
    American Academy of Forensic Sciences (AAFS)   130
    International Association for Identification   131
    American Society of Crime Laboratory Directors
    (ASCLD)   133
How to Avoid Abuse   134
Primary Ethical Issues   135
    Outright False Data   135
    Investigation Not Performed   136
    Data Altered   136
    Conditional or Limited Engagement (Private Experts)   136
    False Testimony   136
    Ignoring Data   136
    Recanting Prior Contra-Positions   136
    Assignments Beyond Competency   137
    Unauthorized Attorney Influence   137
    Reaching Conclusions before Research   137
    Conflict of Interest   137
    Fraudulent Credentials   138
    Contingent Fee (Private Experts)   138
    Abuses of Experts   138
    Abuses by Experts   139
    Asserting Your Rights as a Witness   139
    Countering the Claim of Junk Science   140
Conclusion   141
Review Questions   142
Discussion Questions   142

Appendix A: Federal Rules of Evidence 701 through 706   143
   Rule 701. Opinion Testimony by Lay Witnesses   143
   Rule 702. Testimony by Expert Witnesses   143
   Rule 703. Bases of an Expert   143
   Rule 704. Opinion on an Ultimate Issue   144
   Rule 705. Disclosing the Facts or Data Underlying an Expert   144
   Rule 706. Court-Appointed Expert Witnesses   144

Appendix B: A Proposed Code of Conduct   147
   Carol Henderson
   American Academy of Forensic Sciences Jurisprudence
   Section Code of Professionalism   147
      Preamble   147
      Terminology   148
      Rules   .   148

Appendix C: An Expert's Bill of Rights   151
   Harold Feder
   The Expert Witness Bill of Rights   152
   Asserting Your Rights as an Expert Witness   156

Appendix D: Frye v. United States   159

**Appendix E: Daubert v. Merrell Dow
Pharmaceuticals, Inc.   161**

Appendix F: Kumho Tire v. Carmichael   173

Appendix G: General Electric Company v. Joiner   185

**Appendix H: Expert Testimony in the Wake of
Daubert, Joiner, and *Kumho Tire*   193**
   Sidney W. Jackson III
   Frye v. United States   194
      54 APP. D.C. 46; 293 F. 1013 (1923)   194
   The "General Acceptance" Rule of *Frye*   194
   Frye Overruled: *Daubert v. Merrell Dow Pharmaceuticals, Inc.*   194
      509 U.S. 579; 113 S. CT. 2786 (1993)   194
   Post-*Daubert: General Electric Co. v. Joiner*   195
      118 S. CT. 512 (1997)   195
   Kumho Tire Co. v. Carmichael   196
      119 S. CT. 1167 (1999)   196
   How Courts are Implementing *Daubert, Joiner,* and *Kumho Tire*   199
   Recent Federal Decisions   199
   Conclusion   201

Appendix I: Resources for Private Experts   **203**

    Sample Interrogatories and Request for Production to
    Expert Witnesses   203
        Sample of Interrogatories and Request for Production
        to a Party Concerning Expert Witness   203
    Cross-Examination of Expert Witnesses   206
        Harold A. Feder
        Some Typical Questions and Answers   206
    Sample Engagement Letter (For Private Experts)   208
    Mediation and the Expert Witness   210
        Harold A. Feder
        Introduction   210
        Step 1   210
        Step 2   211
        Step 3   211
        Negotiating Techniques   211
        Settlement Plan Checklist   212
        Step 4   213
    Report Writing for Federal Rules of Civil Procedure
    Rules 16 and 26   214
        Harold A. Feder
        Rule 26—Federal Rules of Civil Procedure—Rule 26(B)(2)
        A, B, C   214
        Rule 16(A)(1)A (1)E and (B)(1)C of the Federal Rules of
        Criminal Procedure   214

Glossary and Important Terms   **215**

Bibliography   **225**

Index   **227**

Foreword

What does it mean to succeed as an expert witness? Is success measured by whether the side that summoned you to the witness stand prevails at trial? By recommendations that you make a convincing presentation to judge and jury? By the size of the fee you command in the marketplace or the promotions and awards bestowed upon you in the public sector? My own belief is that none of these are benchmarks of success.

Forensic science and by extension, expert witnesses, are at crossroads. The extraordinary power of DNA to identify the guilty and exonerate the falsely accused is one factor driving the wave of new graduate programs and expansion of undergraduate departments in forensic science. But while DNA typing may be a "truth machine," all too frequently, the truth revealed in post-conviction DNA testing is that years earlier, less powerful (by today's methods) or misapplied forensic science had been presented at trial by the "successful" expert witness to secure what turned out to be a false conviction.

Television's fictionalization of crime scene investigation is so successful that the public seems to prefer crimes be investigated by technicians in white lab coats rather than by old-fashioned gumshoes in rumpled, coffee-stained sport jackets. But is the forensic community's reliance on TV misplaced when the consortium of national forensic organizations parades the TV actors before Congress to lobby for crime lab funding?

Finally, the national mobilization to combat terrorism and defend the homeland lends urgency and patriotism to the justice system; the "righteousness" of the cause, however, may inadvertently compromise the integrity of the result. In the identification sciences, "matching" the suspect to the crime sample can help win the war on terror much the same as it played an important role in the war on crime. But, since experts utilize subjective human judgment, expectation and suggestion can influence outcome. Indeed, one lesson from the DNA post-conviction exonerations is that examiner and confirmation bias are involved in too many erroneous hair, toolmark, and bitemark inclusions, as well as mistaken findings of homicide and arson when the cause was ultimately proven to be accidental. In the aftermath of the 2004 terrorist attack on a commuter train in Spain, the FBI erroneously claimed that the fingerprint of an Oregon attorney with ties to the Islamic community, but no criminal record, "matched" a fingerprint found on a plastic bag containing detonators found near the Madrid crime scene. In the affidavit used to justify the arrest of the lawyer, the two FBI examiners swore they were 100% certain of the match. The Spanish police insisted that the FBI was wrong: An Algerian terrorist was ultimately linked to the fingerprint. Without the persistence of the Spanish police, the FBI would not have reconsidered its findings. One irony of any mismatch is that whenever an innocent man is falsely charged or convicted, the real criminal or terrorist remains at liberty to commit further acts of violence. Faulty forensics may wrongly exclude the factually guilty.

For years, the dominant argument for not regulating experts and forensic sciences was that every time an expert steps inside the courtroom, his work is vigorously peer reviewed and scrutinized by the opposing counsel. A forensic scientist might occasionally make an error at the lab bench but the "crucible" of the courtroom cross examination would expose it at trial. The "crucible," however, turned out to be utterly ineffective. In not one of the forensic science scandals of the last 20 years were the transgressions of experts revealed by counsel at trial.

Although forensic science is used most commonly in crimes of violence, and state courts receive almost 200 times more criminal prosecutions than federal courts, the overwhelming majority of challenges to the admissibility of expert testimony occur in civil cases in the federal system. When the courts in the 1990s moved from the *Frye* standard of admissibility to *Daubert*, they obligated judges to assume the role of "gatekeepers" and to exclude proffered scientific evidence unless it rested on scientifically valid reasoning and methodology. But since most criminal defense lawyers lack the training, skill, time, and money to mount credible challenges to speculative expert testimony, there is nothing for a gatekeeper to tend to. If the "crucible" is a fiction and the judicial system fails to provide meaningful controls to assure the integrity of the process, other remedies must be found further upstream.

Since an expert's conclusions should be predicated on first principles of science, one lesson of the DNA revolution is to require a basic research model that will test the core assumptions in each expert's discipline. Whereas DNA typing rests on a stable foundation extensively rooted in research well documented in the literature, many of the forensic sciences have not been put through the same paces. Basic research takes money and independence, more than agencies such as the National Institute of Justice can provide. Given the urgency of international developments and the success story of DNA, I think it likely that the federal government will rise to the occasion.

Another lesson of DNA typing is the necessity that other disciplines develop methods to provide meaningful frequencies of attributes and characteristics. New protocols need to be established to minimize unintentional bias. Essential principles of statistics, long overlooked by experts, need to be incorporated to substitute random match probabilities (the kind used routinely in DNA) for the uninformative and often misleading terms "match," "similar," and "inclusion." The published probabilities coupled with known error rates, based on external blind proficiency tests, could then be presented in court. The final downstream fix is to establish reasonable parameters for the content of expert reports and live testimony so as not to distort the probative value of the evidence. An expert's job is not simply to answer *all* the questions propounded by the attorneys on both sides. If a question is inherently misleading or scientifically irrelevant, the expert has an affirmative duty to alert the court and put the testimony back on track.

At the beginning of the twentieth century, a critical awareness and creative energy ignited a movement to modernize clinical laboratory medicine. One hundred years later, the time is right for a comparable transformation in forensic science. It is an exciting time for everyone who is part of this community. Succeed by being thoughtful and rigorous scientists. Succeed by being honest, objective, and ethical expert witnesses.

Peter Neufeld
Partner, Neufeld Scheck & Brustin, LLP
New York, New York

Foreword

Our justice system is an adversarial one. We allow each side in a dispute to present its case, and then we ask a jury of peers (or in some cases a judge) to determine which side prevails. In criminal cases, the state must prove a defendant's guilt beyond a reasonable doubt. In civil cases, a plaintiff must prevail by a preponderance of the evidence. To borrow from what Winston Churchill once said about democracy, this is a pretty terrible system, except for all of the others one might imagine.

The problem is that an adversarial system is heavily reliant on the power of persuasion, which isn't always the same thing as a pursuit of the truth. There are any number of factors that can drive the outcome of a jury or civil trial more than the facts of the case. Among them, who has the better attorney, who has more funding to hire investigators and experts. How sympathetic the jury finds the plaintiff or defendant, or even how likable a jury finds the opposing attorneys.

This book addresses the issue of expert witnesses. Ideally, expert witnesses give us more informed juries, which helps those juries arrive at the truth. Unfortunately, as with other aspects of the justice system, the adversarial system can aide expert witnesses in subverting the truth rather than facilitating it. For example, both prosecutors and defense attorneys have long complained about the so-called CSI effect. The complaint is that the CBS franchise of TV shows about forensic analysts has conditioned jurors to expect far more of forensic expertise than forensics allows for. The complaint is that because of these shows and others like them, jurors today crave certainty from expert witnesses, and they're skeptical of anything short of that.

But a conscientious expert witness—particularly one whose expertise is in the hard sciences—tends to speak in terms of probability, not certainty. Prosecutors argue that this makes it more difficult for them to win convictions. (This complaint should be weighed against the fact that in most jurisdictions, prosecutors typically win 80–90% of the time.) On the other hand, defense attorneys argue that the CSI effect makes jurors less skeptical of expert witnesses, particularly in areas of forensics that are presented to jurors as science but in which the methods of analysis haven't been subjected to scientific scrutiny—particularly in pattern-matching fields like bite mark analysis, shoeprint, and tire tread analysis, and hair fiber analysis.

This brings up another way in which expert testimony can inhibit the search for truth in our justice system—the courts are not very good at distinguishing legitimate expertise from artifice. As the author of this book explains, the two prevailing cases that tend to govern how the courts assess the reliability of expertise—standards known as Frye and Daubert—are vague and too open to interpretation. But there's a more profound problem than even that—these rulings assigned the task of distinguishing valid expertise from charlatanism to judges.

Judges are trained to perform legal analysis, not scientific analysis. We wouldn't think of asking a judge to, say, come up with a game plan for an NFL (National Football League) team, or draw up the blueprints for a vacation home. Yet we regularly ask them to gauge the legitimacy of fields and experts in which the judges have no expertise at all, whether its forensics, complex accounting methods, psychology, or really any field that might be relevant in a criminal or civil trial. Typically, judges tend to first look to what other courts have done. That makes sense for someone trained in legal analysis because that's how our legal system tends to operate. Our system operates on precedent, which establishes reliability, predictability, and in most cases, some semblance of equality before the law. (You are tried under the same rules, procedures, and policies as those before you.)

But with expertise—especially scientific or science-ish expertise—this can present huge problems. Lawyers on all sides will tend to push the limits of expertise to get experts on the witness stand who will give testimony favorable to their side. If the other side challenges an expert's credibility, the judge will tend to look to previous courts for guidance. If there's no previous case law on point, judges tend to err on the side of letting the evidence in, and letting competing experts fight to persuade the jury.

This is misguided for several reasons. First, the fields for which you can find credentialed experts willing to take diametrically opposing opinions are the most subjective fields, and therefore tend to be those least scrutinized by the scientific community. For example, most cases involving bite mark evidence will feature expert witnesses on both sides, one or more of whom claim the bite mark matches or "includes" the defendant, and one or more of whom will claim the mark "excludes" the defendant, is indeterminate, or isn't a human bite mark at all.

The very fact that you can find experts willing to take such diametrically opposing opinions, for example, is a good indication that the field isn't scientifically reliable. Contrarily, you'll rarely find two experts who diametrically disagree over the number of common markers in two DNA profiles.

The other problem is when you have competing experts, the set of skills it takes to persuade a jury is not necessarily the same set of skills it takes to be a careful and conscientious analyst. Juries can be persuaded by charisma, charm, and extraneous factors like how much an expert was paid. In criminal trials, they also tend to be skeptical of hired defense experts than of prosecution experts, who tend to be public employees. In fact, it may well be the case that the experts juries find most persuasive are the least scientific, given that, as previously explained, juries tend to crave the sort of certainty that science eschews.

These two mistaken ways with which judges often handle challenges to expert testimony—relying on what previous courts have ruled and, if there's no controlling case law, letting it all in and letting the jury sort it out—can then perpetuate an unfortunate feedback loop. Once a judge lets flawed expertise in, he creates a precedent, which future judges then rely on should that particular sort of expertise be challenged at a later date. Those future judges will rely on that ruling because most judges aren't likely to feel confident enough in their scientific expertise to overturn a precedent, or even to rule against the prevailing opinion from other judges in other jurisdictions. So the same mistakes get repeated in court after court, in jurisdiction after jurisdiction, not because of corruption or bias or maliciousness, but through passiveness and attrition.

This book is not about these flaws in the system I've just described. It isn't a polemic speculating about how those flaws happened, nor does it offer a prescription for how to fix them. If all expert witnesses followed the guidelines in this book, we'd still have a badly flawed system. But it would be less flawed than it is today. And expert testimony would be far less of a contributor to those flaws.

This is a book about how to be an honest, conscientious, and effective expert witness in spite of the regrettable shortcomings of our courts system. It's about how to be transparent and forthright while navigating the legal landscape we have today, fraught as it can sometimes be. It's an instruction manual that, if followed, will at least give an expert witness the peace of mind to know that he or she is contributing to the search for truth, even if he or she has no choice but to operate in a system in which truth isn't always the priority.

Radley Balko
Journalist with the Washington Post
Author, The Cadaver King and the Country Dentist:
A True Story of Injustice in the American South

Authors

Dr. Max M. Houck is an international forensic expert with over 25 years of experience. Houck has experience in the private sector, academia, and local government, and worked at the Federal Bureau of Investigation Laboratory Division. He has worked as a forensic anthropologist, a trace evidence analyst, and a researcher, and has managed millions of dollars in grants and awards. He was the inaugural Director of the Department of Forensic Sciences in Washington, D.C., overseeing 150 employees and managing the forensic science laboratory, the public health laboratory, and crime scene sciences for the nation's capital. Houck has worked on a number of mass casualty scenes, including the Branch Davidian investigation and the September 11, 2001 attack on the Pentagon. Widely published, Houck has dozens of peer-reviewed journal articles and is the author and editor of numerous books. He is co-author of the best-selling *Fundamentals of Forensic Science, Science of Crime Scenes*, and *Success with Expert Testimony*, among others. He is the editor of the Advanced Forensic Science series of books. Houck is also founding co-editor of *Forensic Science Policy and Management*. Houck has served on numerous committees, including for the National Academies of Science, NIST, Interpol, The Royal Society, the Director of the FBI, and the White House. He is a popular public speaker and has given presentations at NASA, the Max Planck Institute, and Oxford Roundtable, as well as keynote talks at numerous international conferences. His research topics include management, leadership, and policy implications for forensic organizations. Houck has bachelor's and master's degrees in anthropology from Michigan State University. He received his Ph.D. in Applied Chemistry Summa Cum Laude from Curtin University in Perth, Australia. He is a Fellow of the Royal Society of Chemistry. Houck is the Director of the Forensic Studies & Justice program at the University of South Florida St. Petersburg.

Christine Funk started her career in the Minnesota Office of the Public Defender in 1994. In 1995, she was assigned her first forensic DNA case. Not a scientist by training, she struggled to understand the complexities of forensic evidence. Over the years, her forensic caseload expanded to include arson, broken babies, drug chemistry, forensic biology, and bite marks, as well as the study of false confessions and eyewitness identification in the context of complex litigation. In 2013, Funk moved to Washington, DC, to become General Counsel for the Department of Forensic Sciences. This experience provided additional insights as to how forensic science fits within the criminal justice system. In 2017, Funk returned to Minnesota, where she writes about issues pertaining to the law and forensic science, provides representation to indigent clients, and consults with criminal justice stakeholders, as well as those writing about forensic science—from investigative pieces to movie scripts to a television pilot. Previously, Ms. Funk has served on the Legal Resource Committee for the Organization of Scientific Area Committees, the Board of the Minnesota Innocence Project, the Forensic Laboratory Advisory Board for the state of Minnesota, and the White House Subcommittee to the Subcommittee on Forensic Science in Education, Ethics, and Terminology.

Harold A. Feder (1932–1995) was a trial lawyer with 35 years of trial experience. Most of his cases involved the use of experts. Feder was a fellow of the college of Law Practice Management and the American Academy of Forensic Sciences, a member of the Association of Trial Lawyers of America, past president of the Colorado Trial Lawyers Association, and an active member of the American and Colorado Bar Associations. Feder wrote and lectured extensively on legal matters, including expert testimony, throughout the United States and Canada for over 20 years. He wrote *Succeeding as an Expert Witness* in 1991; the text was revised in 1993, 2000, and 2008.

Expert Witnesses
An Overview

1

Key Terms

Appellate court
Burden of proof
Civil law
Complainant
Criminal justice process
Criminal law
Depositions
Discovery
Expert
Federal Rule of Evidence
Grand jury
Jargon
Jury of peers
Lay witness
Opinion
Petit jury
Prosecutor's information
Sixth Amendment of the Constitution of the United States
Technique
Work product

It is the job of the law, and not science, to determine how science is to be used in the courts. But in another sense, our passivity has served both ourselves and the legal system poorly. It is the job of science, and not of law, to determine what is good science and what is not.[1]

Introduction

Succeeding as an expert witness requires a basic understanding of who and what experts are. The U.S. legal system permits certain witnesses to render

[1] Thornton, J. Courts of Law v. Courts of Science: A Forensic Scientist's Reaction to Daubert, *Shepard's Expert and Scientific Evidence Quarterly*, 1994 (3): 475–485, page 476.

opinions based on data rather than merely reciting information. These opinions are sought to explain past, present, and future events. You may be or already are such a witness. In this book, you will learn why experts are unique and how they are selected to be witnesses. An expert is a special, often controversial, position in our court and hearing procedures. Federal Rule of Evidence 702 defines Testimony by Experts:

> If scientific, technical, or other specialized knowledge will assist the trier of fact [judge or jury] to understand the evidence or to determine a fact in issue, a witness qualified as an expert by knowledge, skill experience, training or education, may testify thereto in the form of an opinion or otherwise, if (1) the testimony is based upon sufficient facts or data, (2) the testimony is the product of reliable principles and methods, and (3) the witness has applied the principles and methods reliably to the facts of the case.

This may seem to be a moot description—what's the big deal? Contrast Rule 702 with Rule 701, Opinion Testimony by Lay Witness:

> If the witness is not testifying as an expert, the witness testimony in the form of opinions or inferences is limited to those opinions or inferences which are (a) rationally based on the perception of the witness, and (b) helpful to a clear understanding of the witness' testimony or the determination of a fact in issue, and (c) not based on scientific, technical, or other specialized knowledge within the scope of Rule 702.

If you are guessing that a "lay witness" is everybody who does not possess "scientific, technical, or other specialized knowledge," you are correct. In religious organizations, all persons who are not members of the clergy or any monastic order are called "laypersons" and collectively make up the laity. The term in the law, in the context of any specialized profession, is used to refer to those who are not members of that profession, in this case, scientists, technicians, or other specialists. If you are not one of these specific people, your testimony must be limited to any facts—what you have experienced with your five senses—or opinions drawn from those experiences.

Experts, on the other hand, are given a special license in testimony: they can testify about their professional opinion based on their education, training, and experience in a specific topic. A recent article described an expert as:

> a person who, by virtue of training and experience, is able to do things the rest of us cannot. Experts are not only proficient in what they do, but are also smooth and efficient in the actions they take. Experts know a great many things and have tricks for applying these things to problems or tasks. Experts are good at plowing through irrelevant information in order to get at basic issues or actual problems. Experts are also good at recognizing problems as instances

of ones with which they are familiar, generalizing alternative solutions and making good choices among the alternatives.

A few examples may help clarify the difference between laity and experts. Here are some statements of testimony designated either with L for laity or E for expert.

L: The man I saw leaving the bank was tall, about 6′.
E: The individual in the bank surveillance video is between 5′11″ and 6′2″ based on the photogramametric calculations I performed.

L: The woman was wearing a blue sweater.
E: The victim's sweater was composed of dark blue round polyester and blue bi-lobed acrylic fibers.

L: The guy looked like he was bleeding.
E: The victim has suffered a contusion, one and a half to two inches in diameter over his left orbital at the juncture of the left temporal bone.

It is not only the wording characteristic of a particular group (jargon), in this case, experts, that makes these examples expert testimony, it is the knowledge, skills, and expertise behind the statements and the interpretations that result from them. The expert's knowledge of methods (photogrammetry), skills at applying them (how did the expert determine the fibers were polyester and acrylic?), and expertise in applying them (practicing as a medical doctor) are what differentiate them from the average layperson. You might know a doctor or a scientist and perhaps understand what they do a bit better than others, but you are not in a professional position to make scientific or medical judgments the way they do. It is not just the knowing, however, that makes an expert. There is, philosophically, a real difference between someone who knows something and an expert:

> A technique is a standard method that can be taught. It is a recipe that can be fully conveyed from one person to another. A recipe always lays down a certain number of steps which, if followed to the letter, ought to lead invariably to the end desired.[2]

Should something go wrong, the recipe does not provide the tools for understanding and remediating the problem. It takes a true understanding of how the technique works and why to correct problems or, in fact, to improve. An internal corrective mechanism has been offered as one of the ways to distinguish science (astronomy, for example) from nonscience (astrology).[3]

---

[2] Barrett, W. *The Illusion of Technique* (Garden City, NJ: Anchor/Doubleday Press, 1979), page 22.
[3] Kuhn, T. *The Structure of Scientific Revolutions* (Chicago: University of Chicago Press, 1962).

What kind of education and training make someone an expert? Table 1.1 lists a few of the extensive topics that may require expert testimony. As you can see, many of these topics would require a good deal of education and training for a sufficient level of expertise to offer professional opinions in a courtroom.

Our society reveres those with specialized knowledge. Those who abuse that reverence for personal or professional gain, however, are as despised as the real experts are admired. For this reason, Rule 702 adds that the expert's testimony must be "based upon sufficient facts or data" and be "the product of reliable principles and methods" as well as having been reliably applied. For this reason, federal courts advise their juries concerning expert witnesses:

> The rules of evidence ordinarily do not permit witnesses to testify as to opinions or conclusions. An exception to this rule exists as to those whom we call "expert witnesses." Witnesses who, by education and experience, have become expert in some art, science, profession, or calling, may state an opinion as to relevant and material matter, in which they profess to be expert, and may also state their reasons for the opinion.
>
> You should consider each expert opinion received in evidence in this case, and give it such weight as you may think it deserves. If you should decide that the opinion of an expert witness is not based upon sufficient education and experience, or if you should conclude that the reasons given in support of the opinion are not sound, or that the opinion is outweighed by other evidence, you may disregard the opinion entirely.[4]

It is a hallmark of the U.S. justice system that, although they cannot testify the way experts can, the "laity" do make up the juries and have the final say in the case being tried.

History of Experts in Trials

Expert scientific witnesses have a long history of service to the courts. The modern expert witness was a specific creation of the late eighteenth century, but the birthing was awkward and contentious. As Golan says, the expert witness was "a freak in the new adversarial world, an incompatible and inharmonious, yet indispensable and influential, figure in the modern adversarial courtroom."[5] At the beginning of the eighteenth century, an English court would have been recognizable to our modern eyes, but only

---

[4] Devitt, E.J. and Blackmar, C.B. *Federal Jury Practice and Instructions*, 3rd ed., Vol. 1 (St. Paul, MN: West Publishing Company, 1977), §15.22, page 482.

[5] Golan, T. *Laws of Men and Laws of Nature: The History of Scientific Expert Testimony in England and America* (Cambridge, MA: Harvard University Press, 2004), page 7.

Table 1.1   A Few of the Issues That May Require Expert Testimony

Accounting	Fraud
Actuarial evaluations	Grievance procedures
Administrative law	Handwriting analysis
Air, soil, and water quality and contamination	Health or zoning code violations
Application of federal regulations	Immigration issues
Appraisals	Juvenile matters
Appropriateness of warrant and warrantless searches	Labor laws
Aquifer and watershed sources	Land use regulations
Arson	Lost economic opportunity
Assessing damages	Materials testing
Assessment of causation	Mine safety
Banking or business activity	Motorized vehicle collision and dysfunction
Banking practices and legal requirements	Network security
Blood pattern analysis	Odontology
Boundary disputes and title defects	Patent, copyright, and trademark
Causes of fire, flood, or other casualty	Pathology
Chemistry	Personal injury of all types
Child custody and visitation matters	Photography/videography
Child or spousal abuse	Pornography issues
Clean-up procedures and costs	Propriety of claim procedures and damages
Construction defects	Psychiatric and psychological evaluations
Contract meaning and interpretation	Questioned documents
Crime scene reconstruction	Questions of wrongful termination
Criminology	Revocation of professional licenses
Customs matters	Safe working conditions
Damages	Securities regulation and violation
Digital evidence	Shoe prints/tire tracks
Discrimination	Source of mineral specimens
DNA	Surgical procedure
Domestic relations	Taxation
Drugs	Toxicology
Dynamics of machinery	Trace evidence
Employment compensation	Value of property for tax purposes
Environmental and ecological damage Explosives	Value of statutory benefits
Fingerprints	Wages, hours, and conditions of employment
Firearms and toolmarks	Workers compensation

barely. The attorneys were marginally involved, the judge was an active participant and questioned the witnesses, and the accused represented themselves. By the end of the century, the judge was reduced to a neutral referee, the attorneys had taken control of the trial process and were the stars of the courts, and the process had taken on the adversarial approach used today. Scientists in that time were considered to be gentlemen and members of an elite, honor-bound guild who put their reputation first and finances second. Perhaps this is why scientists were allowed to testify in proceedings that did not personally involve them during a time when even the slightest personal interest in a legal matter disqualified someone as a witness. Scientists were perceived to be independent, disinterested men of learning who were above the petty squabbles of those in the courts. The experts could, therefore, be counted on to provide and explain impartial objective facts that—although beyond the knowledge of the public—were central to the resolution of the legal dispute. Some of these perceptions carry over into our modern view of the scientist, but we also know that scientists are only too human: they can make mistakes, lie, and even profit thereby. The adversarial nature of the courts played to these weaknesses and led to a loss of reputation for scientists:

> The growing judicial recognition of their status as a special class of witnesses was not all good news for men of science. It may have underlined their critical importance for the judicial process, but at the same time it also perpetuated their marginalization within this process. In moving across professional and institutional boundaries, from the exclusivity of their lecture theaters, workshop, laboratories, and societies to the public courtroom, men of science hoped to present there laws that were not controlled by human whim. Instead, they found themselves manipulated as mere tools in the hands of the lawyers... As witnesses, they found themselves isolated in the witness box, away from the decision-making process. Browbeaten and set against each other, they found that their standard strategies for generating credibility and agreement were unsuitable for the adversarial heat of the courtroom. The result was a continuous parade of leading men of science zealously contradicting each other from the witness stand, a parade that cast serious doubts on their integrity and on their science in the eyes of the legal profession and the public.[6]

In the twentieth century, as the sciences developed from intricate hobbies to defined disciplines of study, so too did the reputation of expert scientific witnesses in the courts. It was no longer enough for a witness to declare expert status; he or she had to demonstrate it through generally accepted practices used by other scientists in that field. The judge became the arbiter of experts, and legal decisions (*U.S. v. Frye*, specifically) followed that assisted in that task. The *Frye* decision, which will be discussed in more detail later, held that the

---

[6] Ibid., 54.

expert must have suitable credentials to offer the evidence and the evidence itself must "be sufficiently established to have gained general acceptance in the particular field in which it belongs." This shift from the person to the process heralded a new way for the legal system to treat science in its midst.

Post-World War II, the scope of the science offered in courts expanded, as did the judges' responsibility to make sure that it was solid and reputable science and not quackery. By the 1970s, *Frye* was the standard by which all proffered scientific testimony was measured. During the 1970s, the Federal Rules of Evidence (FRE), the requirements for using evidence in federal courts, were codified but made no mention of *Frye*. Instead, the FRE offered Rule 702, which was broad and inclusive, not to mention vague; what, for example, constituted "scientific, technical, or other specialized knowledge"? The courts intended for this to be sorted out by the experts and attorneys and determined by the judges.

Civil and Criminal Cases

Criminal law is the body of statutory and common law that deals with crime and the legal punishment of criminal offenses. "Criminal offenses" generally means actions that are counter to the good of society. This differs from civil law in that civil actions are disputes between two parties that are not of significant public concern; "civil law" is also used to describe all law outside of the criminal law context. Criminal law has been seen as a system of regulating the behavior of individuals and groups in relation to societal norms, whereas civil law is aimed primarily at the relationship between private individuals and their rights and obligations under the law. Experts are useful in both kinds of legal cases, but the archetypal forensic scientist who works for a law enforcement agency will work almost exclusively on criminal cases. Private experts face an entirely separate set of additional challenges.[7]

The Criminal Justice Process

The criminal justice process begins with an alleged crime. An accusation is made (by the person aggrieved, the complainant), which is investigated by law enforcement officers, acting as representatives of the government. A formal complaint, also called an indictment, is presented to a group of citizens, called a grand jury,[8] who determine if enough evidence exists for a criminal trial. If so, the indictment is filed with a court in the appropriate jurisdiction. Grand

---

[7] Hamilton, R. *The Expert Witness Marketing Book* (Clearwater, FL: Expert Communications, 2003).

[8] Grand juries have more members than a trial, or petit, jury.

juries do not exist outside the United States and are not universal within it (Connecticut, Pennsylvania, and the District of Columbia do not use grand jury indictments); each state that uses them has its own set of grand jury procedures. Many states use a prosecutor's information as a means of formally charging the accused of a crime. A prosecutor's information details the nature and circumstances of the charges and is a formal criminal charge filed with the court. It is based on information derived from the initial investigation.

The interests of the state are represented by a prosecuting attorney, while the interests of the defendant are represented by a defense attorney or by the defendant, acting as his or her own attorney. The Sixth Amendment of the Constitution of the United States guarantees a criminal defendant:

- The right to a speedy and public trial, in both state and federal courts, by an impartial jury of the State and district wherein the crime was committed (a "jury of peers")
- The right to be informed of the nature and cause of the accusation
- The right to be confronted with the witnesses against him or her (this is where expert witnesses play a role)
- A compulsory process for obtaining witnesses in his or her favor (the subpoena)
- The assistance of Counsel for his or her defense (so-called Public Defenders, if the accused cannot afford counsel)

While the specific process varies according to the local law, the process culminates with a jury trial (as required by the Sixth Amendment), followed by mandatory or discretionary appeals to higher courts.

The prosecution must prove beyond a reasonable doubt that the defendant is guilty of the crime charged; this is called the burden of proof. The prosecution presents its case first and may call witnesses and present other evidence against the defendant. After the prosecution has presented its case, the defense may move to dismiss the case if there is insufficient evidence, or present its case and call witnesses. All witnesses may be cross-examined by the opposing side. After both sides have presented their cases and made closing arguments, the judge gives the jury legal instructions and they adjourn to deliberate in private. The jury must unanimously agree on a verdict of guilty or not guilty. If a defendant is found guilty, sentencing (punishment) follows, often at a separate hearing after the prosecution, defense, and court have developed information based on which the judge will determine a sentence. As with the guilt phase, the burden is on the prosecution to prove its case, and the defendant is entitled to take the stand in his or her own defense, and may call witnesses and present evidence.

After sentencing, the defendant may appeal the ruling to a higher court. An appellate court ("appellate" is the adjectival form of "appeal") is a court that hears cases in which a lower court—either a trial court or a lower-level appellate court—has already made a decision but in which at least one party to the action wants to challenge the ruling. The challenge is based upon some legal grounds, such as errors of law, fact, or due process. American appellate courts do not retry the case; they only examine the record of the proceedings in the lower court to determine if errors were made that require a new trial, resentencing, or a complete discharge of the defendant, as is mandated by the circumstances.

Discovery and Deposition

Discovery is the pretrial phase in a lawsuit in which each party can request documents and other evidence from other parties or compel the production of evidence by using a subpoena or through other discovery devices, such as depositions. Anything that is relevant is available for the other party to request, as long as it is not privileged or otherwise protected. Relevance is defined as anything more or less likely to prove a fact that affects the outcome of the claim. It does not have to be admissible in court as long as it could reasonably lead to admissible evidence. Discovery, however, does not mean everything is automatically turned over. The court may adjust the limits of discovery on the amount of material requested if it determines that the discovery sought is overly burdensome, redundant, unnecessary, or disproportionately difficult to produce with respect to the importance of the case or specific issue. Also protected are tangible (and some intangible) items created in anticipation of the litigation (so-called work product; for example, a memorandum from an attorney outlining his strategy in the case). Protecting work product is considered in the interest of justice because discovery of such work product would expose an attorney's complete legal strategy before trial. Experts whose opinions may be presented at trial are discoverable, but discovery is limited with experts who are not likely to testify during trial. Any material legally privileged (attorney–client, doctor–patient, etc.) also is exempt from discovery.

One of the main tools in the attorney's arsenal is the deposition. A deposition is evidence given under oath and recorded for use in court at a later date; in the United States, depositions are taken outside of a courtroom. The chief value of a deposition, as with any discovery proceeding, is to give all parties in a case a fair preview of the evidence so that a "level playing field" is achieved and no surprises occur in trial (these used to be called "Perry Mason Moments," after the lawyer character in Erle Stanley Gardner's novels). In the event a witness is unavailable for trial, his or her deposition testimony may be read before the jury and made part of the record in the case, with the same legal force as live testimony. It is crucial for expert witnesses to prepare for depositions just as they would court testimony—in some states, depositions can be offered into evidence even if the witness is available! In any case, one party can use a deposition to impeach (or contradict) the witness's testimony in open court. While depositions may be more common in civil cases, some jurisdictions routinely use them (Florida, for example).

What you say in a deposition may come back to haunt you on the stand. Some depositions are videotaped in anticipation of the unavailability of a witness at trial, so that, if necessary, the videotape may be played for the judge and jury. A deposition is designed to accomplish certain specific objectives:

- Gather information
- Uncover inconsistencies in testimony
- Document statements, processes, and work product
- Assess your ability as a witness

The examination is usually done by opposing counsel, with few if any questions by your sponsoring attorney. The setting is generally informal, scheduled in advance, and conducted in the presence of a certified court reporter; recording by video is common. You may also assist the examining attorney at deposition of opposing experts by assessing their qualifications and capabilities, and framing questions for them. Before your deposition, you should review the following:

- Technical and factual data from the case
- Your scientific and technical materials
- Pleadings on file in the case
- Products of discovery, such as interrogatories, document production, and depositions
- Standard scientific works relevant to the subject
- Appropriate legal authorities

Agreement of counsel or court approval is usually necessary before you may be deposed. The pleadings must show that the information sought by deposition cannot be obtained by other traditional and less expensive means of discovery.[9] Depositions may be taken either for discovery or in lieu of testimony in court because you are beyond the jurisdictional limits of the court's subpoena power.

As an expert, you should play an important role in pleadings and discovery preparation. You may be called on to word technical parts of a pleading. You can also review discovery requests and responses for completeness and technical consistency. In some cases, you can help uncover a body of technical

---

[9] This is particularly true under the Federal Rules of Civil Procedure and in states that have adopted similar rules. See, for example, Rule 26(b)(4), Federal Rules of Civil Procedure.

data, forms, procedures, protocol, notes, and research materials. It is often essential that you participate at this stage to ensure that requisite scientific and technical information is available before deposition. Preparing for deposition should be a joint effort between you and the attorney.

Preparation for Trial

Before trial, you will assist in preparing exhibits and demonstrative charts, tests, and documents. Any demonstration must be tested before the trial or hearing. Trial exhibits should be shown to opposing counsel in advance of trial, and either stipulation or court order approval should be obtained. These are easy ways to guarantee the admissibility of a key chart, exhibit, document, or demonstration. It is proper for you to ask the attorney calling you if these details have been satisfied. Nothing can be as disappointing as preparing costly demonstrations or exhibits that are rejected at trial because of inaccuracy or lack of foundation. Exhibits and demonstrations must be accurate and technically correct. Note that demonstrative evidence may be excluded because it is deemed "prejudicial," meaning that its value as evidence is outweighed by its shock value or inflammatory nature. Color photographs of mutilated bodies or even technically accurate autopsies are often considered too emotionally disturbing to be useful as evidence.

Unnecessary exhibits and testimony should be eliminated before trial. Your calculations should be rechecked. Data should be summarized whenever possible: have the raw data available in the courtroom, but refer to summaries of voluminous documents or material. New rules of evidence allow this use of summary data.[10] The large amount of raw material you have evaluated before trial can enhance the weight of testimony. The data from which summaries are made must in all cases be available for examination by opposing counsel. Good practice dictates that such information be made available well before trial and be in court for opposition examination.

Preparation for trial is somewhat different from preparation for deposition. The attorney should explain to you the objectives of testimony and the physical setting of the hearing room in detail, including positioning of the parties and attorneys, and the dispute resolution forum.

At Trial

First, the attorney who subpoenaed you will try to have you qualified as an expert by the court. In essence, you present your education, training, and

---

[10]See, for example, FRE 1006.

experience as qualifications for your right to speak authoritatively on the evidence you examined. This will be covered in greater detail in a later chapter.

Think of the people involved in a trial: the judge, the attorneys, the jurors, you. Of all those who play a role in the proceedings, how many are under sworn oath to tell the truth? Just you, the witness. This is not to say that anyone will lie to you with intent, but they could. It may be an omission by accident as well, but it's best to remember you—the witness—are the only one who has sworn to be truthful.

During the trial, you should be aware of the importance of careful testimony, particularly the hazard of inconsistent testimony between deposition and trial. You are admonished to tell the truth and to prepare for deposition or trial testimony by reviewing the facts of the case and your work effort. You should not lose your temper. Speak slowly, clearly, and naturally. If you are familiar with the process, you will not fear the examining attorney or the setting. You must answer only the questions asked, never volunteering information beyond the scope of the question presented. You need not have an answer for every question. Avoid arguing with or second-guessing examining counsel. If you make a mistake, correct it as soon as possible. If a negative or apparently damaging fact or omission has been elicited, admit it and move on quickly. To fence, hedge, argue, equivocate, or become angry only exposes you to further cross-examination and a resultant loss of credibility.

Testimony in court, deposition, or hearing should never be turned into a joke. Exaggeration, underestimation, or overestimation are all indications of unwary and ill-prepared witnesses. You must translate technical terms into common, understandable language at every opportunity. Your demeanor and behavior before, during, and after testimony should be the subject of care. Conversations with opposing parties, attorneys, and jurors must be avoided.

At trial your testimony will be divided into five main parts:

1. Voir dire, presenting your qualifications as an expert to render opinion testimony
2. Direct testimony
3. Cross-examination
4. Redirect and re-cross-examinations
5. The judge retaining or excusing you as a witness

Conclusion

You, as an expert because of your knowledge, training, and experience, are allowed to render opinions about scientific or technical matters during the trial processes. You may be called on to assist in all phases of investigation, preparation, discovery, and trial of contested matters. Your role is to transmit specialized information and knowledge to the fact finder (judge or jury). In many cases, your effectiveness will help determine the outcome. Although your primary role is to provide your direct testimony, anticipation of cross-examination will facilitate your persuasive responses. You should prepare for cross-examination and frame a strategy for answering regarding vulnerable areas. Above all else, be truthful and answer the questions asked of you. Testimony may not always be pleasant,[11] but it is an integral part of modern courtroom procedures.

Review Questions

1. How is an expert different from a lay witness? What can an expert do?
2. What is jargon?
3. When were the Federal Rules of Evidence enacted?
4. What is a technique? Is it the same as a method?
5. What is the difference between criminal law and civil law? What needs do they serve in the criminal justice process?
6. Who or what is a complainant?
7. What is a grand jury? Is it different from a petit jury?
8. What does the Sixth Amendment of the Constitution of the United States provide?
9. What is discovery?
10. What is a deposition? Is it different from a trial? Explain.

Discussion Questions

1. Is the grand jury process necessary? Why or why not?
2. Why is the Sixth Amendment important to you as an expert?
3. Why is the discovery process necessary? Often, discovery is not reciprocal and the defense does not have to divulge all of its information. Why do you think this is so?

---

[11] Seventy-eight percent of the students in one of Houck's court testimony classes said they would rather have their hands slammed in a car door twice than have to testify again. The instructor was one of the highest rated by students in that program, so it is, in fact, a reflection on the testimonial process.

Methods, Testing, and Science

2

Key Terms

Falsifiability
Paradigms
Normal science
Scientific revolution
Hypotheses
Accreditation
American Society of Crime Laboratory Directors Laboratory Accreditation Board (ASCLD-LAB)
International Standards Organization (ISO)
American Board of Criminalistics (ABC)
ASTM, International
Certified reference material (CRM)
National Institute of Standards and Technology (NIST)

Introduction

Typically, a case begins with an event involving people, places, events, and objects. In most cases, you will become acquainted with those four fundamental elements. The combination of people, places, and things in a chance moment of time creates a crime, accident, injury, damage, or event (or absence of an event) that may precipitate the need for forensic services. The unique correlation of people, places, and things within a defined time frame constitutes the unusual element of almost every forensic case. Carl Jung referred to it as synchronicity. It is this incidental nature of the forensic realm that separates it from the nonforensic sciences, which generally call for well-thought-out, carefully planned experiments. Suppose you investigate a body found in a van. In the wheel wells and the tire treads of the van you find pieces of what appear to be soil. Upon further inspection, you identify the particles as bits of roofing tile. It is doubtful your laboratory has a prepared protocol for the analysis of roofing tiles.

What methods, then, are best applied? What standards exist? How do you source the tiles to the house or location they came from, manufacturer or production batch? Given the "incidental synchronicity," to coin a phrase, of forensic science, how do we know what to do in any given case?

Accreditation, Certification, and Standardization

Accreditation is the process by which a laboratory establishes a baseline of minimum safeguards showing its services are offered with a certain degree of quality, integrity, and assurance that consistent procedures are applied in each case. The accreditation process is extensive, rigorous, and demanding for the laboratory that undertakes it. The laboratory and its staff first undergo a comprehensive self-study and evaluation with a long checklist of requirements. Once the laboratory implements the procedures called for on the checklist, it then applies for accreditation. The accrediting agency sends out a team to perform an on-site evaluation by trained members of the accrediting body. If the laboratory passes evaluation, it becomes accredited. Accreditation is maintained through periodic review, both internal and external.

It is important to remember that accreditation says nothing about the competence of the individual forensic scientists who work at the laboratory. Being accredited means the laboratory meets certain minimum criteria for the facilities, security, training, equipment, quality assurance and control, and other essentials.

Certification is a voluntary process of peer review by which a practitioner is recognized as having attained the professional qualifications necessary to practice in one or more disciplines of forensic science. In most jurisdictions, certification of individual analysts is not required at this time.

The American Board of Criminalistics is one entity that offers certification and specialty certifications in forensic biology, drug chemistry, fire debris analysis, and trace evidence. Other entities or professional agencies offer certification for their sciences, such as the American Society of Forensic Questioned Document Examiners, the International Association of Identification, and the Society of Forensic Toxicologists.

Standardization plays a major role in helping laboratories become accredited. "Standard" is a word that has at least two very different meanings in forensic science. A standard can take two forms. It can be a written standard, which is like a very specific recipe, that has to be followed exactly to get a result considered acceptable. The ASTM, International (American Society for Testing and Materials, International) has long published standards for a wide variety of sciences, including forensic science (in Volume 14.02). These standards are written by groups of experts in the field who come to agreement on the acceptable way to perform a certain analysis. More recently, the Organization of Scientific Area Committee for Forensic Science (OSAC) has established a registry for forensic science standards for forensic science disciplines.

A standard can also be a physical thing, such as a sample of pure copper. Physical standards like this are called reference materials because scientists refer to them when analyzing other samples—if a specimen is 99.999 percent pure copper, then its properties are known exactly, as is how it ought to react in an experiment. If the reference material has been tested extensively by many methods, it can be issued as a certified reference material (CRM). CRMs come with certificates guaranteeing their purity or quality. The National Institute of Standards and Technology (NIST) is the main agency of the U.S. government that issues CRMs.

What Is Science?

One of the most important people in the history of science was a lawyer. Sir Francis Bacon, who rose to be Lord Chancellor of England during the reign of King James I, wrote the book *Novum Organum*. In it, Bacon details his theory of the scientific method: the scientist should be a disinterested observer of the world with a clear, unbiased mind free from preconceptions that might influence his or her understanding. With sufficient observations, patterns will emerge out of the data and the scientist can make specific statements as well as generalizations about nature. This may sound straightforward, but attempts to apply this method establish its shortcomings. No serious scientific thinker or philosopher, nor your average lay person, accepts Bacon's theory that science works through the collection of unbiased observations. Everything about the way people do science—the words, the instrumentation, the procedures—is framed by preconceived ideas and our experience about how the world works. It is impossible to make observations about the world without knowing what is and is not worth observing. People are constantly filtering their new experiences and observations through those things they have already experienced. Complete objectivity is impossible.

With that understanding, Sir Karl Popper, a noted philosopher, proposed that all science begins under a prejudice, a theory, a hypothesis—in short, an idea from a specific viewpoint. Popper worked from the premise that a theory can never be proved by agreement with observation—you do not know if the next observation will support or refute it—but it can be proved wrong by disagreement. This asymmetric nature of science makes it unique among ways of knowing about the world: good ideas can be proven wrong to make way for even better ideas. Popper called this aspect of science "falsifiability," the idea that a statement must be able to be proven false if it is to be considered scientific. Popper's view of constant testing to disprove statements biased by the preconceived notions of scientists replaced Bacon's view of the disinterested observer.

Science is a complex endeavor, and Popper's ideas do not completely describe science any more than Bacon's did. While it may be impossible to prove a theory true, it is almost as difficult to prove one absolutely false by Popper's methods. The trouble lies in distilling a falsifiable statement from a theory; additional assumptions that are not covered by the idea or theory itself must always be made. If the statement is shown to be false, we may not know if it was one of the basic assumptions, additional assumptions, or the theory itself that is at fault. This confounds the issue and clouds what the scientist thinks he or she has discovered.

Defining science is not a simple matter. It takes a great deal of hard work to develop a new theory that agrees with the entirety of what is already known in any area of science. Popper's falsifiability, scientists attacking a theory at its weakest point to bring it down, is simply not the way people explore the world.

Thomas Kuhn, a physicist by education and training who later became a historian and philosopher of science, offered a new way of thinking about science. Kuhn wrote that science involves paradigms, consensual understandings of how the world works. Within a given paradigm, scientists add information, ideas, and methods that steadily accumulate and reinforce their understanding of the world. This Kuhn calls normal science. With time, contradictions and observations that are difficult to explain under the current paradigm are encountered. These difficulties are set aside as oddities or anomalies so as not to endanger the status quo of the paradigm. Eventually, enough of these difficulties accumulate and the paradigm can no longer be supported. When this happens, Kuhn maintains, a scientific revolution ensues that dismantles the old paradigm and replaces it with a new paradigm. The shift from Newtonian to Einsteinian physics is a good example of such a revolution.

Kuhn's main point is that while the central issues of theories are tested— and some are falsified—the daily business of science is not to overturn its central concepts. If a theory makes novel and unexpected predictions, and those predictions are verified by experiments that reveal new and useful or interesting phenomena, then the chances that the theory is correct are greatly enhanced. However, science does undergo startling changes of perspective that lead to new and, invariably, better ways of understanding the world. Thus, science does not proceed smoothly and incrementally, but it is one of the few areas of human endeavor that is truly progressive. Falsifiability is not the only criterion for what science is. The scientific debate is very different from what happens in a court of law, but just as in the law, it is crucial that every idea receive the most vigorous possible advocacy, just in case it might be right.

In the language of science, the particular questions to be tested are called hypotheses. Suppose hairs are found on the bed where a victim has been sexually assaulted. Are the hairs those of the victim, the suspect, or someone else? The hypothesis could be framed as, "A significant difference exists between the questioned hairs and the known hairs from the suspect." Notice that the hypothesis is formed as a neutral statement that can be either proved or disproved. After the hypothesis has been stated, the forensic scientist seeks to collect data that sheds light on the hypothesis. Known hairs from the suspect are compared with those from the scene, the victim, and others who are known to have reasonably potentially left hairs at the scene. All relevant data will be collected without regard to whether it favors the hypothesis. Once collected, the data will be carefully examined to determine what value it has in proving or disproving the hypothesis; this is its probative value. If the questioned hairs are analytically indistinguishable from the known hairs, then the hypothesis is rejected. The scientist could then conclude that the questioned hairs could have come from the suspect.

But suppose that most of the data suggests that the suspect is the one that left the hairs there, but there is not enough data to associate the hairs with him. It cannot be said that the hypothesis has been disproved (there are some similarities), but neither can it be said that it has been proved (some differences exist, but are they significant?). Although it would be beneficial to prove unequivocally that someone is or is not the source of evidence (and this cannot be stressed enough), not all evidence can be individualized. The important thing to note here is that evidence analysis proceeds by forming many hypotheses and perhaps rejecting some as the investigation progresses.

Formulating a Working Hypothesis

After investigation and testing have yielded findings, the next step is to formulate a working hypothesis. The following hypothetical case shows how this might be done by the lawyers.

Suppose the prosecution's hypothesis is that the defendant, charged with burglary, was the perpetrator of the burglary. The prosecution further hypothesizes the defendant is the seller of the stolen goods taken during the burglary, to the state's prime prosecution witness. The state's forensic fiber expert was able to analyze and establish that fibers analytically indistinguishable from known fibers from the stolen materials were in both the defendant's van and his home closet. This evidence strongly supported the prosecution's hypothesis the defendant at some time was in possession of the stolen materials. But does it speak at all to whether the defendant committed the burglary and theft of the goods originally?

The defense's hypothesis was that the defendant was not the perpetrator, but offered no exculpatory evidence. Do the fibers alone negate the defense hypothesis? No. However, in the American justice system, the defendant has no obligation to prove anything. Rather, the burden of proof is entirely on the state.

Thus, the question becomes, how significant are the fibers? What if the defense presents evidence there was no burglary, but rather, the defendant purchased the items from the owner, who later claimed, falsely, to have been burgled? What if the defendant provides a legitimate bill of sale for the purchase of similar, not stolen items?

The hypotheses of the lawyers may change, but, in this example, the hypothesis of the scientist remains constant. The theories of the prosecution and defense have no bearing on the analysis of the fibers themselves. At the end of the day, the jury, as the trier of fact, determines the relevance of any given piece of evidence.

Use of a Standard Protocol

One essential investigating device is the standard protocol, where one exists. Comparison of that standard to your facts may reveal significant oversights or discrepancies. Many scientific, technical, and professional tasks are the subject of standard protocols. Your task as an investigating forensic witness is to locate that standard protocol and examine the case against it. Your conclusion may be that standard procedures were followed. Or you may determine that important steps were omitted. This can provide valuable information about the reliability and reproducibility of the results of the examination.

Additionally, failure to follow a protocol raises questions about potential civil or criminal culpability, depending on the facts and circumstances of a given case. Accredited forensic laboratories are required to have written protocols for the analyses they conduct, either ones they have written themselves or ones they have adopted from standards agencies, such as ASTM or ISO. Of course, these written protocols are only of value if they are followed. When deviations from the protocol occur, this should be documented completely, including why the protocol was deviated from, how the protocol was deviated from, and so on.

Published Method

Scientific literature is a peer-reviewed source of information, methods, and results. When faced with questions on analysis or with particular samples, it is important for a scientist to review the literature on that topic. The scientific literature includes:

- Professional and technical journals
- Dissertations
- Commercial literature
- Manufacturers' product bulletins
- External validation studies

- Relevant test procedures
- Internal validation studies
- Other experimental studies

The expert's own files, including lecture notes, laboratory tests, reports prepared in prior forensic cases, prior depositions in similar cases, and prior testimony may also be useful. The literature survey will vary in each case, however, depending on the field and the specific case. Your own library of reports, surveys, articles, lecture notes, and testimony transcripts should be studied in preparation for testimony.

Toward Admissibility

To increase the probability that your tests, experiments, demonstrations, and models will be admissible, follow the below steps:

- Be thoroughly familiar with the facts of the case. (Note: This is not a reference to the "case" in the civil or criminal justice system. This is a reference to the scientist's "case" in the laboratory.)
- Have accurate measurements available.
- Be familiar with the progression of events that occurred in the laboratory, including decisions made regarding order of testing, the type and nature of testing performed, and so on.
- Use the same materials that were involved in the event under study.
- Meticulously track your tests or experimental steps.
- Record the tests or experimental events carefully.
- Make your demonstrations substantially similar to the actual events at issue.
- Make your models to precise scale.
- Detail all findings, both positive and negative.
- Where no protocol exists, do sufficient research and consultation with peers and supervisors to establish that the test or experimental procedure is scientifically and technically recognized as authoritative.
- When preparing an exhibit, consult with counsel, where appropriate, to ensure the best posture for tendered admissibility.

Be aware all decisions made, to test or not to test, to test in one way instead of another, and so on are subject to questioning by the lawyers. Consequently, your decisions about testing should be well documented.

Destructive testing raises additional challenges because of the risk entailed in destruction of real evidence. Every effort must be made to be conservative of evidence—each item is unique and irreplaceable. Nondestructive testing options should be exhausted before any evidence is consumed in analysis. This is not just a nice idea but an ethical imperative. In addition, depending on the jurisdiction and the posture of the case, destructive testing without permission from the prosecution, defense, or court could result in a determination that test results are inadmissible. The analyst or the lab may also be subject to sanctions for such destructive testing without permission. Consequently, it is critical that each analyst be familiar with current lab policy about destructive testing.

Test results may determine the outcome of a case. Unless the test or demonstration is adequately founded, there may be serious problems concerning admissibility. Always take careful steps to ensure adequate foundation for tests, demonstrations, or models by following generally accepted scientific methods and the protocols in place within the laboratory, documenting each step of the procedure and limiting conclusions to those supported by science. A passing understanding of the rules of evidence also helps the expert prepare scientific, technical, and professional testimony. (Cautionary note: The writers of fictional television have about as much legal education as your average forensic scientist. A scientist should not rely on the same for knowledge of the rules of evidence.)

Conclusion

Investigation is the process by which one gathers the data on which one's opinions and reports will be based. Many ideas and lists can be used to make the process more efficient. Plan your work and work your plan. Learn from others, review the literature, and conduct tests and research to verify that methods work. As you gather the facts, give consideration to graphic displays that will help you later present the material in an understandable and effective way. Constantly strive to translate your findings into nontechnical layperson language. The most complete casework will be of little importance if the result cannot be relayed in a clear, effective, and understandable way.

Review Questions

1. What is falsifiability?
2. What is a paradigm?
3. What is normal science?
4. What is a scientific revolution?
5. What is a hypothesis?
6. What is accreditation?

7. What is ASTM, International?
8. What is a certified reference material?

Discussion Questions

1. Describe the roles of ASTM, ISO, laboratory accreditation, and NIST. How do they matter to you as an expert who testifies?
2. Why is it important to be able to define science? How would you define it?
3. What is the importance of considering hypotheses other than the one(s) presented to you?

The Players

3

Key Terms

Bench trial
Circuit court
Competence
Contempt of court
Defense attorney
District court
Judge
Juror
Jury
Jury trial
Justices of the peace
Mistrial
Narratives
Paradigm shift
Prosecutor
Public defender
Rhetoric
Small claims court
Supreme Court of the United States
U.S. Court of Appeals
U.S. District Court
Voir dire

Introduction

Court proceedings are not a frivolous matter. After all, peoples' lives and livelihoods are at stake. In civil court, typically it is money that is at stake. In criminal court, it is liberty, including both potential jail or prison time, as well as supervision on probation or parole, that is at stake.

Despite these high stakes, it may seem, however, that some participants, particularly the attorneys, enjoy "the challenge of the hunt." As an expert witness, it can be daunting to have attorneys wax rhetorical while you are required to "just answer the question." Additionally, as lawyers are not, as a general rule, scientifically trained, difficulty may lie in the inartful presentation of lawyers' questions. A trial is not a game, but gamesmanship, including skill, strategy, and long-term planning, is involved. Those who might think it a game do not understand the roles the participants must play, and that includes themselves.

This chapter discusses the roles of those professionals involved in the trial process: the attorneys, the judge, the jury, and, finally, the expert.

The Attorney's Role

Attorneys in the U.S. justice system are advocates, relics of the champions of jousting fields of the past. As such, their duty is to put forward a set of facts and proofs that support their position—in short, a narrative. Occasionally, zeal for the cause may shade professional and intellectual independence. As a starting point, it is not improper for the advocate to give you a wish list stating the most desirable conclusions from the attorney's viewpoint. This does not mean, however, that you must support that view. In fact, wish list aside, your scientifically based conclusions will inform the attorney of the actual (rather than desired) state of affairs. Your integrity, reputation, and personal and professional self-esteem, in addition to the prohibitions against perjury, require that the conclusions you reach and opinions you espouse be supportable based on the available body of facts and operative knowledge. Follow the scientific method regardless of the path it forces you to take. Experts' findings assist the attorney first in evaluating the strength or weakness of their case. Even where an expert isn't called to testify at trial, or the case doesn't go to trial, the expert plays a valuable role.

The role of the attorney is to represent his or her client, be it the People or a person. A prosecutor's goal in trial is to seek justice. A defense attorney's goal in trial is to vigorously defend the constitutional rights of the defendant. A lawyer does this by creating narratives, verbal accounts of events intended to prove or disprove a certain point—what Welsh has called a "strong representation."[1] The arguments of the attorneys are not, in themselves, evidence. Rather, the arguments presented to the jury are offered as a guide to the jury. Jurors are called on to rely on their own recollection of the witnesses' testimony in coming to their decision. Attorneys, when arguing their client's case, "subordinate the facts to a conclusion that makes a difference," and that conclusion "purports to review all the facts…because, in the opinion of the person making the representation, the facts when considered rightly all point in one direction." An adversarial position is presupposed in this view in that

---

[1] Welsh, A. *Strong Representations: Narrative and Circumstantial Evidence in England* (Baltimore: Johns Hopkins University Press, 1992).

one must take a stance to argue a particular point: either the defendant is or is not guilty of the crime of which he or she is accused. Legal narratives are often complex and specific. Defenses can include, but are not limited to:

- The defendant didn't commit the crime.
- No crime was committed.
- The defendant committed the crime but has a defense such as self defense, defense of others; prevention of a felony; mental illness; entrapment; and so on.

The activities in question in a legal case are often unseen by unbiased viewers. In eighteenth-century England, the diminishing respect for personal testimony (people do lie, after all) and the growing use of circumstantial evidence[2] led to the predominance of the attorney as representational narrator. "Objective" physical evidence—in conjunction with the enhanced respect of scientists as a professional class—became the new weapon of the trial lawyer. Ironically, the evidence became almost as important as the trial itself. The narratives became more complex, requiring explanation of the myriad facts and interpretations of those facts involved in the expert evidence. The accused was no longer capable of defending him- or herself:

> People need not go about telling their stories and hoping for the best; instead, the stories should be managed with a careful view to the consequences. This management obviously takes ability and experience and, above all, hard work and therefore can best be left to professionals—and a professional representation is thought to be an impressive performance in it own right.[3]

It is not a game, but it is a presentation of selected facts intended to prove or disprove an assertion, and it is best left to someone skilled in that art: the attorney.

When people criticize attorneys for being "shifty" or "liars," they miss the point of what attorneys are supposed to do: provide arguments for or against a particular proposition. Arguments are rhetoric—the art or technique of persuasion, usually in public or legal settings—and it is the method of the lawyer; words are their weapons, grammar their tactics, and arguments their strategy. If you were accused of a crime you did not commit or were a victim of a crime, you would want an attorney who presents the strongest possible case in your favor. The rules of the courtroom are different from those in the law or the laboratory. Scientists will often complain that lawyers will

---

[2] Evidence based on inference and not on personal knowledge or observation. Thus, all physical evidence is "circumstantial evidence," which means it is not weak or a lesser form of evidence.

[3] Welsh, A. *Strong Representations: Narrative and Circumstantial Evidence in England* (Baltimore: Johns Hopkins University Press, 1992), page 9.

"bend the facts" to suit their needs, ignoring the essential difference between lawyers and scientists: lawyers use facts rhetorically as building blocks in an argument; scientists use facts objectively as verifiable observations. Crossing those boundaries carries a price: one commentator has suggested the central flaw in Microsoft's antimonopoly legal strategy was that it handled the case like an engineer would have and it cost them.[4]

In the United States, in most states, lawyers are required to complete a college degree as well as attend and complete law school, which typically is an additional three years of study. Upon completion of the requisite education, in most states and under most circumstances, people must also pass a bar exam before becoming licensed to practice law. Criminal prosecutors are employed by the city, county, district, state, or federal government. While prosecutors may be employed either full or part time, while engaged in prosecution, they act on behalf of the government that employs them.

Criminal defense attorneys work on behalf of people charged with, or being investigated for, crimes. They may work for a law firm, they may be self-employed, or they may work as a public defender. Public defenders represent people who cannot otherwise afford an attorney. Public defense systems vary from state to state, and sometimes even within a given state. In some states, public defenders are state employees. In other states, each county operates an independent system of public defense. In still other states, courts appoint lawyers to represent indigent clients on a state-by-state basis. The public defense system exists because the right to counsel is a constitutional guarantee under the Sixth Amendment. In *Gideon v. Wainwright*, the Supreme Court of the United States clarified court-appointed counsel is covered by the Sixth Amendment for defendants who are "indigent," or cannot afford to hire their own counsel. Regardless of whether the defense attorney is paid by the client, the client's parents, or the government, the defense attorney works on behalf of the client.

The Courts

The courts constitute the judicial branch of government. There are several different types of trial courts. U.S. district courts are the general trial courts of the U.S. federal court system. Both civil and criminal cases are filed in district court. Each federal judicial district has at least one courthouse, if not more. The formal name is "the United States District Court for [name of the district]," for example, "the United States District Court for the Central District of California" (see Figure 3.1). The U.S. courts of appeals (also called

---

[4] Garfield, M. "*New Yorker* author analyzes Microsoft 'Trial of the Century,'" *Davidson News & Events*, January 22, 2001, page 1.

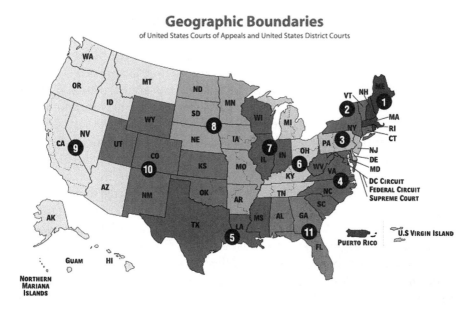

Figure 3.1 The district courts of the United States.

circuit courts) are the intermediate appellate courts in the federal system, which are required to hear all appeals from the district courts within their federal judicial circuit. In state court systems, there is usually a similar system of intermediate appeals and a high court for the state. The U.S. circuit courts were U.S. federal courts established in each federal judicial district. These circuit courts exercised both original and appellate jurisdiction from 1789 to 1912. The original jurisdiction of the U.S. circuit courts is now exercised by the U.S. district courts, and their appellate jurisdiction is now exercised by the U.S. courts of appeals. The "circuit courts" were officially known as United States circuit courts of appeals from 1894, until their name was changed to United States courts of appeals in 1947. The term "circuit" refers to earlier times when a judge and several attorneys would ride on horseback through a jurisdiction (making a circuit), hearing cases at multiple locations.

The Supreme Court of the United States is the highest judicial body in the United States and is the only part of the judicial branch made explicit in the U.S. Constitution. It has the highest appellate authority among both the state and federal courts Congress may create—it is often referred to as the court of last resort. The court consists of nine justices nominated by the president and confirmed by the Senate.

Most forensic scientists who work for local or state jurisdictions will testify in a state court, which has jurisdiction over disputes with some connection to a state. The overwhelming majority of cases are heard in state courts. Cases are heard and evidence is presented at a trial in a courthouse typically in the county seat. A decision in a state court may be appealed (except for an acquittal in a criminal trial due to the Fifth Amendment protection against double jeopardy), and that decision will be reviewed by a state court of appeals. A state Supreme Court will sometimes hear appeals by those still unsatisfied. If this sounds vaguely similar to the federal system, you are correct, but do not make the mistake of thinking the state courts are subordinate to the federal courts. State courts operate in a parallel way to federal courts and hold dominance in the arena of interpreting state laws. States also vary in their court structure and process. While Indiana has 177 superior courts, 90 circuit courts, 5 courts of appeals, and a supreme court, West Virginia has 31 circuit courts and a supreme court of appeals. Other states have no circuit courts, but rather refer to them as district courts. Experts are not expected to understand the varying intricacies of district versus circuit versus superior courts. They are, however, expected to arrive at the proper courthouse for testimony.

Criminal charges brought against a person fall into one of three main categories: infractions (sometimes referred to as petty misdemeanors, depending on the jurisdiction), misdemeanors, and felonies. Infractions are the least serious crimes and include offenses like parking or speeding tickets and building code violations. Infractions typically are punishable with a fine. Misdemeanors are more serious than infractions and include violations such as petty theft, prostitution, vandalism, and trespassing. Conviction of a misdemeanor may involve jail time, as well as probation; classes, such as theft prevention classes, where appropriate; community service; and a fine. The most serious crimes, felonies, include assault, arson, burglary, robbery, murder, rape, and fraud. Some states classify felonies according to their seriousness, and the state's legislature typically determines the maximum punishment allowable for each felony. Imprisonment, for more than a year in some states, or death can be punishments for felonies. Felons often face other sanctions, such as loss of voting rights (suffrage) and exclusion from certain kinds of jobs, ownership of firearms, and public office. Certain felons may also be required to register for some period of time, based on their offense. Finally, depending on the laws of the state, persons arrested for or convicted of crimes may be subject to the collection of DNA samples, to be profiled and placed in the appropriate state or local database.

The Judge's Role

Judges are the leaders of the judiciary branch of government. Judges are to be impartial and not influenced by outside factors, such as political power, money, or fame. Judges are appointed or elected from among practicing attorneys. In rural areas, some states permit nonlawyers to serve as justices of the peace (judicial officers with limited authority, who preside over misdemeanors, traffic violations, etc.) or act as judges in small claims court (courts that hear private disputes where small amounts of money, typically $2500 or less, are at stake). After election or appointment, judges usually receive additional training.[5] Many are expected to attend regular judicial education and instruction sessions.

In their courtroom, the judge is the absolute authority. Phrases such as "If it please the court" and "Your Honor, may I approach the bench?" are not mere formalities—the request is conducted at the discretion of the judge. When a witness is finished testifying, he or she does not leave until the judge excuses him or her. A judge is addressed in writing as "The Honorable Jane Doe" or "Hon. Jane Doe," and in speech as "Judge" or "Judge Doe," or, when presiding in court, "Your Honor."

In the U.S. legal system, in a jury trial, the jury decides questions of fact (guilt or innocence, for example), while the judge decides questions of law. Bench trials in the United States have a single judge who decides issues of both law and fact. Appeals are usually decided by a panel of judges.

One of the powers judges have is the power to punish any misconduct that takes place in the courtroom with a fine, imprisonment, or both. This is called contempt of court. The judge may also punish violations of the court's orders after a hearing when they take place outside the courtroom. An expert witness who gets out of line by refusing to answer questions or does not appear in court when summoned may face contempt of court charges. Additionally, it is quite common for judges to grant motions requesting the witnesses not discuss the case prior to their testimony. An expert who discusses the case with a fellow analyst or another witness risks a finding of contempt. Such conduct could also result in a mistrial.

The appeals process is the first line of defense for judicial oversight. Judges are people, after all, and judicial oversight is provided for cases where, apart from technical matters of the law, the judge may have exceeded or abused his or her authority or was just plain wrong in his or her legal analysis. If the aggrieved does not feel satisfied with the result, he or she would then go to the state supreme court, if the state supreme court is willing to hear the case. Finally, in matters of national consequence or involving federal protections, a party may request a hearing before the Supreme Court of the United States (which rules on whether it will hear a particular case).

The Jury's Role

A jury consists of 6 or 12 citizens who have been sworn to reach an impartial verdict in the case before the court. A person serving on a jury is a juror.

---

[5] For example, the Federal Judicial Center offers training and resources to judges at www. fjc.gov.

Juries determine guilt and innocence and, in some instances, may render sentencing decisions. Those eligible to serve on a jury may never make it to trial; a vetting process, called voir dire,[6] enables the trial lawyers to ask questions of potential jurors to determine if they are biased about issues involved in the case, whether they have prior commitments that may prevent them from serving on a given case, or other legal considerations that may prevent service.

If a jury cannot reach a verdict in a sufficient amount of time (although no limit is set), a mistrial (cancellation of a trial prior to a verdict) may be declared. Depending on the basis of the mistrial, the defendant may or may not be tried a second time. The concept of a jury dates to the Magna Carta (1215), which provided English nobles and freemen the right to a trial by a panel of their peers, rather than solely on the decision of a king or other royalty.

Expert's Role

The definition of an expert was provided previously: someone who has specialized knowledge, skills, and education in an area of relevance to the trier of fact. The influence of the forensic expert in our lives today, helping shape not only future decisions but resolving present controversies over past events, assumes unusually vital proportions. But there are some philosophic impediments the forensic witness must overcome before becoming truly effective.

- If forensic investigation suggests a result scientifically, technically, or factually irrefutable, why all the hassle? Why can't we experts gather around the table and resolve the dispute in a spirit of collegiality and fraternity?
- Why must I as an expert be subjected to rigorous cross-examination when the facts are so clear? After all, I am an expert, I have studied the facts, and I am educated and trained in this area.
- How can there be an expert witness who studies the same facts and reaches a conclusion contrary to mine? The other expert must have had his opinion imposed upon him by opposing counsel.
- How can the attorney ask me to come to a specific conclusion in advance of my analysis? I refuse to have my profession insulted or my integrity challenged by an attorney who makes such a quantum leap.

These four misconceptions lie at the root of most fundamental misunderstandings between forensic witnesses and attorneys. It is in the

---

[6] The phrase "voir dire" comes from the Old French for "speak the truth."

very natures of the legal and scientific professions to be at odds, and a great deal of effort by both groups is required for a suitable and accurate outcome. The human aspect of being a scientist or an attorney cannot be forgotten. As Fourth Circuit Court Judge Russell Clawges has said, "If science were completely objective, we wouldn't need the experts."

Example of the Role of Scientist

The identification of human blood is an excellent parable of the way science may be (mis)applied in the courts. In the late 1800s, given a positive test for blood, many defense attorneys would simply argue that it was animal blood and offer a feasible alibi. At the time, few scientists thought that a test for human blood was possible, let alone reliable enough to send a person to jail or prison. Debate about tests for human blood had raged in forensic and pathology circles for nearly 50 years prior. This debate, and its effect on science in the courts, is instructive, as it offers an example of the role of science and its practitioners in the courts.

In 1877, it was well known that the size and shape of red blood cells ("red corpuscles" or erythrocytes) varied by species. Reptiles, birds, fish, and camels have oval erythrocytes, while mammals—except camels—have circular ones. Mammals' erythrocytes, including camels', are non-nucleated, meaning they do not have a membrane-bound subcellular compartment that contains the cell's chromosomes, among other things. Thus, it is a relatively easy matter to use a microscope and determine if a fresh blood sample is mammalian or not (Figure 3.2). The method espoused by many forensic specialists in the late 1880s was to measure the erythrocytes from a fresh sample and, based on an average diameter falling within a known range of variation, determine human from nonhuman blood.

Forensic samples, however, are rarely fresh. Erythrocytes are fragile and susceptible to damage from environmental changes; too wet and they pop, too dry and they shrivel. This made accurate measurement of the erythrocytes nearly impossible. No standard method existed, either. Instead, each expert had his own technique for performing the method. Microscopy at the time was becoming a discipline per se, and most microscopists, as we would now call them, hailed from many different disciplines. Therefore, they were reluctant to gather under the banner of one leader, resolve their differences, and standardize the method. Arguments, some personal, abounded at professional society meetings and in the academic journals. The issue culminated in the Hayden trial of 1879, with two experts hotly contesting the veracity of each other's testimony and intentions. The affair was accurately summed up by the *New York Times*:

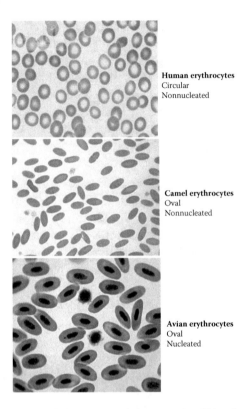

Human erythrocytes
Circular
Nonnucleated

Camel erythrocytes
Oval
Nonnucleated

Avian erythrocytes
Oval
Nucleated

Figure 3.2 Reptiles, birds, fish, and camels have oval red blood cells (erythrocytes), while mammals—except camels—have circular ones. Mammals' erythrocytes, including camels, are non-nucleated, meaning they do not have a membrane-bound subcellular compartment that contains the cell's chromosomes, among other things. It is a relatively easy matter to use a microscope and determine if a fresh blood sample is mammalian or not.

> It is not necessary to impute dishonesty or mercenary motives to the eminent experts in medicine or other branches of science, whose disagreements put the minds of jurymen in a maze, instead of leading them into the light. But there are experts and experts, there are theories and theories, and there are even facts and facts, in every department of science or special knowledge, and lawyers can ingeniously make their selection, giving prominence to some and keeping others out of sight, and twisting and turning until the inexpert mind in the jury box is in danger of losing all faith in science as a witness.[7]

The camps were divided between the microscopists who thought the test faulty or limited and the microscopists who felt it was better to offer some science to the courts. Ultimately, the scientists all agreed upon the facts about human and nonhuman erythrocytes—some mammals could be distinguished by their size

[7] *New York Times*, December 28, 1879, page 6; as quoted in Golan (2004), page 164.

and shape—but not about the meaning of those facts—what we would now call interpretation. Each microscopist saw the same types of samples but prepared them differently, measured them differently, and interpreted their significance differently. Despite this variance, measuring erythrocytes was held to be the premier forensic method for determining human blood until Paul Uhlenhuth's application of antisera to blood identification in 1901. Known as the serological test, it quickly replaced microscopic measurement in forensic science.

The points to remember from this historical example are numerous and important. First, scientific facts are open to interpretation; one set of facts may lead to a variety of conclusions. This variety of conclusions is resolved for scientists in laboratories, professional meetings, discussions, and academic journals. While it is true that experts involved in the same case might gather around a table and come to a consensus conclusion, they also might not. No consensus was achieved in the erythrocyte test. Rather, a completely new test trumped it. If agreement was not achieved after a decade or more of debate and publications, why would it happen in one particular trial? The perceived collegiality and fraternity of academia only goes so far. Scientists are human, and conflicts over scientific findings may persist for tens or hundreds of years.[8] Suspicion of influence by the attorney, or "scientific prostitution" by a greedy expert, need not be the cause of disparate findings.

Another point of interest to scientists is the supplanting of the erythrocyte test by the serological test; this could be seen as a minor example of what Thomas Kuhn calls a paradigm shift. Kuhn's concept was that science does not progress linearly, constantly accumulating new data and knowledge. Periodic revolutions—paradigm shifts—suddenly change the nature of scientific inquiry within a field. One of Kuhn's requirements is that the two theories are incommensurable (the understanding of one theory cannot be gained through a similar understanding of the other). The differences between the erythrocyte test and the serological test are not incommensurable (the size of the blood cell does not affect its antiseral properties), but you get the idea: the new test, because of its accuracy and precision, removed the old test from serious scientific consideration. Perhaps the shift was not a true revolution, but only a coup; nevertheless, it is easy to see how the same facts can be used honestly to render different conclusions.

These scientific debates are manifestly different than legal debates. The trial process, as messy and stressful as it may seem, has been considered the best means of arriving at a decision or resolution of conflict for hundreds of years. The mental obstacle of the question asked earlier, "Why must I as

---

[8] For example, thermal cooling (Kelvin vs. Darwin), the motions of stars (Kepler vs. Greeks), combustion (Priestly vs. Stahl), and the discovery of fingerprints (Faulds vs. Henry); note also that the conflict need not be personal, for example, the miasmatic theory of disease versus the germ theory.

an expert be subjected to rigorous cross-examination when the facts are so clear?" is easily resolved when it is understood that the trial is a legal process and the expert witness is only one small part of that process. The expert assists the trier of fact in interpreting evidence that is beyond the knowledge of the average citizen who is eligible to serve on a jury. Further, the prosecutor carries the burden of proving each and every element of a case beyond a reasonable doubt. If work performed or conclusions drawn by an expert establish or support the existence of an element of the offense, the prosecutor must offer these facts as proof. This proof comes in the form of testimony. Similarly, the defense attorney's job is to make sure the defendant's constitutional rights are protected. If the expert has evidence that calls into doubt an element of the prosecutor's case, they must also offer that evidence to the jury in the form of testimony. Cross-examination is one method of ensuring all the relevant facts and information are made available to the trier of fact. Cross-examination may focus on the limits of the science, the assumptions the scientist made, and the basis for the conclusions drawn. It may consist of attacks on the science, the method, or the scientists themselves. Cross-examination may focus on the relevance of the conclusions in light of various hypotheticals. Without knowing the attorney's theory of the case, it is difficult, if not impossible, to accurately guess the content of cross-examination ahead of time. Knowing cross-examination is part of a trial helps to keep scientists clear about their actions. "Research performed for the purpose of litigation may afford no opportunity for true peer review... cross-examination can perform this function and can in itself be an incentive to perform good, transparent science."[9] The old saying "Pride goes before a fall" is appropriate here: if you are prepared, honest, and humble, you have nothing to fear from a cross-examination.

This leads to the last main point to be taken from the erythrocyte test story: what is useful in a trial may not be—and almost always is not—useful in discovering and expanding scientific knowledge. Trials deal with a specific conflict, have to be concluded in a reasonable amount of time, and need to have a definitive conclusion. An attorney, arguing one version of events, presupposes certain facts that will be useful to him or her. Was the suspect absolutely at the crime scene? If not, how much information points to his or her presence there—a lot? A little? Enough? The attorney needs to know what facts can be used and to what degree they favor his or her argument. The expert needs to make sure that the attorney does so accurately to the limits of the theories, science, and methods employed.

---

[9] National Research Council, *The Age of Expert Testimony: Science in the Courtroom* (Washington, D.C.: National Academy Press, 2002), page 23.

Expert's Role in Court

It has been observed that jurors generally take to ordinary people, but they do not always like and trust experts. In other words, experts tend to depersonalize themselves through their methodology, vocabulary, or general demeanor. The end result is trial presentation by a robot-like creature who has become devoid of human attributes. The good news is that this situation is not inevitable. To be effective and credible, the expert witness must:

- Perform a thorough analysis
- Be personable, genuine, and natural
- Have an ability to teach
- Be generally competent
- Be believable
- Be able to persuade without advocacy
- Be prepared
- Be willing to weather controversy
- Demonstrate enthusiasm
- Listen to the questions presented
- Be willing to consider other alternatives, regardless of which attorney is asking the question or posing the hypothesis
- Admit when they are wrong

Without these qualities, the potential expert witness should not even contemplate stepping into the courtroom.

Thorough Analysis

As an expert, you should be aware that expert opinion testimony must be based on a reliable foundation and be relevant to the case at issue. You must be prepared to show that the professional, scientific, or technical premise on which you rely has a scientifically valid basis.

Ability to Teach

Testimony is an opportunity to teach. Think back to high school or college: recall a favorite instructor or coach. Recollect the qualities that made you want to learn more from that person. Visualize those attributes, and emulate that person. A good teacher-expert is:

- Well-informed and prepared in his or her subject matter
- Apt to use demonstrative aids to enhance understanding

- Not intimidating or pompous
- Ready to use an example or analogy
- Questioning and humble
- Honest about gaps in his or her knowledge or information
- Friendly, human, and has a sense of humor
- Able to communicate complicated subjects in lay terms

Competence

Demonstrated ability and competence in the subject field is a mandatory element of effective expert testimony. Competence is demonstrated by thorough knowledge in the field; appropriate experience or credentials, as demonstrated by publications and presentations, as well as competency and proficiency tests, where appropriate; a currency of information; an ability to perform as well as teach; and an ability to recognize problems, elect alternatives, and make good choices among them. Competence is the demonstrated ability to do something at the expected level of performance.

Believability

You have to believe to be believable. You are not merely a mirror of the position established for you by an attorney. You are presented with a problem, afforded the opportunity to investigate and evaluate the facts, and asked to reach a supportable conclusion. Your conclusion was reached independently and is based upon available data. You are believable because you understand your science and your methods, and can communicate those methods and science in a manner jurors can understand. This provides confidence in what you are saying. On the other hand, if the conclusion you espouse is not supported by the available data, or if you refuse to consider alternative hypotheses or fail to acknowledge subjective interpretation methods in your field, you will not demonstrate confidence and will not be believable. (Note: insisting on projecting confidence in the face of clearly contradictory facts does not advance juror confidence in your believability.)

Ability to Persuade

Do you remember the last time you changed your mind on any subject? What caused you to do that? Did you read a book, attend a lecture, watch a television program, or exchange ideas with persons who had more information than you? As human beings, we change our minds for various reasons. One of your objectives as an expert witness may be to persuade a fact finder of the reliability of a scientific, technical, or factual proposition.

Your task is to persuade without becoming an advocate, to convince without argument, and to encourage a conclusion based upon irrefutable data presented in an interesting way. Effective persuasion is subtle. A person is most strongly convinced if he or she can mentally develop the ultimate conclusion on his or her own rather than it being spoon-fed by the persuader.

Enthusiasm

Enthusiasm for the task at hand, the subject matter, and the conclusion can be demonstrated in many subtle ways. Facial expression and body language tell a great deal about the witness's enthusiasm for the subject. Tone of voice and inflection can suggest boredom or conviction. If you are not interested in what you do and have done, why should the jury be?

Conclusion

A general understanding may help alleviate some of your fears of the adversary system and our dispute resolution process. If the evidence in a particular case is subject to only one conclusion and is cast in terms of absolute proof, the matter will probably not proceed to trial or hearing, unless no reasonable offer has been made for the defendant to consider. It is often the case involving questionable evidence, doubtful outcome, or conflicting exhibits and testimony that requires adversarial presentation. That presentation and its ultimate objective, the justice process, will be aided immeasurably by your service as a forensic witness. As a reminder, justice is for the philosopher, truth is for the sage. However, it is a wise and practical society that endeavors to use the adversarial system and your expert testimony to assist the justice system.

Review Questions

1. What is the difference between a bench trial and a jury trial?
2. What is the difference between a trial court and an appellate court?
3. What could cause you to be in contempt of court? What are the consequences?
4. Which is the trier of fact: the judge or the jury? Explain.
5. Is a justice of the peace the same as a judge? Explain.
6. What is a mistrial?

7. A prosecutor works for _____, while a defense attorney works for _____.

8. Is rhetoric different from a narrative? Explain.

9. Place in the proper order, most local to most national: small claims court, Supreme Court of the United States, U.S. Court of Appeals, U.S. District Court.

10. What is voir dire?

Discussion Questions

1. Do scientists and attorneys both engage in narratives? If so, how are they different; if not, why not?

2. When asked if it would make him nervous to use an expert who would sell his opinion for the right price, an attorney responded, "It doesn't because you know what the son-of-a-bitch will say."[10] What does this say about the professional cultures of attorneys and scientists?

3. One participant, an attorney, in the National Research Council's workshop on expert testimony said, "Science can sometimes get it wrong.... Science is not always value-free, and most importantly... when lawyers accept the validity of an established scientific paradigm uncritically, they do risk making the same mistake as scientists." What do you think "the same mistakes" are? How can those mistakes be prevented or corrected?

---

[10] Prichard, F. *Experts in Civil Cases: An Inside View* (New York: LFB Scholarly Publishing, LLC, 2005), page 88.

The Legal Context

4

Key Terms

Deposition
Discovery
Exculpatory evidence
Federal Rules of Civil Procedure
Federal Rules of Evidence
Interrogatories
Privileged

Introduction

This chapter discusses some of the most important tools in the legal system's kit to ensure all parties have all and the same information. Discovery, depositions, and the Rules of Evidence (either Federal or state specific) are not only for attorneys—the well-prepared expert would do well to review these tools and understand what will be expected of him or her. Discovery, depositions, and the Rules of Evidence are both a sword and a shield.

Discovery

Discovery has been defined as "compulsory disclosure, at a party's request, of information that relates to the litigation."[1] Discovery can involve any material that is relevant to the case, excepting information that is privileged (protection for communications between certain parties, such as a client and attorney, that keeps them confidential), information that is the work product of the opposing party, or certain kinds of expert opinions. Under most rules of civil procedure, discovery tools include statements on oral or written questions, written interrogatories, production of tangible items, property, physical and mental examinations, and requests for admission.

---

[1] *Black's Law Dictionary* (St. Paul, MN: West Publishing, 2014), citing Fed. R. Civ. P. 26–37; Fed. R. Crim. P. 16.

In criminal cases, discovery includes material in information either in the possession of the prosecutor or in the control of the prosecutor. It may include police reports, witness statements, laboratory reports, the defendant's statement, charts, graphs, photographs, tangible objects such as items collected at a crime scene, and so on. How this information is obtained by the defense varies by jurisdiction. All prosecutors, however, are bound by the *Brady* decision of the Supreme Court of the United States. Prosecutors are bound to disclose exculpatory evidence, which is evidence that tends to negate the defendant's guilt. Withholding evidence "casts the prosecutor in the role of an architect of a proceeding that does not comport with standards of justice" (*Brady v. Maryland*, 373 U.S. 83, 88 [1963]). The facts in *Brady* involved a statement given to police that the police did not provide to the prosecution. Nonetheless, the Supreme Court held failure to disclose that evidence was a violation of the defendant's right to a fair trial. Experts, in particular experts who work for the government, should be mindful of the prosecution's obligation to disclose evidence to the defendant. Under no circumstances should an expert fail to disclose information to the attorney he or she is working with. It will be up to the lawyer, not the expert, to decide whether something is subject to discovery in any given case.

In layperson's terms, discovery is the sometimes laborious process you go through to learn the underlying facts surrounding a matter in dispute. Certain devices are available by rules of procedure or practice in the various jurisdictions to help uncover underlying facts. Some lawyers think that discovery is the key to really getting to the factual basis for litigation. Others consider discovery the bane of their existence and the weight that is driving the justice system to unfathomable depths. Regardless of an attorney's point of view about the process, the exchange of discovery allows attorneys the opportunity to evaluate the strengths and weaknesses of their case. This frequently leads to case resolution prior to trial.

All procedural rules must be liberally construed to secure just, speedy, and inexpensive dispute resolution.[2] The Federal Rules of Civil Procedure (Fed. R. Civ. P.) govern civil procedure in the U.S. district courts. The Fed. R. Civ. P. are promulgated by the U.S. Supreme Court and then approved by Congress. The federal courts use the Fed. R. Civ. P. as their rules of procedure in civil cases (where the dispute is typically over money). States, although they produce rules that apply in their own courts, have largely adopted rules that are based on the Federal Rules. In the Federal system, civil discovery is governed by Fed. R. Civ. P. Title V, "Depositions and Discovery," Rules 26–37 (see Table 4.1).

Discovery and inspection in federal criminal cases are generally governed by Federal Rules of Criminal Procedure (Fed. R. Crim. P.) 15 and 16. As with

---

[2] Federal Rules of Civil Procedure, Rule 1(a).

Table 4.1   Title V of the Federal Rules of Civil Procedure, Rules 26–37, That Govern Depositions and Discovery

V. Depositions and Discovery

Rule 26. Duty to Disclose; General Provisions Governing Discovery

Rule 27. Depositions to Perpetuate Testimony

Rule 28. Persons Before Whom Depositions May Be Taken

Rule 29. Stipulations about Discovery Procedure

Rule 30. Depositions by Oral Examination

Rule 31. Depositions by Written Questions

Rule 32. Using Depositions in Court Proceedings

Rule 33. Interrogatories to Parties

Rule 34. Producing Documents, Electronically Stored Information, and Tangible Things, or Entering onto Land, for Inspection and Other Purposes

Rule 35. Physical and Mental Examinations

Rule 36. Requests for Admission

Rule 37. Failure to Make Disclosures or to Cooperate in Discovery; Sanctions

the civil rules of procedure, the states have their own versions of the rules of criminal procedure. While many rules mirror the federal rules, each state's rules may vary in one way or another from the federal rules.

The idea behind the rules of discovery is best stated in the rules themselves. According to Rule 26 of the Fed. R. Civ. P.:

> 1. Scope in General. Unless otherwise limited by court order, the scope of discovery is as follows: Parties may obtain discovery regarding any nonprivileged matter that is relevant to any party's claim or defense and proportional to the needs of the case, considering the importance of the issues at stake in the action, the amount in controversy, the parties' relative access to relevant information, the parties' resources, the importance of the discovery in resolving the issues, and whether the burden or expense of the proposed discovery outweighs its likely benefit. Information within this scope of discovery need not be admissible in evidence to be discoverable.

The rules typically should be construed "to secure the just, speedy, and inexpensive determination of every action and proceeding."[3] Similarly, the Federal Rules of Criminal Procedure are designed "to be interpreted to provide for the just determination of every criminal proceeding, to secure simplicity in procedure and fairness in administration, and to eliminate unjustifiable expense and delay."[4]

---

[3] Federal Rules of Civil Procedure, Rule 1.
[4] Federal Rules of Criminal Procedure, Rule 2.

Discovery affects experts in two distinct ways. First, experts are an important source of information to support the case. Second, an expert's work, investigation, and opinion may be the subject of discovery effort by opposing counsel.

The Discovery Components

Under the federal rules of civil discovery that attend most court proceedings, the following general devices make up the discovery arsenal:

- Written interrogatories, or questions to an opposing party or witness
- Verbal deposition, or the informal process of taking sworn testimony from witnesses before trial
- Requests for production of documents; tangible things; entry onto land or other property to inspect, measure, survey, photograph, test, or sample the property or object
- Physical and mental examination of parties and examination of premises
- Requests for admission, designed to eliminate issues from trial

The rules of civil discovery differ from rules of criminal discovery. The constitutional guarantee against self-incrimination limits discovery from defendants in criminal cases. This is based on the Fifth Amendment to the Constitution, which holds that defendants in a criminal case cannot be forced to testify against themselves or give evidence against their own interest.

The Republic's founders were concerned about forced confessions, so much so that protection from self-incrimination is deeply ingrained in our criminal law practice. Because of the fear of forced self-incrimination, the prosecution in a criminal case has limited access to the files, records, documents, and projected testimony of a criminal defendant prior to trial.

Certain identifying items, such as DNA profiles, hair, urine, handwriting, breath, fingerprints, footprints, or voice exemplars, have been carved out as acceptable prosecution discovery products. Search warrants issued "upon probable cause" allow law enforcement access to the files, premises, and person of a criminal suspect or defendant.

Defendants are allowed to probe government files in preparation for trial. Both the Federal Rules of Criminal Procedure and state rules typically allow some discovery by defendants. For example, the government must disclose statements of the defendant, including, in some jurisdictions, the defendant's grand jury testimony, the defendant's prior criminal record, documents, other objects that are intended to be evidence at trial, and reports of examinations and tests, as well as a written summary of the anticipated testimony of expert witnesses.

The government does not have to disclose internal government documents, inspections, or reports in connection with an investigation or prosecution of criminal case, or statements made by government witnesses or prospective government witnesses, except as provided by detailed statutory exceptions.[5]

Under the Federal Rules of Criminal Procedure, a defendant must provide copies of documents that are intended to be used at trial if the defendant has asked for production from the government. The same is true for reports of examination and tests, provided the defendant intends to present that evidence at trial. Defense memos or documents created in connection with the investigation or defense of the case by the defendant, the defendant's attorney, or their agents, which include experts, need not be produced.

Under the Federal Rules and in some states, depositions may be taken if exceptional circumstances are shown and it is in the interests of justice. In other states, depositions are taken in criminal cases as a matter of course.

The rules of the relevant jurisdiction specify what objects the defendant may obtain under criminal procedure disclosure rules. While discovery rules vary by jurisdiction state to state, typically, the following are subject to discovery in criminal cases:

- Arrest reports
- Investigative reports
- Statements of witnesses
- Statements of the accused (whether written or oral)
- Grand jury transcripts (in some jurisdictions)
- Tangible evidence
- Results of physical, mental, and scientific tests
- Results of experiments or comparisons
- Books, papers, documents, photographs, or other tangible things that will be evidence in the case
- Access to buildings and relevant places
- Record of prior criminal convictions of the accused or co-defendant
- Tape and transcripts of electronic surveillance
- Electronic data

In addition, in some jurisdictions, the following materials may be produced only by court order (in other jurisdictions, no such order is required. In still other jurisdictions, some of the below is accessible only under certain, specific circumstances):

- Material in possession of other governmental agencies
- Defendant's expert reports or statements

[5] 18 U.S.C. 3500

- Physical or mental examination of defendant or other witnesses
- Scientific experiments or comparisons

Almost all rules of discovery, civil and criminal, make mandatory a continuing duty on the part of a responding party to update responses based on additional or newly discovered information. All discovery rules, both civil and criminal, typically have sanction provisions by which the court can enforce its orders and require compliance.

The Expert and the Discovery Process

The expert's initial attitude may be, "Well, discovery is nice for the attorneys and the litigants, but it doesn't have anything to do with me. I'm a scientist. I'll do my work and research the way I've always done it, without cumbersome rules of procedure that require continuous jumping through ever-diminishing hoops, and let the attorneys worry about discovery." However, the rules do indeed apply to experts. Because the rules vary from jurisdiction to jurisdiction, and because the rules are subject to change, an expert should never presume to understand the rules of discovery.

It is important to distinguish the discovery process from standard professional or technical information-gathering procedures. Scientists gather information based upon an organized plan of investigation and inquiry; their use of investigative protocols and procedures, case plans, and action plans creates a process for getting their work done. The steps followed to complete the investigation and/or testing enable the facts and information on which your expert opinion will be based to be collected in an orderly and logical way. Customary and routine testing, investigation, and consultation with others provide the needed facts.

Discovery, on the other hand, is structured and driven by the time deadlines imposed by court or procedural rules. Each item of discovery is undertaken in a set manner, with or without court intervention, by attorneys representing the parties. The discovery process is ultimately subject to supervision of the court. What discovery and standard expert investigation have in common is that, in each case, facts are gathered that ultimately will shape the expert's opinions and hence possibly the legal outcome.

Criminal Case

A unique burglary ring was discovered in a suburban community. The leader of the gang was a young mother of two. The woman was a cult leader who conducted bizarre rituals in the basement of her modest home. Actively working in the burglary operation for her under her direction and supervision were her husband, her husband's brother, and a societal dropout who had recently joined the group.

The focal point of the ritual activity of the group was a satin-lined casket, which was the first item they had stolen. Criminal charges against them included many counts of burglary. In addition, the three adults were charged with contributing to the delinquency of the fourth member of the ring, who was a minor. According to the investigative reports, the cult leader motivated her followers by dispensing drugs and sexual favors, sometimes in group settings.

Each defendant was tried separately from the others. An investigator criminalist engaged by counsel for the brother-in-law discovered the existence of statements in the prosecution's files from other defendants. Appropriate motions were made under the rules of criminal procedure to require the prosecutor to produce the statements for examination prior to trial.

The investigator also discovered that numerous items of stolen property were to be used as exhibits at the trial. Again, a motion made to the court required the prosecutor to allow the defense counsel to inspect the items before trial.

In addition, the client advised the investigator and counsel that all the accused persons had made statements to the investigating and arresting officers. Those statements had not been transcribed, although the investigator determined that one of the arresting officers had made extensive notes of conversations with the accused. The trial court granted a defense motion to reveal the officer's notes to defense counsel prior to trial.

On the prosecution side, a number of stolen items carried fingerprints that matched prints taken from various crime scenes. The police obtained a warrant to secure fingerprints from each to compare with those on the items of stolen property and at the crime scenes. Some of the items of stolen property had been recovered from a garage some distance from the cult leader's home. Police had taken custody of items in that garage without a search warrant and without any showing of probable cause. Appropriate motions were made, and the evidence was suppressed by court order following a hearing.

Civil Case

A number of years ago, a soldier at Fort Dix, New Jersey, became ill. His illness was tentatively diagnosed as swine flu. From that one case, never actually confirmed, the full power of the U.S. Public Health Service swung into action. The entire government was mobilized. Private contractors were authorized to manufacture millions of doses of swine flu vaccine. The government indemnified the manufacturers because vaccine testing procedures were abrogated due to the perceived threat to the public health.

There was some evidence that the government concluded it had no place to store the vaccine. It was determined to literally "warehouse" the vaccine in the bodies of the people of the United States rather than incur the expense of physical storage. Testing procedures had not yet been completed.

The press, radio, and television carried warnings of the dangers of swine flu and urged mass inoculation. The surgeon general of the United States made pleas. As a result, millions of persons were inoculated.

Then epidemiologists started to note cases of a disease called Guillain-Barré syndrome (GBS), a neurological impediment that had from mild to fatal effects on its victims. Not much was known about GBS except that it affected the central nervous system and resulted in paralysis or weakness of various parts of the body. The attacks were unpredictable, and treatment was not well established. Massive amounts of physical therapy and drugs were prescribed for the sufferers; some never recovered.

The victims of GBS were correlated with persons who had received the swine flu vaccine. It became obvious that the swine flu vaccine was the cause of the GBS outbreak. Tort litigation was commenced in many federal districts against the U.S. government and the vaccine manufacturers. The government admitted causal connection for a certain group of victims, and Congress passed a law making the government fully responsible for the claims and further indemnifying the drug manufacturers.

A multidistrict litigation panel of the federal court system was convened. Judge Gerhard Gesell of the U.S. District Court in Washington, D.C., was the supervising jurist of all swine flu vaccine cases. A claimants committee undertook a first wave of discovery against the drug manufacturers and the government. Many experts were engaged to track the relationship between the swine flu vaccine and the onset of GBS. National forensic experts worked closely with a plaintiff's steering committee to frame the discovery questions that were asked of the federal government and the drug manufacturers. Some discovery areas included:

- Diagnosis of swine flu
- Actual cases of swine flu
- Components of the swine flu vaccine
- Vaccine test procedures followed
- Test procedures that were known to be applicable, but were not used
- Warehousing by inoculation of the vaccine without adequate testing

A number of physicians, primarily neurologists, engaged by victims throughout the country further guided the discovery process against both the drug manufacturers and the federal government. After extensive research into the disease process as compared with the vaccine components, they testified as to epidemiologic information, time relationship between inoculation and symptom onset, uniform treatment procedures, morbidity, and available physical and drug therapy.

Depositions, interrogatory responses, and requests for production of documents, as generated by the attorneys and guided by experts, allowed many patients to reach significant settlements. In addition, some won substantial damages after trial.

The expert becomes involved in formal discovery in four ways: as a consultant who assists in generating questions for cross-examination, as an advisor in responding to the opposition's questions, as the person responding to written and verbal questions prior to trial, and, finally (perhaps most common), when attorneys request evidence to support their conclusions. Not all experts will actively participate in the discovery process. Typically, where an expert is acting as a consultant to one side or the other, to assist in formal discovery in a meaningful way, the expert must be:

- Professionally and technically competent
- Knowledgeable about the real world
- Conversant with current literature, practice, and procedure
- Familiar with the facts of the case
- Able to develop a working hypothesis
- Innovative in digging out information from the opposition
- Well schooled in the art of brevity
- Informed about the legal rules that govern the discovery process

Drafting written questions that the opposing party must answer fully and under oath, outlining areas of inquiry and constructing specific questions for use during deposition of the opposing witnesses or experts, guiding the attorney to a better understanding of your science, or performing an independent evaluation of the conclusions of another are all tasks the expert may be asked to conduct.

Preparing for Deposition or Trial Testimony

Getting ready for deposition is in many respects a preparation for a mini-trial: the same steps are required for both events. Deposition is sworn testimony outside of a courtroom. At trial, the sworn testimony is provided in court, before a judge and jury. Jury testimony will be addressed further in Chapter 5; however, the tips for deposition testimony are also true for trial testimony. It is helpful, in approaching the deposition or trial, to understand the opposing attorney's potential objectives. In general, these may include:

- To gather additional information
- To assess your demeanor as a witness
- To demonstrate to your client and attorney the extent of knowledge and expertise the opposition possesses

- To attempt to impeach you
- To lock you into a position

It is valuable, if painful, to practice giving deposition on videotape. The attorney can ask some questions—both open-ended and closed questions, to allow the expert to review his or her demeanor during depositions. The benefit of observing physical mannerisms and methods of answering questions for purposes of self-improvement is crucial. Certainly, not every case warrants videotaped deposition preparation, but for cases that do, the results of rehearsal can be dramatic.

Do not attend a deposition without substantial preparation. Following is a checklist of things to do before and during your deposition:

- Review your entire file
- Carefully check the accuracy of your final report
- Confer with the attorney
- Dress as you would for trial
- Get a good night's sleep before the deposition

There is a fundamental rule in discovery matters that you probably already know. Talking too much in discovery, revealing more than is required, waxing eloquent or acting egotistical, telling all you know about the entire subject—all can be detrimental to the case.

Some examples of good and bad answers to deposition questions will help you prepare. First, the bad answers:

Question: Please state your name for the record.
Answer: My name is Harvey Witness. I live at 1224 Main. My phone number
         is (707) 555-8811. My consulting company is known as Witness
         Consulting.

Comment: Obviously, the witness has violated a cardinal rule of deposition examination: he gave more information than was actually requested. See what that technique does for Mr. Witness later.

The witness has violated several cardinal rules of deposition examination. He did not listen to the question he was asked. He responded with much more information than he was asked to provide. And he tipped off the opposing counsel that he will likely continue to listen carelessly to questions and respond with excessive detail. This can be detrimental to an expert's client's case.

Question: Did you inspect the parking lot?
Answer: I did and I will tell you there is no way that the parking lot complies
         with the Uniform Building Code, the architect's design, or the
         National Safety Council requirements.

Comment: The correct answer would have been "Yes." Mr. Witness's answer opens up a whole series of questions about items that Mr. Witness may (or may not) have fully examined or be qualified to testify about. In his desire to be the consummate expert, Mr. Witness tries to tell all he knows. If he had not disclosed the three items on which he relied, examining counsel might never have asked about them. It might turn out that the three items do not support Mr. Witness's conclusion, and some backpedaling would then be required at trial. Further, attorneys have ethical obligations in regards to discovery. If the answer provided is not addressed in some fashion in the expert's summary of findings provided to opposing counsel, this could potentially result in a mistrial if the expert volunteers this information for the first time at trial.

Question: Mr. Witness, do you have an opinion as to what caused Mrs. Wally to fall in the parking lot?

Answer: Yes, I do. She fell because the concrete parking bumper she tripped over was not painted the required color. It was dark between the cars, she had her arms full of groceries. She followed her daughter into the parking lot and the daughter stepped over the parking bumper. Mrs. Wally failed to see the concrete bumper, tripped, and fell. There is absolutely no question in my mind that failure of the store to paint the parking bumper yellow was the direct cause of the fall.

Comment: Here Mr. Witness has done quite a number of things wrong. First, instead of just answering the question with a simple "Yes," he proceeded to explain everything he knew about the subject. Each piece of information he volunteered constitutes a trail for the skillful examiner to follow. The next thing he did wrong was to state his opinion in absolute terms. He forgot that many things were sufficient to have caused Mrs. Wally to fall in the parking lot, none of which are necessarily what Witness examined. He also forgot that all he has to state is his opinion, based upon a probable—not an absolute—basis. Rarely are things "absolute." Consequently, the expert loses credibility by taking this position. Trying to help one side "win" by overstating the strength of the evidence could have dire consequences to the expert's future viability. He also opened up the defense tactic of "contributory or comparative negligence" by noting that his client failed to see what her daughter clearly saw.

Question: Is it possible, Mr. Witness, that you've made a mistake in your opinion?

Answer: Absolutely not. I can't image how you could even suggest that. I did my work. I made my measurements. I studied everything there was to study. I've been in this field for 35 years.

Comment: Mr. Witness has violated several more rules of good testimony procedure. He has gotten angry with the attorney and become defensive and argumentative. He has spoken in absolutes. In all respects, he has done no service to himself or his client.

After proper schooling and some video practice, Mr. Witness becomes a much improved witness.

Question: Mr. Witness, do you have an opinion as to why Mrs. Wally fell?
Answer: Yes.
Question: What is the basis for your opinion?
Answer: My investigation of the case.

Comment: At this point, examining counsel has a choice. The answer can either be accepted or probed further. A good examiner would probe further, asking for details about education, documents reviewed, when the scene was visited, and so on, but if it is getting late and the witness seems to be in control of the examination, the attorney may move on to something else. That would be beneficial to Mr. Witness's client and his position as a testifying expert. He can tell all he knows at trial, not at deposition.

Question: Mr. Witness, in light of all the circumstances of this case and with
                a view toward your testimony at the time of trial, just what is it that
                you are saying and how do you explain your position at this time?
Answer: I don't understand your question; it is really two questions.
Question: Which part did you not understand?
Answer: If you could break the question down into separate questions, I'll try
                to answer each one as accurately as I can.

Comment: This shows Mr. Witness's understanding of the process of complex and compound questions. Numerous questions, some of which were vague and unclear, were built into the attorney's long and rambling question. Mr. Witness did right by politely asking the attorney to break the question down into separate parts.

Question: Mr. Witness, did you talk with anyone before coming into this
                deposition room today about your testimony?
Answer: Yes.
Question: Who did you talk to?
Answer: I talked to Ms. Booth, the prosecuting attorney.
Question: What did she tell you to say?
Answer: She told me to be truthful in all respects.
Question: Did you rehearse your testimony?
Answer: No, but I did prepare for today.

Comment: The attorney can make little response to this question-and-answer series. He should move on to something else. From that response, Mr. Witness has done right again and has been truthful and honest in his answer.

Question: Mr. Witness, what do you think could have been done to remedy this parking lot situation?
Answer: Are you asking for my opinion?
Question: I want to know what you think.
Answer: My opinion is that, in all probability, standard lighting and painting would have avoided the situation.

Comment: The attorney is trying to obtain a guess or speculation. Mr. Witness, persists in rendering his opinion. In trial, that opinion will be enhanced and embellished based on reasonable scientific and technical probability.

Question: Mr. Witness, are you absolutely certain the parking bumper was not painted yellow at the time of Mrs. Wally's fall?
Answer: I'm reasonably certain that was the situation.
Question: Isn't it possible that the paint wore off between the time of her fall and the time of your inspection?
Answer: My inspection of the scene occurred on July 15 and the incident occurred on July 8. I doubt the paint would have worn off in seven days.

Comment: The attorney is attempting to instill doubt and lock Mr. Witness into an absolute position, knowing that given the rules of human conduct, there are few absolutes. But because the witness framed the answer in terms of his investigation and reasonable probability, he avoids the trap. His documentation of the scene and his investigation support his position resolutely.

Question: Is it not true, Mr. Witness, that part of the responsibility for this fall must be squarely placed on Mrs. Wally for not having watched her step?
Answer: It's not my place to decide that issue.

Comment: Here Mr. Witness has shown his careful preparation of the case and his recognition of the legal principles involved. His field of expertise and technical examination do not extend to the ultimate weighing of comparative fault or contributory negligence. He knows that matters of claimant's contributory or comparative negligence are jury questions, not for determination by the design-and-construction expert.

Question: Is it correct that the amount of light available at the site of Mrs. Wally's fall is measured by your "guesstimate"?
Answer: No, that is not correct.

Question: Well, how is the light measured?

Answer: By use of standard test equipment that measures light intensity in terms of candlepower.

Comment: At this point, Mr. Witness is tempted to, but did not, go into techniques of measurement, description of standardization equipment, recognized scientific procedures, methods by which lighting was tested, and precautions that he took to make sure the test was done at the same time of day Mrs. Wally fell. If examining counsel wishes to go into those items, he will. If not, the matter is best left for sponsoring counsel to explore at trial.

Your deposition may be preceded by a required written report and a series of written interrogatories. Examining counsel has the right to select any reasonable means of discovery. Written interrogatories may be used; these are formal written questions that require an answer. (A useful example of sample interrogatories and requests for production to expert witnesses appears in Appendix H of this text.)

Some of the questions may appear almost harassing, and others may seem irrelevant; some questioning will sound like a fishing expedition. All are allowable and standard operating procedure in deposition for opposing counsel to attempt to accomplish the above objectives. There are six areas that demand the expert's attention in preparation for deposition:

- Conversations conducted to prepare you for deposition may be discoverable.
- The lawyer who attends the deposition with you may not be able to instruct you as to whether you can or cannot answer questions.
- What items to volunteer in your answers must be carefully reviewed with counsel.
- If you have published or testified to something inconsistent with your position, be sure to discuss this with counsel in advance.
- Be open and receptive to suggestions from counsel about your behavior, attitude, and posture during testimony.
- Prior drafts of your reports may be required to be produced in some jurisdictions.

When you attend your deposition, your overall air of quiet confidence and control will be immediately apparent. (Do not confuse arrogance with confidence! Confidence stems from knowing you have proper education, training, and experience, and that your review of your work confirms your conclusions.) When you enter, take a moment to survey the room. You may wish to select a seat that requires others in the room to shift their position. You may want to sit with your back toward the glare of outside windows.

The papers and materials you use to refresh your memory during or before testifying may be ordered produced. Of course, if you have prepared a report that has been provided to the other side, that is the best memory refresher to use. Do not hesitate to ask for a recess if you are tired, if the questions appear to be coming too fast and furiously, or if you otherwise need a break. Recall that your words are being recorded. Long pauses are not. If you only need a moment or two to collect your thoughts, take a moment to sip your water, search your file, or just sit quietly to reflect upon the question. Do not allow counsel to rush you if you need a moment. There is nothing wrong with saying, "I need a moment to consider the question."

The deposition room often, but not always, represents a full-court press. There should be no off-the- record or informal discussions with counsel. They are a trap for the unwary and inexperienced expert. When the deposition is concluded, do not ask the attorney who hired you how you did; you will learn soon enough. Remember that any discussions you have with counsel during the recess may be inquired into by the examining attorney. Your posture will tell a great deal about how you approach the task, so walk into the room standing tall. Avoid fraternizing with anyone in the room. Sit erect, maintain eye contact, be alert.

Take some time to evaluate the method and manner of approach of the examining attorney. Is the approach aggressive and tenacious, or does he try to "nice guy" you to death? Your early analysis will be important, both for deposition and trial. The attorney might vary his style to throw you off base. Be alert to changes in demeanor. Treat everyone at the deposition politely. Jokes or flippant comments are inappropriate. Maintain your professional demeanor at all times, but do not appear cold.

You have reviewed your facts and file. You are comfortable with your subject matter. You know more about the case than anyone else in the room. You display an air of competence and composure, no matter how you feel internally. Your demeanor should be that of a person who is familiar with the spotlight and sufficiently accustomed to it to be comfortable there.

Now begins the examination: How many hours have you devoted to the project? What have you done? Who have you seen? What tests have you performed? What do they show? What did the attorney tell you about the case? Produce every communication you have had with the lawyer. What other experts have you consulted? What did they say? What texts or periodicals did you review? Which are authoritative, in your opinion? Your skillful yet precise answers will keep the examination on track. Listen to the question asked. Answer that question, and that question only. Do not volunteer additional information. Do not presume you know where the attorney is going and jump ahead to offer the answer you anticipate they may be seeking. If the lawyers want more information beyond the question immediately before you, know they will get to it eventually.

The attorney will address your conclusions or opinions. "You concluded the children's milk was poisoned?" "In coming to this conclusion, did you consider the following facts… " "Are you aware of a recent study published in *insert peer reviewed journal here*? Did you consider the findings of that study when coming to your conclusion?"

During the deposition, do not look to the attorney who engaged your services for assistance. Your eyes must be focused on the examining attorney, no one else. Think about it. What will the opposition think of you as a witness if you have to keep looking to counsel for aid? The other side will know that, come the time of trial, you will not be able to stand up to the rigors of examination. Further, at trial, the attorney may either comment on your conduct to the jury, or stand between you and counsel, removing your safety net. Either strategy may be employed once opposing counsel realizes your weakness.

At the conclusion of the deposition, gather any papers, say polite goodbyes to everyone in the deposition room, and leave. You will have ample opportunity to confer with counsel later. After doing well, the human tendency is to immediately review the successful event ("Man, I nailed that chain of custody question!"). Suppress that tendency. Doing poorly will also carry its own burden. A professional will leave the room as if he or she has done well. As in questioning, do not provide information that was not requested—if you leave the room looking arrogant or beaten, that may tell the opposing attorney something he or she did not know.

Request a copy of your transcript. A transcribed copy will be made available for review. Examine it to correct typographical errors, not to make substantive changes you have thought of since the deposition. Make the minimum number of corrections or changes possible, because the changes you make can become the basis of cross-examination at trial. An important "yes" when "no" was the right answer will be hammered hard on the stand. After the transcript is reviewed, your signature is required to approve the transcription as offered or with modifications. If you do not examine the transcript, then most local rules provide that the deposition may be filed without your signature, with approval being assumed. Therefore, always review the transcription for transmission or typographical errors.

Your deposition presents a challenge and an opportunity. The challenge will become less severe in direct proportion to the degree of your preparation; the opportunity is to display your ability as a witness, not to display all the knowledge you have amassed on the subject of this or any other case. Your calm, cool demeanor and confident professionalism should permeate the entire deposition experience.

Federal Rules of Evidence

The Federal Rules of Evidence are the rules that govern the admissibility of evidence in the U.S. federal court system. Although the FRE apply only in federal courts, the states have adopted similar—or even identical—rules. Prior to the adoption of the FRE in 1975, case law (unofficial common law) formed the basis of the rules of evidence. The U.S. Supreme Court drafted versions of the FRE in 1969, 1971, and 1972. Congress then studied the FRE, ultimately allowing them to become federal law in 1975, with modifications by the Supreme Court. The rules of evidence in broad measure tend to admit evidence that is helpful, reliable, trustworthy, and assists the jury in determining whether a party has proved or disproved an issue in a case.

The FRE are divided into eleven articles, with each article containing one or more rules. The articles are:

- General Provisions
- Judicial Notice
- Presumptions in Civil Actions and Proceedings
- Relevancy and Its Limits
- Privileges
- Witnesses
- Opinions and Expert Testimony
- Hearsay
- Authentication and Identification
- Contents of Writings, Recordings, and Photographs
- Miscellaneous Rules

General Rules Regarding Witness Testimony

There are over 60 rules of evidence, many of which have multiple subsections. The purpose of the rules of evidence is to "administer every proceeding fairly, eliminate unjustifiable expense and delay, and promote the development of evidence law, to the end of ascertaining the truth and securing a just determination" (FRE Rule 102, 2017). Below follows a brief discussion of some of the relevant Federal Rules of Evidence as they relate to testimony. Note that these rules may vary in form and substance at the state level. People are considered competent to be witnesses unless the rules of evidence or rules of the court or statutes provide otherwise (FRE 601). Generally, witnesses may not testify unless they have personal knowledge of the matter in issue, with one major exception, and that is regarding experts, who may render opinions even if they did not have personal knowledge of the facts at the time the case arose (FRE 602). Oath or affirmation is customarily given to testify truthfully. This oath is issued in a form "designed to impress that duty on the witness's conscience" (FRE 603).

The credibility of a witness may be attacked by any party, and that includes the party who called the witness in the first instance (FRE 607). Opinion and reputation evidence going to the credibility, or lack thereof, of a witness may be admitted, but only to show past character for truthfulness or untruthfulness. This evidence is allowed only if the witness has been attacked as to credibility or reputation. Specific instances of conduct of the witness supporting or attacking credibility may not be used to attack credibility, except in very narrow circumstances (FRE 608).

A witness may be impeached by proving conviction of a serious crime for which imprisonment in excess of a year is called for; however, before admission, the court must perform an analysis of the probative nature of the conviction. If the witness has been pardoned or the conviction annulled, the conviction is not admissible (FRE 609). Religious beliefs of a witness are not admissible to bear on the credibility of the witness (FRE 610).

Generally, the court controls the method and order of questioning. Leading questions should generally not be used on direct examination except as foundation testimony. The contrary is true on cross-examination, where leading questions are permitted. Leading questions may also be used for hostile witnesses, an adverse party, and witnesses associated with an adverse party (FRE 611). Writings may be used to refresh the witness's memory. If used, such writing may be inspected by the adverse party (FRE 612). A witness may be examined concerning a prior statement, but that statement does not have to be shown to the witness. However, upon request, the party must disclose the statement to opposing counsel. When a party seeks to introduce extrinsic evidence of a prior inconsistent statement by a witness, the witness must have the opportunity to either explain or deny the statement (FRE 613).

A court may call witnesses on its own motion. In this circumstance, both parties are entitled to cross-examine the witness. The court may also examine or cross-examine a witness regardless of who called the witness (FRE 614).

Finally, and perhaps most importantly, courts have the power to exclude witnesses so they cannot hear another witness's testimony. There are exceptions to this, including, under the federal rules, the presence of a person, such as an expert, who is essential to a party's case [FRE 615 (c)].

Rules Regarding Expert Testimony and Opinion Testimony

Generally, only experts may testify as to opinions or inferences, except if lay opinion is tendered based upon the perception of a witness (for example, speed, intoxication, mental state), such testimony would be helpful to a clear understanding of the witness's testimony, and the testimony is not based on specialized knowledge, such as scientific or technical knowledge, which is governed by Rule 702 (FRE 702).

When a witness is established as an expert based on knowledge, skill, training, experience, or education, he or she is permitted to render an opinion if the following criteria are met:

- The expert's knowledge will assist the trier of fact to either understand the evidence or come to a determination about a fact that is in issue in the case; and
- The testimony is based on "sufficient facts or data;"
- The conclusions or opinions are based on principles and methods considered reliable; and
- The reliable principles and methods were "reliably applied" in the case at bar (FRE 702).

Facts on which an expert bases an opinion can be facts the expert has been made aware of by another, or facts or data personally observed. The expert can rely on hearsay if the hearsay is of a type experts "reasonably rely on ... in forming an opinion on a subject" (FRE 703).

Experts may, for the most part, give opinions about the ultimate issue to be decided by the trier of fact. This opinion is not automatically objectionable simply because it goes to the ultimate issue. However, there are limits on such testimony (FRE 704).

The expert may testify in terms of opinion and give reasons therefore without first testifying to the underlying facts or data, unless the court requires otherwise. However, the underlying facts or data are still subject to cross-examination (FRE 705).

In certain cases, the court can appoint experts either on its own motion or at the request of the parties. Court-appointed experts can be called and cross-examined by either party. The compensation for expert witnesses appointed by the court is determined by the court in accordance with rules of court or local statutes. Nothing about this rule prevents either party from calling their own experts if they choose (FRE 706).

Federal Rules of Evidence 702 and 703

Experts should be most familiar with Rules 702 and 703, as they pertain directly to them. These rules in their entirety are below.

Rule 702

A witness who is qualified as an expert by knowledge, skill, experience, training, or education may testify in the form of an opinion or otherwise if:

a. The expert's scientific, technical, or other specialized knowledge will help the trier of fact to understand the evidence or to determine a fact in issue.
b. The testimony is based on sufficient facts or data.

c. The testimony is the product of reliable principles and methods.

d. The expert has reliably applied the principles and methods to the facts of the case (FRE 702, 2017).

Rule 703

An expert may base an opinion on facts or data in the case that the expert has been made aware of or personally observed. If experts in the particular field would reasonably rely on those kinds of facts or data in forming an opinion on the subject, they need not be admissible for the opinion to be admitted. But if the facts or data would otherwise be inadmissible, the proponent of the opinion may disclose them to the jury only if their probative value in helping the jury evaluate the opinion substantially outweighs their prejudicial effect (FRE 703, 2017).

In Rule 702, you will notice the core of the issues visited later by the courts in *Daubert*, *Kumho*, and *Joiner*: What are sufficient facts or data? What does "reliable" mean? How do we know if a method is reliable? How can we tell if that method has been applied reliably in the case at hand? For the expert witness, these can be frustrating questions in that scientists will answer them one way, but the courts may answer them another. A good rule to follow is to stick to the science that supports your professional discipline and let the courts decide what they want. You will be held accountable for your science, not your knowledge of legal decisions.

Review Questions

1. What is discovery?
2. What is a privileged communication?
3. The Federal Rules of Civil Procedure govern what and are created by whom, and who approves them?
4. What is the difference between discovery in the civil and criminal courts?
5. What is a deposition?
6. What is an interrogatory?
7. Why should you request a copy of a transcript of your deposition?
8. What are the Federal Rules of Evidence, when were they adopted, and what was used before they were adopted?
9. Which Federal Rules of Evidence are the most important for the expert to know?
10. How do the Federal Rules of Evidence define an "expert"?

Discussion Questions

1. How is deposition similar to testimony in court? How should one prepare for deposition?
2. Does the definition of an expert, according to Rule 702, seem specific or vague? Why do you think it has been defined this way?
3. What is the purpose for the difference between civil and criminal discovery?

Testimony

5

Key Terms

Jury education

Introduction

Arguably, testimony is the most important thing a forensic scientist does, second only to the quality of his or her work. Testimony is also unique. Think of various situations where spoken communication is important, such as conversation, lectures, plays and movies, speeches, and songs. Testimony, unlike any of these forms of spoken communication, is:

- Highly structured
- Interactive, but mostly on someone else's terms
- Narrowly focused
- Of indeterminate length
- Directed by someone else's agenda
- Limited in scope based on Rules of Evidence, procedure, case law, constitutional protections, and pretrial rulings

Some attorneys, in an attempt to either calm or throw off a witness, will say, "We're just going to have a little conversation, here." The wise expert will ignore this oversimplification and stay attentive because nothing could be further from the truth. Expert testimony does seem simple at the outset—answer the questions and tell the truth. It is not, however, that simple. Rather, testimony may be one of the most difficult forms of spoken communication humans conduct for a number of reasons. First, expert testimony requires a simplification of very technical information to an audience who does not necessarily have any knowledge of the topic. This "translation" is targeted at a specific concept or concepts in a particular case. However, the concept and case are actually larger and editing is necessary.

The lawyer and the expert must come to understand that they will always feel a need to say more about a technical concept that is being translated by the expert for the fact finder. But this is the impossible goal of a perfect translation, and in the courtroom there is practically never enough time to realize this dream. It is crucial that the expert and the lawyer come to agreement about what amount of testimony is enough to make clear the meaning that must be communicated.... A successful presentation allows the fact finders to trust in the expertise of the witness and to apply his translation of the scientific and technical concepts and findings to the issues that the fact finders must decide.[1]

Second, the rules governing testimony are layered and intricate, spanning English grammar and vocabulary through scientific methodology and into federal, state, or local laws, and even "house rules" of particular judges or jurisdictions. Finally, the question-and-answer format is almost always done in an adversarial setting. In addition to rules regarding the form and nature of questions, opposing counsel is entitled to object if they feel the question, the answer, or the potential answer is somehow beyond the limits of what is appropriate. A simple conversation? Hardly.

This chapter covers some basics on testimony itself. The two main forms of testimony, direct and cross, will be handled in separate chapters.

Your Report

Although testimony is verbal, it starts with written words: your report. Your report should demonstrate organization, clarity, neatness, and completeness. Its contents will depend on the scope of your analysis and form the basis for your testimony. The following recommended list of items for inclusion is intended to suggest possible areas to consider:

- The name, business address, and official title of the expert
- Contact information for the examiner or relevant contact person, depending on lab policy
- The name and address of the expert's agency or business affiliation
- The date the report was issued
- The case identification information (laboratory number, case number, etc.)
- General description of the items examined
- The methods and instrumentation used to examine and analyze the submitted items
- The results of the examinations and analysis
- Any interpretations or statistics that are relevant to the results
- A statement of the disposition of the evidence
- The signatures of the examiner and any reviewers of the report
- The limits of the science
- Measurement uncertainty (where applicable)

[1] Smith, F., and Bace, R. *A Guide to Forensic Testimony* (Boston: Pearson Education, Inc., 2003), pages 108–9.

The format of the report should roughly follow that of a standard scientific paper—Introduction, Materials and Methods, Results, Conclusions, and Discussion. You will find that most laboratory reports do not, however, have this structure. The reports may read as simply as:

> Item 1 was found to contain cocaine, a controlled substance. The net weight was 5.24 grams.

This terse approach to writing forensic reports does not tell the reader much. Unlike a scientific paper in a peer-reviewed journal, a forensic science laboratory report is not primarily intended for other scientists—most of the readers of a forensic science laboratory report are law enforcement officers, attorneys, and judges, all of whom may have little to no training in science. This lack of training requires a special effort to make the reports readable, intelligible, and concise. Many laboratories have traded completeness and documentation of procedures for a protective style: if a scientist does not tell how he analyzed something, perhaps no questions will be asked. Forensic science laboratory reports should be summations of analyses, but should also be transparent as to methods, instrumentation, and results.

The DNA revolution in forensic science led to a very different style of report writing for the biological forensic sciences:

Item 1
Human DNA was isolated from the swabbings of the waistband (Item B). The DNA obtained from the swabbings of the waistband (Item B) was amplified with the polymerase chain reaction (PCR) method and typed for 20 STR genetic markers and amelogenin, a gender-specific genetic marker, using the [lab-appropriate] amplification kit.

An STR DNA profile that is a mixture of DNA from at least two individuals was detected from the swabbings of the waistband (Item B). This mixture includes at least one male contributor.

This language may be followed by language such as:

- Assuming DNA from only two individuals in this mixture, a major female contributor can be determined at X number of genetic markers. Female suspect A is the source of the major female DNA from this Item.
- A major profile can be determined. Female suspect A cannot be excluded as a possible contributor of DNA from this Item.
- The minor STR data obtained is suitable for exclusionary purposes only due to the limited amount of statistical information available. Based on the STR DNA types detected, the possible contribution of DNA from the male suspect is inconclusive.

- The minor STR data obtained is suitable for exclusionary purposes only due to the limited amount of statistical information available. Based on the STR DNA types detected, the male suspect is excluded.
- The sample was amplified and typed at D1S1656, D2S441, D2S1338, TPOX, D3S1358, FGA, D5S818, CSF1PO, D7S820, D8S1179, D10S1248, THO1, vWA, D12S391, D13S317, D16S539, D18S51, D19S433, D21S11, and D22S1045.

Item 2

Human DNA was isolated from the swabbing of the hat (Item A). The DNA obtained from the swabbing of the hat (Item A) was amplified with the polymerase chain reaction (PCR) method and typed for 20 STR genetic markers and amelogenin, a gender-specific genetic marker, using the [lab-appropriate] amplification kit.

A single-source STR DNA profile was detected from the swabbing of the hat (Item A). Statistical calculations were performed using population statistics from databases of unrelated African American, Caucasian, and Hispanic individuals.

The probability of randomly selecting an unrelated individual with a matching DNA profile D1S1656, D2S441, D2S1338, TPOX, D3S1358, FGA, D5S818, CSF1PO, D7S820, D8S1179, D10S1248, THO1, vWA, D12S391, D13S317, D16S539, D18S51, D19S433, D21S11, and D22S1045 as obtained on the hat swab (Item A) is approximately:

 1 in 310 sextillion in the Caucasian population
 1 in 38 septillion in the Black population
 1 in 83 sextillion in the Hispanic population

Although the jargon could be cleared up a bit and the prose made more readable, this is the way more forensic reports should look. In preparing your report, use internal quality assurance and final check procedures. Recheck all calculations; make sure technical terms are used correctly. Review the report for typographical errors, grammar and syntax, and clarity. The sequence of pages, exhibits, and attachments should be verified. Finally, make sure your report is distributed only to the proper recipients. All too often, experts rely on technical and administrative review to "catch" errors before a report leaves the laboratory. Experts should be mindful any errors in the work product will forever be attributable to them and them alone, regardless of who was supposed to provide a second read.

Preparation for Testimony and Communicating with Attorneys

The title of this section may suggest an oxymoron, in that some think it is impossible to communicate with attorneys. Communication with the attorney who engaged your services, with opposing counsel, and with judges and administrative hearing officers is critical to the success of any expert witness. One of the fundamental difficulties in communicating with attorneys involves the fact that they sometimes use language differently than scientists. Further, just as scientists use some words differently than the majority of the population, so, too, do lawyers. Contrary to popular belief, legal language is not used to delay, deceive, or confuse—words are used to the specific limit of their intended resolution. A simple example may suffice. In an investigation, a person who seems to be culpable for the crime in question will be referred to as a suspect; in the courtroom, however, that person is almost always the defendant. His or her status has changed and that must be reflected in the words used to describe it. Sometimes, however, the original, uncharged suspect may be referred to in court as the "third-party perpetrator," if another person was subsequently charged with the crime and the defense theory is the original suspect committed the offense. As in any profession, particular terms have specific meaning; a little understanding will help the translation.

Experts have isolated problems in communicating with attorneys:[2]

- Lawyers are too busy to discuss the case.
- They do not know technical language.
- They do not listen to experts.
- They are too aggressive and adversarial.
- It is hard to get them to return phone calls.
- They oversimplify complex issues.
- They require yes or no answers.
- They contact the expert at the last minute.

Experts also suggest the following ways in which attorneys could improve the situation:

- Give the expert more time.
- Plan and organize better.
- Make an effort to learn the fundamentals, through reading, seminars, and meetings with scientists. Recognize competence includes understanding science.

Notably, lawyers also identify common communication problems:

- Scientists spend too much time attempting to explain minutiae that have little to do with the case.
- Scientists use words and phrases that are too technical for lawyers to understand in a short amount of time.

---

[2] Prichard, F. *Experts in Civil Cases: An Inside View* (New York: LFB Scholarly Publishing, LLC, 2005).

- Lawyers do not understand science, and scientists do not make it easy for them to do so.
- Lawyers only want to focus on the area of testing they believe is relevant, and scientists frequently want to discuss other things not relevant to the lawyer's theory of the case.

Communication between you and the attorney carries dual responsibility. You must translate technical terms and concepts for the attorney. The attorney must translate the legal vocabulary for you. A clear understanding of objectives and goals given to you by counsel will sharpen your focus. Development of one or more working hypotheses will enhance mutual understanding. To improve communication, you and the lawyer must focus together on what is to be accomplished. Opposing attorneys may try to suggest that you have been told what to say by the attorney who called you, that you have been "coached." This is why ground rules are important. (See Chapter 3.) You must not compromise your scientific integrity to satisfy an attorney. Having previously had a discussion on that subject allows you to testify truthfully about it if your integrity is challenged. Discussing the case ahead of time only makes sense, and it is easy to counter the implication of bias:

Q: Did he go over with you the questions he was going to ask you by the time you took that chair to testify?
A: We reviewed the matters that I would be testifying on, yes.
Q: He told you the questions he was going to ask you, didn't he?
A: I didn't know the specific wording; I knew generally what he was going to ask, yes.
Q: And you told him what your answers would be, didn't you?
A: That's normal to review in a pretrial; yes, sir.
Q: You told him the answers, didn't you?
A: That's what I stated; yes.[3]

Do not let an attorney make a simple, sensible process like pretrial conference sound like a conspiracy. One of the easiest ways to avoid this, for those working in government labs, is for the lab policy to include meeting with any and all attorneys who ask for such a meeting.

Most technical, professional, and scientific fields boast a text or series of books that constitute the core knowledge for that field. Experienced trial lawyers will regularly ask you for such texts. Failing that request, take the initiative and make that material available to the attorney. The attorney

---

[3] Bodziak, William, O. J. Simpson civil trial, November 27, 1996.

should make available to you enough information about the judicial process and your role in it for you to function effectively.

The main points during a case about which you could communicate with the attorney are:

- Understanding the overall case
- Getting to know each other's literature and vocabulary
- Drafting of interrogatories, requests for production, and deposition questions
- Preparation for deposition, both yours and the opposition
- Issuance of a final report
- Preparation for trial
- Development of direct examination questions
- Assistance in preparation of cross-examination
- Creation of exhibits
- Trial testimony
- Other trial assistance

At each of these points, confirm with counsel your understanding of what is being said to you, either verbally or in writing. Ask counsel to do the same for you. Repeating communications is an excellent way to ensure accurate understanding. Before trial, you may assist in preparing exhibits and demonstrative charts, tests, and documents. Any demonstration must be tested before the trial or hearing. The lawyers generally must show trial exhibits to opposing counsel in advance of trial. Where the parties disagree as to the relevance or admissibility of an exhibit, the court typically makes a determination well in advance of trial. Consequently, "surprise exhibits" shouldn't be created by the expert and only shown to the lawyers on the day of testimony. These are easy ways to guarantee the admissibility of a key chart, exhibit, document, or demonstration. It is proper for you to ask the attorney calling you if these details have been satisfied. Nothing can be as disappointing as preparing costly demonstrations or exhibits that are rejected at trial because of inaccuracy, lack of foundation, or lack of notice. Exhibits and demonstrations must be accurate and technically correct. Demonstrations must be substantially similar to the subject under litigation to be admissible.

Preparation for trial is somewhat different from preparation for deposition. The attorney should explain to you the objectives of testimony and describe the physical setting of the hearing room in detail, including positioning of the parties and the attorneys. The attorney should tell the expert where to position him- or herself at court. Entering the courtroom during another witness's testimony can have dire consequences. The attorney should outline the functions of the witnesses, attorneys, jury, or other fact finders.

Preparation for Testimony without Communicating

There are a number of steps to follow if you are heading for trial or hearing without an opportunity to confer with counsel. Beginning these steps presupposes that you have done everything right to that point.

Consider how you will present your topic and report. Usually, identifying questions will come first, such as who you are; your relevant background, training, and experience; what your assignment was; what you did; and how you did it. Your observations and tests will come next, and, finally, your opinions and reasoning. Other lawyers prefer a method on direct exam referred to as "front-loading." This method asks for the expert's opinion up front. The lawyer then asks questions about your observations, your tests, and your reasoning behind your opinion.

Decide when and how you will use easily understood examples to illustrate your testimony for maximum effectiveness. Because you have not spoken with the attorney, do not plan to rely on visual aids or models to illustrate your testimony. It is unlikely these will be admissible.

If you cannot tell your results in three brief sentences, you do not know your material. Spend time encapsulating your analysis, findings, conclusions, and opinion into three brief statements. Practice delivering those three statements to neighbors, friends, and family members. Do they understand? Don't just presume they understand. Ask them to repeat the concepts back to you. If they cannot articulate your results, refine further.

Become familiar with the trial setting. If possible, visit the place where your testimony will be taken. Locate the witness chair and your path to it. In particular, determine the location of electric outlets and walls or screens for projection. Determine how any visual aids or exhibits may be projected. Test all of your equipment thoroughly before you use it in trial.

You should have been provided with copies of interrogatories you helped answer or draft. Review them prior to trial. Review tests, examinations, and pretrial preparation that were the subject of formal discovery response. Take particular time with the transcript of your deposition and those of concurring and contravening experts, if available. Study all these documents for strong and weak points. This will help you anticipate cross-examination.

Because you are not the lawyer, you will have no control over the order of the questions presented to you. You will only have control over how you present the evidence in response to questioning. Whether you appear well organized on the witness stand will tell the trier of fact a great deal about your confidence, competence, and credibility.

Leave nothing to chance. Practice, practice, practice.

You need to know when you will testify. Trials and hearings are sometimes delayed by sickness, unavailability of witnesses, or emergencies.

If the attorney has not informed you of whether and when you will testify, make every attempt to contact his or her for guidance.

Demeanor, Dress, and Deportment

When you testify, you represent more than yourself. You are representing your laboratory, your government, and your profession. In this instance, less is more. Although it pertains to a con artist addressing his victim (a "mark"), the following advice from the 2001 movie *Ocean's Eleven* is still valuable for the expert witness on the stand.

RUSTY: How are you going to stand?
LINUS: [Hands clasped in front of him]
RUSTY: No good. And don't touch your tie. Look at me. OK. I ask you a question and you have to think of the answer, where do you look?
LINUS: [Looks down]
RUSTY: No good. You look down, they know you're lying. [LINUS looks up] And up, they know you don't know the truth. Don't use seven words when four will do. Don't shift your weight. Look always at your mark but don't stare. Be specific but not memorable. Be funny but don't make him laugh. He's got to like you and then forget you the moment you've left his sight. And for God's sake, whatever you do, don't, under any circumstances—
[Off screen]: Russ!
RUSTY: Yeah?
[Off screen]: Can you take a look at this?
RUSTY: Sure. [walks off]

Whatever the unspoken advice Rusty intended to give Linus, the previous statements are all valuable to remember. Good expert witnesses know that they are the conduit for the information the court needs to hear. The trial and testimony is not about them, per se, but about the evidence, how it was handled and analyzed, and what it means.

Even if you do not care how you look personally, all those whom you are representing do. You owe it to them, at least, to look presentable and professional. Further, courts frequently have dress codes for professionals. You should dress like you are on a job interview. You can express your "special" personal style after work and on the weekends. Dressing properly for court is easy and does not have to be expensive. Court is not the time to express yourself through your wardrobe. The center of attention is the evidence, not you. The basics are easy and apply equally to men and women:

- Black, navy, or gray suit (matching jacket and slacks/skirt) that is a solid color or pinstriped.
- White or blue shirt/blouse.
- Black shoes (and belt for men)—polish them.
- Clean, trimmed fingernails.
- Empty pockets—no jingling change or bulges.
- No gum, candy, or cigarettes.
- Briefcase or portfolio.
- Less is more. Keep your look simple.

A few other specific dos and don'ts:

- Men
  - Silk necktie with an unobtrusive pattern (no clip-ons).
  - Neat, clean, trimmed head hair; avoid facial hair.
  - Wedding ring and college ring only.
  - No earrings or other visible body piercings.
  - Cover tattoos.
  - Dress shirts do not have short sleeves.
  - Socks should be a shade darker than your suit.
  - Full-length overcoats should be worn in winter.
  - Avoid cologne.
- Women
  - Always wear a suit—no dresses.
  - No stilettos or boots; flats or modest heels only.
  - Hosiery at or near skin color.
  - No more than one ring per hand.
  - Your hair should be neat and out of your face.
  - One pair of earrings only; remove other visible piercings.
  - Cover tattoos.
  - Skirts should hang at least to the knee.
  - Skirts should be straight, not pleated or gathered.
  - Cleavage has no place in the courtroom.
  - Carry only a briefcase to the witness stand; no purses.
  - Other than noted, no additional jewelry.
  - Avoid perfumes.

This may seem overly conservative, and that is the point: court is a serious event and the impression you give the jury will reflect the nature of your work—serious and professional. Recall you are testifying both by your words and your demeanor. Dress the part.

At Trial

At trial, your testimony will be divided into three phases and four main parts:

- Phase 1
  - Your qualifications as an expert to render opinion testimony (voir dire)
- Phase 2
  - Direct examination
  - Your work and how it was performed
  - Findings of fact based on your analysis
  - Your expert opinions and interpretations
  - The reasons that support your conclusions
- Phase 3:
  - Cross-examination concerning facts in evidence, your direct examination, your file, your conclusions, your laboratory, and/ or your science

Your qualifications are based on your education, training, and experience. A series of typical questions is offered below; it may and should be altered as your career advances.

- Please state your name.
- How are you employed?
- Where did you work prior to your current position?
- What is your educational background?
- Are you a member of any professional organizations?
- Do you have any publications?
- Have you received any specialized training in your field?
- Have you taken any competency tests?
- Have you taken any proficiency tests?
- What is the nature of your work? What are you authorized to do?
- Why are these types of examinations or analyses conducted?

At this point, the sponsoring attorney may ask the court to qualify you as an expert in a specific type of examination or discipline. The opposing attorney may want to question you regarding your qualifications in an attempt to discredit or even disqualify you, lay foundations for questions to be posed later, or just "rattle your cage." Alternatively, the opposing attorney may stipulate to your qualifications; he may prefer the jury not hear how much of an expert you are. It is also possible the opposing attorney may stipulate to your qualifications because they simply do not care about your testimony. Remember, it is always possible the opposing counsel doesn't find your testimony relevant to their theory of the case. Don't take this personally. For example, if a defendant is claiming self defense, the defendant won't care whether you have matched his fingerprints to the weapon or the victim's DNA to the defendant's clothing. These are points the prosecution may feel compelled to put into evidence, but the defense may have already acknowledged this evidence.

If the judge determines that you have sufficient qualifications for what you are about to testify to, he or she will accept you as an expert in that particular area. Listen closely to the decision, as it will be the boundary for your expertise in this case. Being qualified as a textile fiber analyst does not necessarily mean you are qualified to testify about fabric damage. Once qualified, your direct examination begins, typically with jury education, the instruction of the jury in the necessary technical and scientific concepts and details to understand the expert's testimony sufficiently to aid in deliberation. A word about boredom. At some point in your career, you may cease to find the polymerase chain reaction as fascinating as you once did. However, when you are testifying, it is your job to present this evidence (if asked) to the jury in a compelling way. Just because it is boring to you doesn't mean it is boring to the jury. They are likely hearing this for the first time.

Your opinions may be based on facts found, tests conducted, or a series of hypothetical questions based on facts, evidence, and proof developed at trial. During the trial, you should be aware of the importance of careful testimony, particularly the hazard of inconsistent testimony between deposition and trial. You are admonished to tell the truth and to prepare for deposition or trial testimony by reviewing the facts of the case and your work effort. You should not lose your temper. Speak slowly, clearly, and naturally. If you are familiar with the process, you will not fear the examining attorney or the setting as much. You must answer only the questions asked, never volunteering information beyond the scope of the question presented. Remember that most questions asked by the other side can be answered "Yes," "No," "I don't know," "I don't remember," "I don't understand the question," or by a simple factual answer. You should not memorize your story or testimony. Avoid such phrases as "I think," "I guess," "I feel," "I believe," or "I assume." These are weak and insufficient to meet scientific and technical burdens of proof of reasonable probability.

Taking a breath—slow inhale, relaxed exhale—before answering a question is always a good idea. Taking a sip of water can also slow the pace and give you a chance to consider your answer. Let the attorney finish the question, allow a beat, then answer. Don't get anxious and jump in before the question is finished:

Attorney: Do you agree with me that the quoted text I just read to you—
Expert: Yes!
Attorney: —is inaccurate?
Expert: Uhm…

Pausing allows you to appear deliberate and gives you time to digest the question and frame an answer. Be careful of trap words such as "absolutely" or "positively"; be cautious about estimating time, space, and distance. If technical information is involved, give specifics—not estimates—in the answer. Refer to files or notes to refresh your recollection.

Avoid fencing, arguing with, or second-guessing examining counsel. If testimony could be reduced to two words, they would be patience and awareness. Patience helps you to remain calm and not rise to perceived suggestions or jibes by an attorney. To fence, hedge, argue, equivocate, or become angry only exposes you to further cross-examination and a resultant loss of credibility. It also draws attention to the weakness. One way to handle the situation is to answer the question and then add: "But please let me explain." The examining attorney will probably not let you do that. But the attorney for whom you are working may ask you to explain on redirect examination if they think it is important. You should not deny having had prior discussions about testimony in the case if such is the fact. If you make a mistake, correct it as soon as possible. If a negative or apparently damaging fact or omission has been elicited, admit it and move on quickly.

You should never answer too quickly or look to counsel for assistance. Testimony in court, deposition, or hearing should never be turned into a joke. Exaggeration, underestimation, or overestimation are all indications of unwary, ill-prepared, or overly confident witnesses. Translate technical terms into common, understandable language at every opportunity. Your demeanor and behavior before, during, and after testimony should be the subject of care. You should know the hazards of discussing testimony in hallways, restrooms, or public areas around the hearing room. Conversations with opposing parties, attorneys, and jurors must be avoided.

Review Questions

1. What is the most important aspect of a forensic scientist's work?
2. How is testimony different from other forms of spoken communication?

3. Testimony is based upon what?
4. How are forensic laboratory reports similar to journal research papers? How are they different?
5. Is it possible to testify without having consulted with the attorney calling you?
6. What are the three main phases of testimony?
7. What should the expert always do before answering a question during testimony?
8. If you make a mistake or misstatement on the witness stand, what should you do?
9. Should you express your personal style on the witness stand?

Discussion Questions

1. What is so important about dressing conservatively in court?
2. Why should you know what the courtroom looks like before you testify—why should that matter?
3. Go through the points you would discuss with an attorney about a hypothetical case; what must you make sure he or she knows? What can you disregard safely?

Direct Examination of Experts

6

Key Terms

ADDIE model
Bailiff
Best evidence rule
Compound question
Credibility
Direct examination
Hearsay
Hostile witness
Leading question
Objection
Past recollection recorded
Recollection refreshed
Redirect examination
TOM I. PASTA

Introduction

The primary objective of effective expert testimony is to present yourself as a well-organized, informative, and credible person. The fact finders need not become amateur experts because of your testimony. They only need to be convinced you are a believable person with something important to say, who will materially assist them in doing the job of deciding the case. Whether the case is decided in support of your position is not the true measure of the effectiveness of your testimony. The true test of testimonial excellence is whether you were credible. One of the best opportunities you have to establish that trait is through direct examination. Lawyers have a saying about trials, "You are responsible for the effort—not the result." Scientists would do well to embrace this mantra. You are judged not by the verdict of "guilty" or "not guilty," but rather by your testimony, your approach to testing, your documentation in your file, your preparation, and your demeanor.

Credibility is the believability of a statement, action, or source, and the propensity of the observer to believe that statement made by the expert. In public speaking, Aristotle considered the credibility of the speaker, in essence his or her character, to be one of the forms of proof. Social science research and psychologists have generally found that there are multiple dimensions of credibility, but three key aspects are competence, trustworthiness, and dynamism.

You must be professionally competent and have done a thorough job of analysis, investigation, and reporting. Your individual style and demeanor must be developed. The jury must be able to trust you and your work—do not assume they will trust you just because you are an expert. You should display enthusiasm without advocating. Pattern yourself after your best teachers and be prepared to illustrate your testimony graphically or with demonstrations. Prior to actually testifying, mentally visualize your best possible performance as a witness. Use of the word "performance" is intentional, because in a way you are performing a key role in a real-life drama. Younger experts, in particular, are cautioned. Do not take the stand as your favorite television forensic scientist or your personal forensic scientist hero. Take the stand as you. Emulate the skill set—not the character—of those you most admire. Your credibility will be established by effective use of teaching skills. Testimony is not a game, but gamesmanship is involved. A key to good testimony is to stay within your expertise, as in this example from the cross-examination of a forensic pathologist:[1]

Q (by the defense attorney): Okay. And you would agree that's blood, correct?
A: I would agree that that looks like blood, yes.
Q: All right. And for a person to have bled in that particular manner, the person has to be above it, correct? Bled down on that horizontal bar, true?
Opposing Counsel: Objection. Lack of foundation, Your Honor.
The Court: Overruled.
The Witness: I—
Q (by Mr. Baker): You can answer.
A: It looks to me
Q: Can you answer my question? I didn't ask—
Opposing Counsel: If the Court please—
Q: (by defense attorney): I didn't ask what it looks like to you.
A: I'm not a blood splatter expert.
Q: Would you agree that the person who left the blood there had to be above the area where the blood is dropped on the horizontal rail of the fence and then puddles into the dirt area?
Mr. Medvene: Objection. Asked and answered. The witness said he's not a blood splatter expert and he wasn't put on for that purpose.

---

[1] Dr. Werner Spitz, O.J. Simpson civil trial, November 12, 1996.

The Court: You can answer yes or no. He testified in direct examination with regards to blood flow.

The Witness: The origin of this blood could be from a higher level. It could be from the same level.

Notice that the pathologist, although not an expert in bloodstain pattern analysis ("blood spatter") can testify about general blood flow; it was determined to be within his expertise on direct and it was allowed previously. Understanding the rules of law is critical in this situation. Experts are advised: anywhere you are willing to go on direct, you will be legally compelled to revisit, if asked on cross-examination. You are not allowed to pontificate or opine for one side, and then, when the other side inquires, claim you are not qualified to comment.

The same witness testifies at a different point in the trial:

A: My opinion of this is that it supports my conclusion that there is a single assailant with a single weapon.

Q: Well—

A: Because if there is a transfer, then there are others, of course. There is blood of one victim on the weapon, and then there will be blood on the same weapon from the next victim.

Q: Doctor, you, if that were true, there would be minuscule—that is, a small amount of—blood transferred because it would only be blood transferred by the knife, correct?

A: I cannot discuss that. I am not an expert in blood spatter. I have no expertise. I have no training. I have not read about it and I think that if I'm going to go into the detail of how much is enough, I will be misleading you and the jury and the judge.

Note the witness clearly and firmly sets the boundary.

There are several ways to present and enhance all of these factors, including positive and open body language, emphasis of key points, establishing the main points early, summarizing the main points at the conclusion of your testimony, and recognizing the need for common-sense explanations.

Direct Examination and Strong Narratives

Direct examination (also called "examination in chief") is the questioning of a witness by the attorney who called him or her in a court of law. Direct examination is offered to provide evidence in support of facts that will satisfy or refute one or more required elements of the attorney's case. Much of direct testimony lays the foundation for what is to come or establishes facts for other witnesses; to that end, it may not be very exciting:

Q: And it was in or from that general area that you obtained these known fiber
    samples from the carpet?
A: It would have been underneath there, yes.
Q: Did you label and appropriately package and preserve those items?
A: Yes, I did.
Q: What item number did you give them?
A: Item no. 25.
Q: Did you collect other evidence while you were at that house at that
    particular day and time?
A: Yes, I did.

The basis of direct examination is what Andrew Welsch calls a strong representation.[2] Strong representations or strong narratives are factual, carefully managed narratives based upon evidence that endeavors to prove something more encompassing than personal, direct examination. First-person accounts can vary, especially in emotionally charged events.[3] As science expanded, and the faith the public had in it, physical evidence overshadowed eyewitness testimony.

Because the criminal event at issue resides in the past, the narrative is supported by the residual evidence of those events—what has been termed "proxy data." This is the essence of circumstantial evidence: the evidence of things not seen. The strong narrative is devoted to the truth, but is carefully crafted with words subtly put together (such as the difference between the vague "The hairs matched" and the more exact "The questioned hair exhibited the same microscopic characteristics as the known hairs and therefore could have originated from the same person"). Facts, however, do not explain anything by themselves. If you know the temperature outside is 82°, that alone explains nothing. Are you in Augusta, Maine, or Augusta, Georgia? Is it August or April? Is that Fahrenheit or Celsius? Ultimately, facts must be subordinated to the conclusion. The expert's conclusion and the significance of the evidence are more important to the trier of fact than any one fact. Finally, a strong narrative must purport to be true and conclusive, but only to the extent that it is capable of being. Each inference in the narrative supposes a possible sequence of events, but not necessarily the right one. However, the more exhaustive the procedure for ruling out wrong inferences, the stronger the sequence of cause and effect will appear. The conclusion drawn cannot be ruled out.

[2] Welsh, A. *Strong Representations: Narrative and Circumstantial Evidence in England* (Baltimore: Johns Hopkins University Press, 1992).
[3] National Institute of Justice. *Eyewitness Testimony: A Trainer's Manual for Law Enforcement* (Washington, D.C., 2003).

Important Points to Remember

The essence of trial competence centers around projecting an image of credibility from beginning to end. Accuracy of citation, precision in factual presentation, articulate organization of graphic materials, and an organized presentation of testimony and documentary evidence are all required. As part of that credibility effort, you must project an ambiance of honesty, integrity, and believability. Given that both sides in a dispute tend to present often competing views of the same evidence, you must stand forth as a beacon of believability. Additional traits that are beneficial to an expert witness include being honest, open minded, well mannered, fair, polite, dynamic, and positive. You must be a good listener and project yourself as a reliable source of information. You must also testify as to the limits of the science. You must admit readily when you failed to consider something, when asked. If new information changes your conclusion, or a new hypothetical could change your hypothetical conclusion, you must be willing to readily admit this.

One national authority on the subject of forensic engineering, Marvin M. Specter, founding president of the National Academy of Forensic Engineers, suggests how these factors, traits, characteristics, and techniques can be projected in the testimonial process, initially displayable on direct examination.

- Convey the fact that you are a professional, dedicated to accurate and detailed work.
- Avoid any impression that you are a "hired gun" by not being drawn into biased or exaggerated statements.
- Emphasize the specialized task you performed in the case, and that your testimony represents professional work and careful analysis.
- Be ready to bolster your opinion with recognized technical publications.
- Do not be afraid to expose the weakness of your case to counsel.
- Remember that the courtroom is a serious place; your task is of utmost significance, as someone's liberty is at stake.

Some points only experience teaches. They are enumerated here to highlight mistakes and observations of experienced expert witnesses and trial attorneys. Knowing about these seemingly minor admonitions will further serve your goal of increased credibility during direct examination. A descriptive vignette will illustrate salient suggestions.

As you walk in, display common courtesy to all with whom you come in contact. You never know who is a juror, hearing officer, attorney, or judge. Do not discuss who you are and certainly not why you are present with persons you do not know. Contact with opposing experts, regardless of your degree of friendship with them, should be minimal; a casual greeting will suffice. Potential fact finders observe hallway demeanor.

Depending on the jurisdiction and the judge's preference, the bailiff,[4] the lawyer offering the witness, or the court clerk calls the name of the witness. How you carry yourself transmits subtle messages to the audience, so walk with eyes forward, upright posture, and a confident stride. Make sure your voice, on the occasion of your first "I do," when asked if you will tell the truth, comes across loud and clear. Use your voice tone, volume, and modulation to maintain interest, vary the presentation, and keep everyone awake. Conversational normalcy is the order of the day, but make sure you can be heard clearly throughout the room. Your illustrative drawings and charts should stand alone and be self-explanatory. If called on to draw or write on a board or chart, keep your handwriting legible, and as a good performer, never turn your back on the audience. When testifying about a chart, photo, map, or other visual aid, recall a court reporter is taking down your testimony. The purpose of this is to create an accurate record of the testimony. Do not point to documents and refer to "here" or "over there." Rather, use descriptions such as, "In the upper left corner of the document" or "the curve of the second 'r' in the word 'terrible'."

When asked to examine a document, stop talking because you cannot read and talk at the same time. During any recess, politely maintain your distance from everyone. If you need to confer with counsel, do so out of sight of fact finders and opposition. Be particularly cautious of casual conversation in hallways, restrooms, and dining areas. If approached by a juror, do not engage in conversation. Report the encounter to the lawyer immediately. Throughout your testimony, you must be conscious of proper breath control, upright posture, and elimination of distracting or nervous mannerisms, such as facial expressions, verbal tics such as "ummmmm" or "okay," eye rolling, clicking a pen open and shut, or physical tics (tapping fingers or feet).

When a witness is asked a question, the opposing attorney can raise an objection, including (but not limited to) the following reasons:

- Nonresponsive
- Best evidence rule
- Compound question
- Present recollection refreshed
- Past recollection recorded
- Hearsay
- Leading question
- Argumentative or inflammatory

---

[4] Bailiffs are the law enforcement arm of the court. They keep order in the court, serve legal process or other court documents, and take charge of juries when the court is not in session. Also, bailiffs will provide general security for the courthouse and its visitors and staff.

- Asked and answered
- Calls for speculation
- Irrelevant, immaterial, incompetent
- Lack of foundation

The rules of evidence provide for structure during court proceedings. Attorneys make objections when they believe the other attorney or the witness has overstepped the bounds of appropriate behavior. When an attorney objects, as the witness, your job is to stop talking immediately. Typically, you will know an objection is being made because the other attorney will preface their remarks with the word, "Objection." However, this is not always the case. As a general rule, any time you are speaking, or about to speak, and an attorney starts talking, this is your cue to stop talking. Leave it to the lawyers and the judge to sort out the appropriateness of a question or a response. Do not substitute your judgment for that of the court. At best, you will annoy the judge. At worst, your conduct could cause a mistrial. Remain silent until you are told by either the judge or the lawyer asking you questions that you may respond or not respond.

Below is a brief description of some of the most common objections.

An objection of "nonresponsive" is somewhat unusual in that it objects not to the question asked, but rather the answer provided. As the word implies, an objection "nonresponsive" indicates the attorney is objecting to the fact the witness did not answer the question that was asked. For example, if the question is "Do you own a watch?" the answer, "It's 4:30," is nonresponsive. If asked, "Did you perform testing in this case?" answering, "It was arson," is nonresponsive. The remedy for providing a nonresponsive answer typically is the jury is instructed by the court to disregard the answer. Repeatedly ignoring the question presented could result in additional sanctions imposed on the witness.

There may also be an objection to the answer, typically that the answer is nonresponsive to the question (Q: What time is it? A: Cheesecake).

The best evidence rule is a common-law rule of evidence that dates to the eighteenth century. The general rule is that secondary evidence, like a copy or facsimile, will not be admissible if the original document is available. In the eighteenth century, a copy was usually made by hand by a clerk, and the best evidence rule was predicated on the assumption that there was a significant chance of error or fraud in using a copy. In the digital age, the rule is more difficult to justify. The likelihood of actual error (as opposed to mere illegibility) through photocopying or scanning is slight because most are legible and authenticated. Further, the question remains as to what the original of an electronic communication, like email, really is.

A compound question is one that contains several components. In trial, a compound question will likely raise an objection because the witness may be unable to answer the question unambiguously. For example, if an attorney cross-examining a defendant asked, "Isn't it true that you shot your spouse in the head, then volunteered for the local battered women's shelter?" the question could not be answered with a simple yes or no. All or part of the question could be true:

- The defendant did shoot his spouse and volunteered.
- The defendant did shoot his spouse but did not volunteer.
- The defendant did not shoot his spouse but did volunteer.
- The defendant did not shoot his spouse or volunteer.

Compound questions are objectionable for several reasons, including the risk they will confuse either the witness or the trier of fact. One risk, for example, includes the risk the witness may be responding to only part of the question. Both "and" and "or" can create this problem. Once objected to and sustained, an attorney will be given the opportunity to rephrase the question into several questions, such as:

- Isn't it true you shot your spouse in the head?
- On the day your spouse was shot, did you volunteer at the homeless shelter?

Put this way, there is no ambiguity or uncertainty about what is being asked or answered.

The hearsay rule is a rule of evidence that defines hearsay and provides for both exceptions and exemptions from that rule. The hearsay rule was designed to prevent testimony by people who heard another person say something, who cannot be cross-examined on the substance of what they heard but only that they heard it. Since hearsay statements are being used to prove the truth of the matter asserted, it can be terribly damaging if the opposing party cannot cross-examine the person who uttered the statement. Technically, forensic laboratory reports are hearsay when used by themselves in court. The United States Supreme Court addressed the use of forensic laboratory reports in *Massachusetts v. Melendez-Diaz* and *New Mexico v. Bullcoming*. Broadly speaking, forensic reports are not in and of themselves admissible. However, given the volume of work performed in any given case, not to mention in the laboratory overall, it is not uncommon for a witness to forget one or more details in the file. When this happens, there are two methods lawyers can use to attempt to admit the facts contained in the file.

An attorney may attempt to refresh your present recollection (referred to as present recollection refreshed). For example, imagine you examined evidence in the lab, wrote a report, and have reviewed the file prior to testifying. You are now in court, testifying about the evidence you examined. However, imagine you cannot recall whether you examined two shotguns and a rifle, or two rifles and a shotgun. You knew the information when you reviewed the file. An attorney may attempt to refresh your recollection as follows:

Q: Did you have the opportunity to examine the evidence in the laboratory?
A: Yes.
Q: Did you write a report based on your examination of the evidence?
A: Yes.
Q: Did you review the file before court, including your report?
A: Yes.
Q: I'm going to ask you to take a look at your report, specifically, the third paragraph on the second page. Do you see that part of your report?
A: Yes.
Q: Please read that part of your report to yourself and let me know when you are done.
A: I'm finished.
Q: After reading your report, does that refresh your recollection of the types of firearms you examined at the laboratory?
A: Yes.
Q: Please tell the jury about the firearms you examined.

Sometimes, however, no amount of file review will jog a witness's memory. In that case, an attorney may be able to get the information in under past recollection recorded. Assume that you used a specific setting on an instrument in your analysis. On the witness stand, you cannot remember the exact number, however, the number is part of the standard protocol.The attorney may ask,

Q: At the time you performed the testing, did you follow the standard protocol?
A: Yes.
Q: Did you document that setting in your notes?
A: (after confirming in notes) Yes.
Q: Does that refresh your recollection?
A: No. I still do not have an independent recollection of this setting.(Note: the attorney first tries to refresh the witness's recollection. However, just because the witness does not independently recall the information doesn't mean the information isn't admissible. The examination continues…)
Q: Did you document that setting at the time you did the testing?
A: Yes.
Q: Is it fair to say the purpose of documenting such information is so you or another person will be able to look at the notes and determine what steps you took?
A: Yes.
Q: At the time you were documenting the testing you performed, did you take care to make accurate notes?

A: Yes.

Q: Is this a record of information you recorded in the past, closer to the time of testing?

A: Yes.

Q: And what was the setting?

A: According to my notes made on the day of the analysis, that value was 28.4.

A leading question is one that suggests the answer. For example, "You were at the scene of the crime on the 7th of December, were you not?" It suggests that the witness was at the scene on the day in question. The nonleading form of this question would be, "Where were you on the 7th of December?" In essence, nonleading questions are open ended. Leading questions typically call for a yes or no answer.

Whether a leading question is proper depends on the relationship of the witness to the attorney asking the question. An attorney may ask leading questions of a hostile witness or on cross-examination, but not typically on direct examination. An exception to this rule occurs if a witness has been declared a hostile witness. If the court declares the witness "hostile," the attorney may ask the witness leading questions during direct examination.

When the attorney is finished with direct examination of you, he or she will "pass the witness," often by saying "No further questions" to the judge, or "Your witness" to the opposing attorney.

Trials are supposed to be fact-finding missions for the jury. As such, argument is reserved for closing arguments, where each lawyer takes the facts presented at trial and argues about their significance, meaning, or whether the evidence rises to the legal level of proof required, be it beyond a reasonable doubt or a preponderance of the evidence, depending on whether it is a criminal or civil trial. Questions that are argumentative are objectionable. For example, "You examined the evidence?" "And this was at your so called independent laboratory?" The question makes the argument the laboratory is not, in fact, independent. This argument should be saved for closing argument.

Once a question has been asked and answered, attorneys should move on to another line of questioning. Sometimes, attorneys will repeat a question to highlight the answer, such as, "I want to make sure I understood your testimony. You stated you cannot determine, in this case, whether the fire was intentionally set?" This question, in and of itself, is acceptable. Usually, when a question is objected to as asked and answered, it is because an attorney is seeking a different answer than the one provided. It might look like this:

Q: You said you couldn't determine if the fire was set?

A: Correct.

Q: So it might have been set?

A: Correct. I couldn't determine that.

Q: If someone did set it, you couldn't tell?
A: Yes.
Q: And it's also possible it wasn't set?
A: Correct.

At some point, the attorney for the other side will object to this line of questioning as "asked and answered." Whether the objection will be sustained after the second question, the third, or the fourth is up to the judge.

When attorneys ask about a hypothetical, they set the parameters. When a question calls for speculation, no such parameters have been set. Questions such as, "What was the shooter thinking when he fired into the crowd?" and "How long do you think it took him to travel five miles on foot?" call for speculation, as there are variables that cannot be known to the witness. Did the person run five miles? Walk five miles? Walk three miles, run one mile, and take a nap before jogging the final mile? Without a video or eyewitnesses, this calls for speculation, not fact, and is therefore objectionable.

Witnesses are cautioned, even if there is no objection, to consider carefully any question that calls for you to speculate about things such as what was going on in someone else's mind, how long it took to travel a distance without a valid measurement, and so on.

Similarly, when an attorney objects as the question assumes facts not in evidence, the question fails to set the parameters of a hypothetical. For example, assume a trial wherein labor and delivery are at issue. At the time of the question, there has been no information about the length of the woman's labor. The question, "Couldn't several days of unattended labor result in sepsis?" assumes several days of labor. An attorney may object because of this. However, the question can easily by modified to an acceptable question by couching it as, "Doctor, assume a hypothetical wherein a woman labors alone for several days. Could this result in sepsis?"

Relevancy is a judicial determination. What is important to one person or case may be of no consequence in a different circumstance. For example, the color of the car driven away from the crime scene may be relevant. The color of the car driven by the person who dropped the evidence off at the lab probably is irrelevant.

Before witnesses can testify about certain things, lawyers must lay foundation. This includes providing the basis for admitting an expert's opinion, as well as establishing foundation for items of evidence. To lay foundation for an expert opinion, a lawyer must establish the witness's credentials, whether based on education, training, experience, or a combination of these or other factors. To lay foundation for evidence, lawyers must ask the following:

- Do you recognize this?
- What is it?

- How do you recognize it?
- Is it in the same condition (or substantially the same condition) as when you examined it?

Attorneys must also establish a chain of evidence prior to taking testimony about an item of evidence. If an expert is asked about an area where no expertise has been established, or an expert is asked about an item of evidence where it hasn't been established they examined the evidence or that it is in the same condition, an attorney may object due to lack of foundation.

Redirect Examination

Once the attorney is finished with direct examination, the attorney representing the other side is allowed to cross-examine the witness. (Cross-examination is discussed further in Chapter 8.) When the attorney is finished with direct examination of you, he or she will "pass the witness," often by saying "No further questions" to the judge, or "Your witness" to the opposing attorney.

Redirect examination occurs after cross-examination. This allows the attorney an opportunity to ask the witness to explain or qualify any answers obtained on cross-examination. Redirect examination is limited to topics discussed on cross-examination. If an attorney attempts to bring up a new area for testimony, the opposing attorney may object to that line of questioning as beyond the scope of cross-examination.

Experts frequently express frustration when an attorney either chooses not to redirect or alternatively doesn't hit every point the expert thinks should be addressed. Experts are reminded, attorneys have theories and themes of their case, which may have little or nothing to do with one or more of the finer points of the cross-examination of an individual witness—even if that witness is an expert. For example, imagine a man is on trial for beating his wife to death with a lead pipe. Imagine further that the defendant is arguing self defense. Whether a defense attorney misstated the finer points of the polymerase chain reaction, while demonstrably wrong, is of no consequence to the state's theory, which focuses on the defendant's duty and ability to retreat, not on how DNA testing works. Thus, rather than risk alienating the jury on a technical point of no consequence, most attorneys will simply, wisely, maintain their focus on the legal issues at hand in the case and choose not to redirect on that issue.

Elements That Enhance Direct Examination

Experts and attorneys agree that certain elements make for a better witness and better testimony. Those elements include:

- The ability to coordinate verbal testimony with documentation
- Communicating basic and complex ideas in a simple manner

- Supporting opinions with admitted evidence
- A serious but pleasant demeanor
- An observable comfort level with the material and the courtroom experience

Coordination of testimonial media involves a smooth blend of verbal testimony with charts, drawings, exhibits, and other tangible items to support the testimony. That blend becomes smoother with practice, rehearsal, and improved timing. You should build to your conclusions in a linear sense, accumulating facts and results that lead to your conclusion. It is a building block philosophy: since A, B, and C are already established, D must be true. If prior adverse expert testimony has established certain facts or conclusions, the more of those facts and conclusions that you can use to bolster your opinions, the stronger and more reliable your opinion. Be willing to agree to the truth—just because another or opposing expert said it does not make it false.

You become a better expert witness by observing others. Watch, listen, and read. Visualize yourself as that witness: How would you handle that question or use that chart? Review your own depositions with an eye toward improving the sharpness of your answers. Watch video of yourself testifying, if possible. Look for opportunities to sharpen your skills, your style, your technique, and your presentation. The goal is to become a more competent, persuasive, and believable witness and a more reliable resource for the justice system. Better testimonial skill is one aspect of that effort, and it is first displayed on direct examination.

Be a Teacher

The testament to your skill as an expert witness is your ability to teach. An analysis of what it takes to become a good teacher is instructive. Your instructors from high school, college, and graduate school may stand as good or bad examples of how to teach. Remembering what it is like to be a student is also key—avoid bad habits of bad teachers. Some qualities of persuasive and effective teaching are applicable to the courtroom arena. Good teachers are well informed, enthusiastic, provocative, and intellectually curious. They use examples and illustrations. They have a sense of humor. They engage their audience through eye contact. They are dedicated to their work. Good teachers engage the student with quality information, arranged sensibly and logically in a way that encourages mental or physical participation.

Creating Instructional Materials: A Global Approach

Perhaps the most common model used for creating instructional materials is the ADDIE model. In this model, each step has an outcome that feeds into the subsequent step: analysis, design, development, implementation, and evaluation. In the analysis phase, the particular instructional problem is clarified, the goals and objectives of the learning are detailed, and the learning environment and learner's existing knowledge and skills are identified. Questions that are addressed during the analysis phase include:

- Who is the audience and what is their background?
- What question is before them?
- What types of learning constraints exist; for example, how long will the teaching last?
- What are the delivery or media options?
- How much time does the instructor have to prepare?

The design phase deals with learning objectives, how the quality of the teaching will be assessed, presentation media and activities, content, subject matter analysis, and lesson planning. The design phase should include a logical, orderly method of identifying, developing, and evaluating a set of planned strategies targeted for attaining the project's goals. Each element of the instructional design plan needs to be executed with attention to details. These are the steps used for the design phase:

- Document the project's instructional, visual, and technical design strategy, if any.
- Apply instructional strategies according to the content type.
- Create storyboards or outlines of the instruction for use in practice for testimony.
- Design the media and presentation characteristics to be used, after consultation with the attorney.
- Create and rehearse a prototype

The development phase is where the instructors create and assemble the content created in the design phase. The instructor works to develop or integrate technologies, "debug" the procedures, and review and revise the instruction plan based on feedback. During the implementation phase, the instruction is delivered according to plan. The media are deployed and the lessons provided through the chosen technologies.

After delivery, the evaluation phase consists of two parts: formative and summative. Formative evaluation is present in each stage of the ADDIE process. Summative evaluation consists of tests designed for criterion-related referenced items and providing opportunities for feedback from the users. In testimony, feedback typically comes from three sources: yourself, the attorney who called you, and any reviewers in the courtroom.

Experts should welcome feedback at all stages, as it makes them better witnesses. Experts may gather preliminary feedback from colleagues, coworkers, family, and friends by practicing their delivery of information prior to testifying.

Creating Instructional Materials: A Concrete Approach

An approach for presenting instructional materials developed by the U.S. Navy is represented by the acronym TOM I. PASTA, which includes nine main parts:

- Title
- Objective
- Materials
- Introduction
- Presentation
- Application
- Study
- Testing
- Assignment

You can use this format when you take the witness stand for direct examination to teach what you have learned about a case to the judge, jury, or hearing panel. However, do not attempt this approach (or any approach) cold. Practice this approach ahead of time.

Presenting Complex Data

Statistical data and expert testimony can be difficult for juries, judges, and hearing panels to understand. The reasons are simple:

- The material is complex.
- The topic is foreign.
- The relevance of the testimony is not clear.
- The presentation is boring!

The presentation of statistics can be interesting if you take certain proactive steps. Studies have shown that lengthy statistical data can be vitalized by a single hypothetical case example.[5] For instance, if a statistical

---

[5] Goodman, J., Greene, E., and Loftus, E.F. "What Confuses Jurors in Complex Cases: Judges and Jurors Outline the Problems," *Trial*, November 1985, pages 65–73.

chart demonstrates a particular conclusion, that drab numerical summary can be brought to life by use of "factitious" example. If the summary chart of a thousand events suggests a particular incidence of drug reaction, the expert on direct could proceed as follows:

Q: Doctor, you are familiar with the chart, Exhibit A, isn't that correct?
A: Yes.
Q: How is it you are familiar with the Exhibit?
A: I prepared it for purposes of this trial.
Q: What does a chart like that really mean?
A: It means that if I see 1000 patients, only 1.2 or, say, a maximum of 2 will ever experience the drug reaction that occurred in this case. In other words, the chance of this adverse reaction occurring is quite remote.

To present statistics clearly, you must explain what the statistics are based on. Explain how the information was gathered. Explain how the information provides scientific or technical credibility to a proposition by numeric probability. Illustrate your presentation with lively, clear, and persuasive visual aids when possible. Finally, relate the statistics to the facts of the case at issue. Numerous studies have shown that people, including educated professionals, interpret and intuitively understand frequencies better than percentages; that is, people intuitively understand what "about 1 in 1000" means better than "0.012%."[6] To present complex information takes time, thought, and careful preparation—the more complex, the more time, thought, and preparation.[7] Newspapers are written on an eighth-grade level; jurors are no differently situated than readers of the newspaper.[8] Consider modifying your testimony accordingly. Trying to explain mass spectroscopy or DNA extraction, amplification, and analysis to a group of eighth graders is different from discussing them with your colleagues.

Review Questions

1. What is direct examination?
2. What is a bailiff?
3. What is an objection?

---

[6] Gigerenzer, G. *Simple Heuristics That Make Us Smart* (ABC Research Group, Oxford University Press, Oxford, 1999).
[7] Pascal, B., *"Je n'ai fait celle-ci plus longue que parce que je n'ai pas eu le loisir de la faire plus courte"* (I would have written a shorter letter, but I did not have the time), Provincial Letters: Letter XVI (Osgood and Company, Boston, Houghton, 1880).
[8] "Now Juries Are on Trial," *Time*, September 3, 1979.

4. What is a compound question?
5. What is hearsay?
6. What is a leading question?
7. What is the taxonomy of educational objectives?
8. What is the ADDIE model?
9. What is TOM I. PASTA?

Discussion Questions

1. Why should you approach direct examination like a teacher or instructor?
2. Would you handle redirect any differently than direct examination?
3. Explain some complicated aspect of your job to a nonscientist friend or family member. What questions do they ask? What did you leave out or assume they knew?

The Visual Display of Information

7

Key terms

Anscombe's Quartet
Chartjunk
Chewbacca Defense
Data-ink
Demonstration
Enthymemes
Graphic
Syllogism
Trial chart

Introduction

Experts tell us we learn 15 percent from what we hear and 85 percent from what we see. Therefore, you must translate complex principles into visual presentations. You must clearly demonstrate how those principles can be applied to the facts of your case. A list of possible vehicles for visual presentation of technical data is below—these materials must be planned early in your casework:

- Drawings, for use during testimony
- Photographs, including black and white and color enlargements and slides
- Films or videos
- Charts and graphs[1]
- Time-lapse still photography
- Photographic enlargements or overhead projection of critical documents
- Parts, samples, or specimens of tests that were performed
- Microscopic examination of slides

---

[1] See, for example, Rule 106, Federal Rules of Evidence, specifically allowing, if not encouraging, use of such summary charts and graphs.

- Models and mockups of the site
- Computer-generated or enhanced animation to demonstrate movement, time, and sequences of events
- Computer-enhanced displays to portray otherwise difficult-to-observe features
- Digital retouching of photographs (be sure to state that retouching has been done)
- Three-dimensional computer graphics

It is the truly great witness who uses demonstrative and graphic aids for maximum effect, working with counsel to obtain appropriate rulings to allow use or admissibility. A truly poor witness can use graphics that confuse the jury and obscure the evidence.

Visually Displaying Quantitative Information

If you have numeric information, why bother with graphics? Consider the following four sets of numbers.

Anscombe's Quartet

I		II		III		IV	
x	y	x	y	x	y	x	y
10	8.04	10	9.14	10	7.46	8	6.58
8	6.95	8	8.14	8	6.77	8	5.76
13	7.58	13	8.74	13	12.74	8	7.71
9	8.81	9	8.77	9	7.11	8	8.84
11	8.33	11	9.26	11	7.81	8	8.47
14	9.96	14	8.10	14	8.84	8	7.04
6	7.24	6	6.13	6	6.08	8	5.25
4	4.26	4	3.10	4	5.39	19	12.50
12	10.84	12	9.13	12	8.15	8	5.56
7	4.82	7	7.26	7	6.42	8	7.91
5	5.68	5	4.74	5	5.73	8	6.89

This data set is called Anscombe's Quartet.[2] The four sets of data that make up the quartet are similar in many respects. For each of the four sets:

- Mean of the x values = 9.0
- Mean of the y values = 7.5
- Equation of the least-squared regression line is: $y = 3 + 0.5 x$
- Sums of squared errors (about the mean) = 110.0

[2] Anscombe, F. J. Graphs in Statistical Analysis, *American Statistician* 27 (1973): pages 17–21.

- Regression sums of squared errors (variance accounted for by x) = 27.5
- Residual sums of squared errors (about the regression line) = 13.75
- Correlation coefficient = 0.82
- Coefficient of determination = 0.67

However, when the data is plotted, the differences among the data sets are obvious:

Without graphic representation, the patterns of the data sets would be lost. Imagine being an expert who has generated the equivalent of Anscombe's Quartet in your analysis but has not plotted them; you walk into court and the opposing witness has Figure 7.1 presented to the jury. Ouch.

Graphic representations of data can take many forms, from charts to graphs to tables, in an almost limitless array; choosing the best one can be difficult. Edward Tufte, an outstanding expert on graphic displays, states that "data graphics visually display measured quantities by means of the combined use of points, lines, a coordinate system, numbers, symbols, words, shading, and color."[3] According to Tufte, data graphics should do the following:

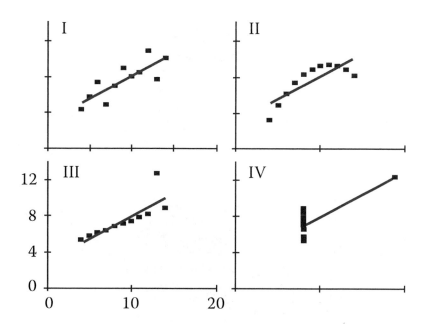

Figure 7.1 Anscombe's quartet graphed.

[3] Tufte, E. *The Visual Display of Quantitative Information* (Cheshire, CT: Graphics Press, 1983).

- Show the data
- Get the viewer to think about the content, not the form
- Avoid distorting what the data has to say
- Make large data sets coherent
- Encourage comparison between data
- Reveal the data on several levels
- Serve a reasonably clear purpose
- Be integrated with verbal and statistical descriptions

Good examples of bad graphics are easily found. European Union scientists now publish roughly the same number of papers as U.S. scientists, according to a survey conducted by Science Watch. The EU's portion of research papers increased from 30% to 36% over the last 16 years, while the U.S. share fell from 40.5% to 36.5% during the same time period. As Figure 7.2 attempts to show, the EU increase and the U.S. decline have intersected; the U.S. share of the world's total research papers exceeds Europe's by only a small margin. Unfortunately, the 3D "wall graph," even with reference lines across the back, is a poor choice for this kind of data. A simple line graph would foster more direct comparisons between regions. The multiplicity of lines, shading, the

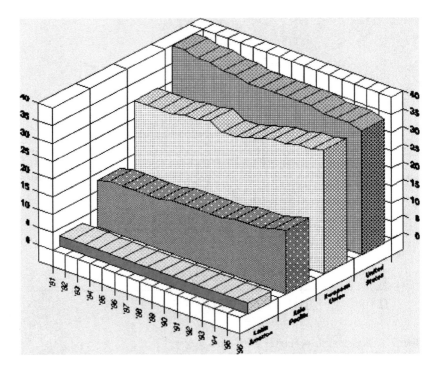

Figure 7.2 A graph purporting to show the publication rates of scientific papers internationally. The format of the graph grossly detracts from the content.

confusing grid in background, and the "false data" of the third dimension—it does not show any real information—all obscure the real message of the data.

Data-Ink

The majority of the ink in a graphic should present the data or information the graphic is intended to show. Data-ink is the nonerasable portion of the graphic, without which the data would cease to be represented. Some graphics use nearly all of their ink on the data, while others apparently hide the data beneath wells of ink. Obscuring data is easier than you might think. Take, for example, this simple data set (23, 34, 47, 51, 68, 71, 99, 105) charted in a popular spreadsheet program:

How much of the ink in this graphic presents the data (Figure 7.3)? What could you remove and still have the data? Most of it, as it turns out (Figure 7.4).

While not an excellent graphic (the spacing could be closer and the axes could be tighter, among other things), it is certainly clearer than the previous "pyramids of power" chart that the software automatically produced. Even a simple bar graph overrepresents the data six times (Figure 7.5).

In any graphic, the amount of data-ink should be maximized and the amount of non–data-ink should be minimized or removed entirely.

Chartjunk

This leads to the next thing to avoid in graphics: chartjunk, unnecessary or confusing visual elements in graphics that detract from the data. Too much

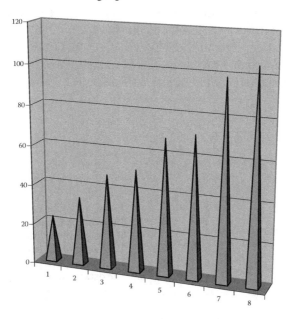

Figure 7.3 Most of the ink in this graphic goes to things other than the data.

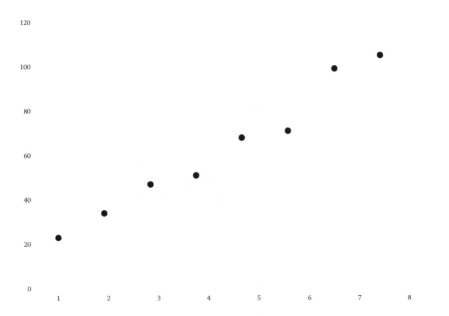

Figure 7.4 Most of the ink in this graphic is devoted to representing the data.

non–data-ink adds to chartjunk, but chartjunk is more than just that. For example, see Figure 7.6.

This graphic is painful to look at; it is, admittedly, an extreme example of overdecorated chartjunk. Someone thought the data alone was boring and needed to be dressed up. This is prevalent in presentations at meetings, symposia, and lectures—the speaker feels the content is not sufficient to hold the audience's attention and therefore makes it "entertaining." Think back on the best lectures you heard as a student. Were they colorful and animated or were they interesting and engrossing? If the data is meaningful and the

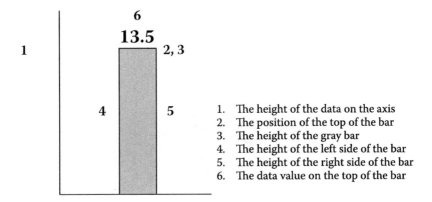

1. The height of the data on the axis
2. The position of the top of the bar
3. The height of the gray bar
4. The height of the left side of the bar
5. The height of the right side of the bar
6. The data value on the top of the bar

Figure 7.5 Even a seemingly innocent bar graph can massively overrepresent the data.

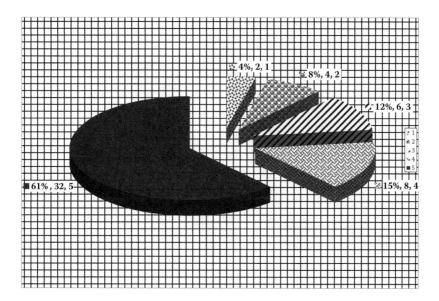

Figure 7.6 This figure is grossly overadorned with useless decoration, including the grid, the numbers, the exploded 3D disk, the patterns of each slice, and the painful visual of it all crammed together.

narrative is good, the data does not need to be enhanced with chartjunk, for example, the image of weather data from 1980 in Figure 7.7.

While March and April were the wettest months, they certainly were not the most humid, and that cold snap in June—brr. Notice how your eye wanders across the data, automatically comparing points and data types. Even though you might think the weather is a dull topic, your brain recognizes this is a good graphic. Imagine having to explain this data to a jury: It could be fun.

Graphs, Graphics, and Comparisons in Court

After all this discussion of what not to do, what is a graphic? A graphic is a visual representation of information or data. Graphics surround us, from maps to charts to graphs and diagrams. What you choose to use to demonstrate your evidence to the jury is largely up to you, so a good understanding of how to arrange information is key to a successful trial chart, the name typically given to visual representations used by forensic witnesses.

The arrangement of the elements of a trial chart is key to getting your point across. For example, you would use the layout shown in Figure 7.8a to encourage comparisons within sets of items (carpet fibers vs. garment fibers, for instance). The arrangement in Figure 7.8b would be to encourage comparisons between sets (evidence found on the suspect and the victim, for example). Finally, the layout in Figure 7.8c promotes comparison of data points. Using B to compare items from the victim and the suspect would

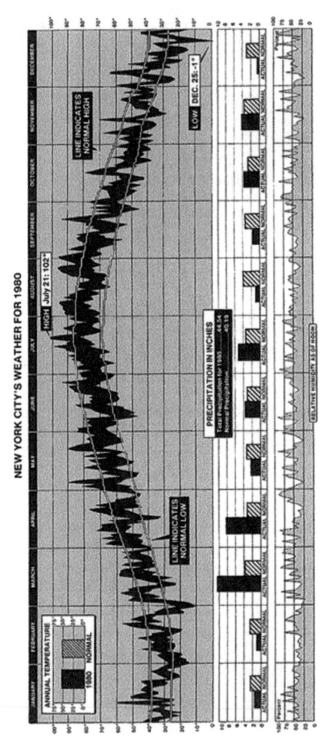

Figure 7.7 *New York Times*, Jan. 11, 1981, p. 32; also in Tufte, 1983, p. 30.

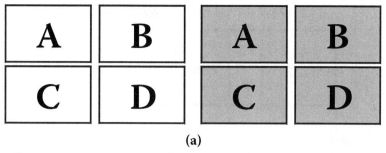

(a)

Encourages comparison *between* sets (A to A, for example)

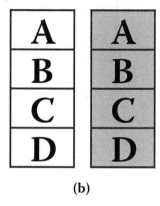

(b)

Encourages comparison of data points

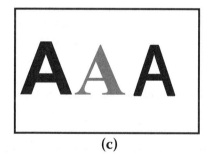

(c)

Figure 7.8 These graphics are examples of layouts that encourage comparisons (a) within sets of items (carpet fibers versus garment fibers, for instance); (b) between sets (evidence found on the suspect and the victim, for example); and (c) of data points.

not help the jury see the similarities or differences between the elements; to compare A with A, they have to visually skip over B.

Using a forensic example, review Figures 7.9 and 7.10 and think of them as trial charts. This is a case of drunk driving, and a breath alcohol result will be presented and most likely challenged as being insufficient compared to the blood alcohol results. How would you improve on these graphics? Take a few

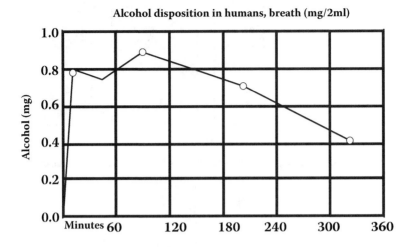

Figure 7.9 A plot of breath alcohol values.

minutes and make some notes thinking about data-ink, chartjunk, and what you want to show the jury (Figures 7.9 and 7.10).

You should have considered some of the following:

- Removing the background grid.
- Removing the axes and the frame.
- Decreasing the font.
- Moving the label "Minutes" to below the values to provide symmetry.
- Removing the data point markers; the trend is more important than any single data point.

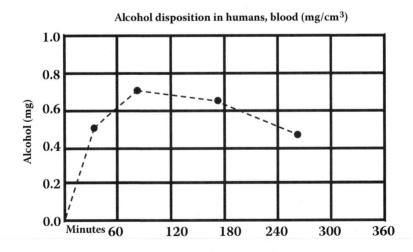

Figure 7.10 A plot of blood alcohol values.

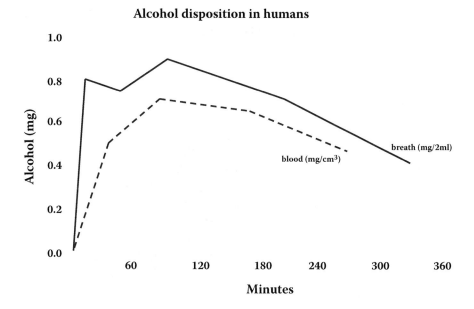

Figure 7.11 A reconfiguration of figures 7.9 and 7.10.

Finally, did you consider combining them into one chart? The key thing you want to emphasize with this data is the difference between blood and breath alcohol results (Figure 7.11).

The jury will now see that, although the method of measuring blood alcohol content may change, the body's response is the same. This graphic will strongly support the verbal discussion of why both methods are useful. Imagine trying to support that argument without any of these graphics.

Demonstrations: If the Glove Doesn't Fit, You Must Acquit

A demonstration, a presentation of activities or events to illustrate how something happens, must be carefully considered before being performed in open court. Inherently more complicated than a static graphic, a demonstration involves the live or recorded action of the events to be displayed. If the timing is off, if something is missing, if the software seizes up, if any of a myriad of things go wrong, the demonstration makes the demonstrator look unprofessional or ill prepared.

The core of any graphic is the information presented in it. For a demonstration, it is the rational chain of events leading to an inevitable conclusion; miss a link in that chain and the argument does not work. Arguments that have unstated assumptions, or links in this analogy, are called enthymemes. The unstated assumption must be true for the premises of the argument to lead to the desired conclusion. This makes it difficult to assess the argument or perhaps even have it be persuasive.[4] An example enthymeme is: Socrates is mortal because he is human. The complete argument[5] would be the classic:

> All humans are mortal (assumed).
> Socrates is human.
> Therefore, Socrates is mortal.

Enthymemes are not necessarily invalid, but they can be illogical yet persuasive. The best modern example of this is the argument Johnnie Cochran offered in defense of O.J. Simpson: "The glove doesn't fit [the defendant], so you must acquit."[6] The glove in question is one found at the scene soaked in the victims' blood and dried by the time it was collected. The prosecutors asked Simpson to try on the evidence glove—not a clean new one as would have been the case prior to the crime—in front of the jury. Simpson's struggling to fit his rubber-gloved hand (for safety reasons) into the dried, shrunken glove left an indelible impression on the jury and one that Cochran fully exploited. The extended argument would be:

> If any evidence does not fit the defendant, then acquittal is required (assumed).
> The glove doesn't fit the defendant.
> The glove is evidence.
> Therefore, you must acquit the defendant.

More is unstated in this argument, even in this extended form, than is stated. For example, how "fit" is determined, which glove is being discussed (the one from the scene, the one the perpetrator used, a clean one, etc.). Hiding premises can be an effective way to deflect criticism of questionable reasoning. Hiding premises is not, however, how you should prepare your court demonstrations.

---

[4] Heinrichs, J. *Thank You for Arguing* (New York: Three Rivers Press, 2007).

[5] This is technically a syllogism, an argument in which one proposition is inferred from the previous two, but a proper treatment of this topic is beyond the scope of this book. The interested reader is directed to Priest, G. *Logic: A Very Short Introduction*. Oxford, UK: Oxford University Press, 2000.

[6] Wonderfully parodied in the South Park episode "Chef Aid." In the episode, Johnnie Cochran defends a character using the Chewbacca Defense, consisting of nonsensical arguments meant to confuse a jury. Cochran states, "I have one final thing that I want you to consider. Ladies and gentlemen, this is Chewbacca. Chewbacca is a Wookiee from the planet Kashyyyk. But Chewbacca lives on the planet Endor. Now think about it; that does not make sense!...Why would a Wookiee, an eight-foot tall Wookiee, want to live on Endor, with a bunch of two-foot tall Ewoks? That does not make sense! But more important, you have to ask yourself: What does this have to do with this case? Nothing. Ladies and gentlemen, it has nothing to do with this case!...If Chewbacca lives on Endor, you must acquit! The defense rests." A workshop was held at the American Academy of Forensic Sciences meeting in 2006 about the Chewbacca Defense.

Each link in your argument should be transparent, clearly stated, and stoutly connected to the premises that precede and follow it. Discuss the demonstration with the attorney ahead of time (no surprises!). Practice and rehearse your demonstrations multiple times to make sure it works properly in the allotted time. Know what materials and resources you will need in the courtroom and either take them or have them ready when you arrive. Demonstrations can be effective, but they can also be disasters if they are not thought through, planned, prepared, and executed properly.

Conclusion

Graphics can greatly enhance your testimony—they can also distract from it. Plan ahead on how to use graphic displays of information to support your testimony. Think about the essence of what you want to show to the jury. Consider the comparisons you want them to make. Are your graphics clear, concise, and free from chartjunk? Have you maximized the data-ink? Review and rehearse any demonstrations you plan to do; rehearse them again and again to make sure they work. You will encounter enough surprises in court without inadvertently creating them yourself.

Review Questions

1. What is Anscombe's Quartet?
2. What is data-ink?
3. What is chartjunk? Find a good "bad" example in a newspaper.
4. What is a graphic?
5. What is a trial chart? Is it different from a graphic?
6. What is a demonstration?
7. What is an enthymeme?
8. What is the "Chewbacca Defense"?
9. What is a syllogism? Is it the same as an argument?
10. Why would you, as an expert, use a graphic in court?

Discussion Questions

1. Take the example of chartjunk you found for Review Question 3. Find the original data or estimate the data as best you can. Reformat the graphic using the principles in this chapter. What did you change? What did you keep (data-ink)? Why?

2. Although it is not covered in this chapter, think about color in a graphic. When do you have to use it, and when could you get away with black and white or gray tones?

3. Take the following data points, decide on a message, and create a graphic from them. Why did you design it the way you did? Did you use raw data or did you use statistics (mean, median, mode, etc.)? Why?

Cross-Examination

8

Key Terms

Foundation
Frontloading
Historic hysteric gambit
Hypothetical questions
Learned treatise
"Yes, but" answer

Introduction

There are some specific things you can do to prepare yourself for cross-examination. Most obvious are those that have been previously discussed in this text. All those devices and ideas serve to enhance your credibility as an expert witness. As your credibility is enhanced, cross-examination threats are diminished.

In truth, most cross-examination "threats" exist only in the minds of the novice witness. Experienced experts are aware they have no dog in the fight. They come to court prepared, with their conclusions based on earnest effort, experience, testing, and data. Being questioned about their findings should not be cause for consternation.

That said, there are specific things you can do to make yourself more ready and less vulnerable to cross-examination. Your résumé must accurately reflect what you have actually accomplished, not what you wish you had done. Do not exceed the bounds of your own expertise. In taking on assignments and in answering questions, do not venture beyond the areas in which you are professionally qualified. The temptation is great to move into areas in which you are not qualified. Your image and credibility will be enhanced by sticking to your field of knowledge, training, and experience. Whatever investigative steps you have taken must be completed and fully documented. The thoroughness of your preparation to testify will be exemplified by your direct examination. Accurate investigation creates a dense fabric of fact that becomes difficult to penetrate on cross-examination. Further, strict adherence to scientific principles, regardless of whose position they favor, often reduces the length of cross-examination. Consider:

Q: Is it possible another gun was used to fire this bullet?
A: It is highly unlikely.
Q: But it's possible?
A: I can't imagine that's the case.
Q: Are you testifying this bullet could only have been fired from this gun to the exclusion of all other guns on the planet?
A: Well, I didn't say that…
Q: So it's possible that another gun fired the weapon.
A: Yes.

This lengthy exchange could have been avoided if the expert had just answered the question with a "yes" the first time. Experts who wish to be considered independent need to display this independence at all times.

Cross-Examination: Friend or Foe?

Most forensic experts dread cross-examination, and with good reason: it can be very unpleasant. In reality, with planning and patience, even a vigorous cross-examination can be weathered with your integrity and results intact. If you are believable, stick to the facts you know and can support, and have done your homework, your abilities will be obvious. Psychological persuasion conveyed by body language, repetition of theme, dress, and demeanor all add to your positive image. The smooth, solid presentation you made on direct examination must be maintained throughout cross-examination. Similarly, the respect shown to one side must be shown to the other. This holds true both in your preparedness, your attitude, your demeanor, and your willingness to answer the questions posed.

Witnesses who are certain of their own effort and preparation with the data to back it up are generally questioned cautiously on cross-examination. The cross-examining attorney quickly senses your truthful and positive answers. Part of the stimulation of a classroom setting is the ability to field questions from students. The skill with which those questions are responded to is often the mark of a great teacher. Your function as an "expert witness teacher" is merely an extension of that exercise. The cross-examiner who probes your qualifications, preparation, conclusions, and opinions will press you for answers.

One of the major opportunities for attorneys in cross-examination is to highlight their theory by reviewing prior testimony. In some cases, prior testimony may be used to further make the point. See below:

Q: You were trying to imply to this jury that that imprint was a Silga sole, weren't you?
A: No. I testified I couldn't determine that.
Q: Oh. Okay. You went a little bit farther than what you testified to in the criminal case, didn't you?
A: No. I said exactly the same thing that I said in the criminal trial.
Q: All right. Let's go to page 32842 of the criminal testimony, lines 12 through 17. 32842.

(Reading)
Q: My understanding is, there was insufficient detail present to call it one way or the other as to those marks, whether they're a footprint or not, in the Bronco?
A: I couldn't associate them with the sole to sole, yes.
Q: That was your answer, right?
A: Yes.
Q: And you weren't trying to imply to this jury that that was a Silga sole when you put the overlay over the board?
A: No, I was not.[1]

Here, the witness is confident in his wording and what he meant; this kind of confidence comes from experience, good methods, and a cool head.

During your professional career, you might have written articles, books, or reports. In addition, you might have testified in deposition or at trial on prior occasions. Your personal library should include reprints of every article you have ever published and every deposition or court transcript of your testimony. The attorney for whom you are testifying is entitled to know about your prior opinions. In addition to alerting you and the parties for whom you act to areas of cross-examination, your prior writings and testimony can supply positive support or rebuttal material for cross-examination. When asked about prior testimony, where the attorney suggests you testified differently, follow these three simple steps:

- Don't panic.
- Take the time to review the facts and testimony referenced.
- Consider whether the current case is the same as or different from the prior case.

All of this should be done prior to responding to the question.

---

[1] William Bodziak, O.J. Simpson civil trial, November 27, 1996.

Know the Attorney's Goals

Laying Foundation

Before discussion about the goals of cross-examination in general, a basic discussion about foundation is in order. An attorney is not allowed to ask you about an exhibit if it has not yet been introduced into evidence. Unless the parties stipulate to a piece of evidence's admission, the attorney seeking to introduce the evidence must "lay foundation" for its admission. Care should be taken to listen to and answer only the questions asked during foundation. The questions are, generally:

- Do you recognize this document/item/report/photograph? This answer to this should be yes or no. That's all.
- How do you recognize it? Perhaps you examined it, wrote it, or took the picture. Limit your response to how you recognize it.
- What is it? It is a report, a gun, a photo. For this question, resist the urge to launch into a paragraph detailing your findings. Just answer with what the piece of evidence is.
- Is it in substantially the same condition as it was when you wrote it/ examined it/read it? Again, the answer should be yes or no. That's it. If it is not in the same condition, wait until asked to explain what is different.

Following this series of questions, the attorney will offer the evidence for admission. Opposing counsel may choose to object to its admission. The judge then decides whether it is admissible. Only after the item is admitted should you be offering testimony about it.

Cross-Examination Techniques

Professor James W. McElhaney suggests eight fundamental techniques attorneys typically employ to cross-examine an expert witness:[2]

- Make the expert your witness; highlighting evidence favorable to their theory.
- Attack the field of expertise; show lack of recognition of the professional field.Attack the witness's qualifications; establish gaps in the professional résumé.
- Expose the witness's bias; give reasons why testimony is slanted.
- Attack the witness's fact basis; investigation was inadequate or the witness did not have access to all the facts in the case.

[2] McElhaney, J.W. Expert Witnesses, *ABA Journal*, 75 (March 1989): pages 98–99.

- Change the hypothetical used on direct; vary the facts to support a different theory if use of the hypothetical question is the basis for expert opinion.
- Impeach the witness with learned treatises and journals; any recognized text, authoritative in nature, can be used to cross-examine.
- Attack the witness head on; find prior contra writings by the witness.

The following cases show how opposing counsel attempts to achieve these goals during cross-examination. Even if the examples are not in your field, notice the pattern, the sequence, and the intent of the questions; these will be instructive to you as you learn about cross-examination.

Making the Expert Their Witness

In an action involving construction of a golf course in a residential neighborhood, the applicant's expert testified that, in his opinion, a perimeter fence around the golf course would not be unsightly. He based his conclusion on the fact that other fences at nearby golf courses, which he had photographed, did not appear to disturb neighborhood aesthetics. Cross-examination was designed to make the witness support the opposition.

Q: Do you agree, Mr. Witness, that the fence will be at least 40 feet high?
A: Yes.
Q: It will be supported by telephone pole–size support columns?
A: That's true.
Q: The fence is to be made of chicken wire, is that correct?
A: That's correct.
Q: And the fence will border residential property for approximately 300 yards, is that also correct?
A: Yes.
Q: Do you agree the chicken wire and telephone pole structure will be twice as high as any of the residences in the neighborhood?
A: I can't say for sure.
Q: Well, the houses are all one-story houses, are they not?
A: Yes.
Q: Is there any other structure like the one you have described anywhere in the neighborhood at this time?
A: No.
Q: And the homes have been there for years, isn't that true?
A: Yes, many years.

The objective of the questioning was to emphasize that the fence was out of character with the residential homes in the neighborhood. In effect, the witness, through the cross-examination, supported the opponents. The adverse effect could have been avoided if other tall structures in the area could have been identified. Of course, it is possible no other tall structures are in the area. If the witness is offering an opinion, such as in this case, the witness should have considered such arguments and addressed them in their report. Even if not included in the report, a good expert will consider counterarguments and be prepared to respond to them. Perhaps the expert would note the chicken wire is mostly air and difficult to see, for example.

Attacking the Expert's Field of Expertise

In attacking your field of expertise, the effort is to show there is little or no scientific, technical, professional, or other recognized basis to support your testimony.

Q: Dr. Jones, your field of expert testimony is environmental epidemiology, is that correct?

A: That's correct.

Q: Is it true, doctor, that there is no college or university in the United States that now offers a degree in environmental epidemiology?

A: That's correct.

Q: As a matter of fact, doctor, isn't it true there is no college or university in the world that offers a degree in environmental epidemiology?

A: That's correct.

Q: Isn't it correct, doctor, that there are no national boards that deal exclusively with the subject of environmental epidemiology?

A: That is correct.

Q: Isn't it correct, doctor, that there are no national associations that deal exclusively with the subject of environmental epidemiology?

A: That is correct.

Q: Isn't it correct, doctor, that there are no professional societies that deal exclusively with the subject of environmental epidemiology?

A: That is correct.

The fact that there is no degree in the subject and no professional association dealing exclusively with the area of expertise does not disqualify you to state opinions. However, the question has now been raised as to whether there is such a specialty field as environmental epidemiology. This is called "frontloading." The sting should have been anticipated and brought out during direct examination, not left for a cross-exam bombshell.

Attacking the Expert's Qualifications

An attack on the witness's qualifications can cover many aspects of the résumé.

Q: Mr. Smith, it appears from your professional résumé you attended the University of Wisconsin. It that correct?

A: Yes, that's correct.

Q: Mr. Smith, in your résumé it doesn't say what degree you received from the University of Wisconsin. Is that because you did not receive a degree?

A: The work toward my undergraduate degree was almost completed when I left the university.

Q: Mr. Smith, isn't it correct that you did not receive a degree from the University of Wisconsin?

A: Yes.

Q: As a matter of fact, Mr. Smith, isn't it correct that you never received a degree from any college or university in the United States?

A: Yes, that's correct.

Q: And isn't it also correct that you have been practicing as a professional engineer without being licensed in any state of the United States to practice that profession?

A: Yes.

While the witness did not attempt to conceal the absence of professional qualifications in his résumé, the cross-examiner is making him seem unqualified to the jury. If the problem had been explored on direct examination, the thunder would have been taken from the cross-examiner. Some attorneys will ask directly, "What will the other side attack you on?" when meeting with experts before putting them on the stand. You should be prepared to answer this question based on prior experience and common sense.

Attacking the Factual Basis for the Expert's Conclusions

In an effort to attack the factual basis of testimony, the attorney could attempt to show any of the following:

- You are not familiar with the scene of the events.
- Your examinations are not really scientific.
- You have not examined the actual product in question.
- You made no measurements.
- The measurements you did make are wrong.
- You carried out no tests.
- The tests you did carry out were not relevant, incorrectly applied, or had no standards.

- You were not in a position to observe the events.
- Your opinion is based on secondhand information.
- Your opinion is based on incomplete information.

Such attacks go nowhere if you have done your homework.

The Use of Hypotheticals

Use of hypothetical questions is still a valid method of examination. The technique on cross-examination is to insert into a hypothetical question facts that could lead you to reach a conclusion opposite to that tendered on direct examination. Pay close attention to the form of the hypothetical question and do not be afraid to hedge your answers. The phrase "Assuming the facts in this case…" is a signal that the attorney wants you to make the same assumptions he is making (but may not be stating), as in the following case.

Case

In an action involving an alleged defective setting of a ski binding that failed to release, a technician rendered an opinion that the binding had been too tight for the weight and ability of the claimant. On cross-examination, the defense attempted to establish that the claimant had lied about his skiing ability and his weight. The following exchange occurred:

Q: Isn't it correct that unless you are advised accurately as to the skier's ability and the skier's weight, you can't make the proper adjustment on the ski binding?

A: That's correct.

Q: If, instead of being an intermediate skier, the claimant was only a beginner, would that make a difference to the installing technician?

A: Yes.

Q: If the skier said he weighed 150 pounds when in fact he weighed 175 pounds, would that make any substantial difference in the adjustment?

A: Of course.

Q: For the sake of my examination, Mr. Technician, I want you to assume that the plaintiff told the ski binding technician he was an intermediate skier when in fact he was a beginning skier. I want you to further assume that the claimant stated he weighed 150 pounds when in fact he weighed 175. Now with that information, what would the proper binding setting have been, assuming those facts?

The objective of the questioning was to create a set of facts that accorded with the defense view of the plaintiff's conduct. As the witness, your job is to consider the question and answer it.

Notice the witness's ease of requesting clarification in the following example of a complex hypothetical question:[3]

Q (by defense attorney): In terms of your examination and determination of where everybody was in this reconstruction. If in fact the internal jugular vein was the first vein severed, and if, in fact, it bled down his left side and down his pants and down into his boot, you would agree that he would still have the ability to fight off an attacker for a period of time, 5 minutes or longer, true?

Opposing Counsel: Objection. Assumes facts not in evidence, Your Honor.

The Court: Overruled. Hypothetical question.

The Witness: Are you asking, if I may, so I can understand the question, are you asking me whether, with a severed jugular vein, he could still fight for 5 minutes? Is that what you're asking me?

Particularly when faced with a hypothetical, clarifying the hypothetical universe is essential to maintaining your credibility.

Using a Learned Treatise

Attacking you by use of an authoritative publication is one of the most effective devices in the cross-examiner's toolkit. This is often referred to as the learned treatise.

Case

In a case involving dissolution of a marriage, a rehabilitation counselor testified for the wife concerning her alleged inability to return to the job market because of the psychological trauma she had sustained from the divorce proceeding. A series of quotes were read from a text to the testifying witness that suggested the type of trauma being used to support the testimony was not supportable.

After four quotes had been read, the witness asked the examining attorney the name of the publication. To the witness's surprise, the attorney told the witness that the quotes had been extracted from his own technical writing published within the preceding year.

The court found the wife able to return to the job market. The lesson is obvious: know what you have written previously—everything you have written—and know it cold, and be aware of what is authoritative.

Rule 803(18) of the Federal Rules of Evidence states that you as an expert do not have to recognize a learned treatise as authoritative to be cross-examined about it. At least in the federal courts, if any expert witness testifies that a particular treatise is authoritative, you, as a testifying witness, may be examined about it.

---

[3] Dr. Werner Spitz, O.J. Simpson civil trial, November 12, 1996.

An Attack on the Expert's Conclusions

A direct attack on your position is difficult to undertake, yet the effort will be made in a proper case. On occasion, you may be tempted to maintain a position of absolute certainty even in the face of overwhelming contradictions. That dogged adherence to a position can destroy your credibility.

Case

> In a case involving valuation of real property, the expert stated that his task was to place himself "on the piece of property 10 years prior" and attempt to determine value in that hypothetical stance. Cross-examination and other evidence revealed that the expert had not contacted the actual buyer, another appraiser, or the zoning official, all of whom had dealt with the property 10 years before. All three of those individuals testified that the expert's opinion of value was substantially incorrect.
>
> Nevertheless, in the face of that overwhelming contravening testimony, the expert stood fast. He maintained that he was in a better position to value the property 10 years after the fact than the three knowledgeable persons had been at the time. Steadfast adherence to an untenable position served to erode the witness's credibility.
>
> This expert can expect to be cross-examined on this incident for years to come.

Testing the Entire Field

The question as to whether you will be allowed to testify may not come up until trial. Under the Federal Rules of Evidence, the trial judge determines the qualifications of witnesses.[4] The test may be whether the scientific principles you rely on are considered reliable enough to support expert opinion. Attacks on your field of scientific expertise should not be overlooked by you as you prepare to testify, if the area of testimony has not yet reached scientific or professional acceptance or recognition. Attorneys may attack a discipline with historical anecdotes that are no longer true, ideas like phlogiston in chemistry or Lamarck's theory of inheritance through acquired traits. The attorney will then try to make your discipline look silly or make modern ideas seem as threadbare as the old discarded ones. This is known as the historic hysteric gambit.[5] The best way to counter this attack is to know the history of your discipline and understand your methods as completely as possible.

However, in some disciplines, particularly in forensic science, the evolution is going the other way. Disciplines that were once considered rock

---

[4] Federal Rules of Evidence, Rule 104(a) (2011).
[5] Brodsky, S. L. *Testifying in Court: Guidelines and Maxims for the Expert Witness* (Washington, D.C.: American Psychological Association, 2004).

solid have been called into question by the National Academy of Sciences 2009 publication "Strengthening Forensic Science: A Path Forward" and the President's Council of Advisors on Science and Technology's Report to President Obama entitled, "Forensic Science in Criminal Courts: Ensuring Scientific Validity of Feature-Comparison Methods." An expert should be familiar with criticism of their discipline.

Among the most dangerous of questions is the hypothetical question. This is a question that proposes an imaginary situation incorporating facts about the case. Hypothetical questions can be answered only in terms of their validity, not if they make sense. For example, a person may ask: "Would you drink the Atlantic Ocean if it were lemonade?" To answer this question, you have to assume that the Atlantic Ocean is made of lemonade, so you have to answer only as to whether or not you would drink it. Saying, "But the ocean is not lemonade," is not an appropriate response; you can only respond with answers like "yes," "no," or "depends on if enough sugar has been added." The attorney states a factual foundation (often based on disputed facts in the case) and asks the expert to draw conclusions based on the hypothetical foundation. The hypothetical question includes only facts already in evidence. Do not assume that the facts are true. Hypothetical questions are slippery things because of the (often unspoken) assumptions being made. Be willing to ask about certain facts and clarify the question.

Reducing Vulnerability to Cross-Examination

Certain areas of weakness attend some expert testimony. Those areas will certainly be the grounds for attack by a cross-examining attorney. Knowing the areas of jeopardy will help you prepare in advance for the cross-examination.

Is your opinion based in whole or in part on judgment as opposed to measurable fact? It is always proper for cross-examination to probe the basis for your well-established conclusions. If that basis is technical and scientific testing, you will not be vulnerable. However, if subjective judgment and opinion are the sole basis for your opinion, you are vulnerable. Consider two examples. A chemical test involves mixing a compound and then adding a measured number of drops of reagent to turn the compound from pink to blue. The exact number of drops necessary to cause the color change constitutes a specific scientific measurement. No judgment or opinion attends this test. The results can be documented with laboratory protocol and photographs. In a more subjective example, valuation of motor vehicles requires an orderly examination of each vehicle against a 50-point checklist. Each item on the checklist is graded from 1 to 10. Each of the 50 items requires judgment based upon observation. True, an expert's observation is more valid than that of the average person. However, judgment is the key word. This valuation would be considered a major area for cross-examination.

Is your opinion based upon input from others? You are to testify as an orthopedic surgeon. The issue is the extent of a fracture sustained in a fall. The radiologist's report suggests to you a compound comminuted fracture with 30 bone fragments at the fracture site. You testify to that effect. However, by cross-examination, it is established your testimony is based on the radiology report. As an orthopedist, you may not be able to identify 30 bone fragments from the x-ray, but ordinary practice allows you to rely on the radiologist's report. You must be ready to defend your reliance as customary in your field.

Cognitive bias cannot be denied. Instead, be prepared to describe the steps taken to reduce the potential impact of cognitive bias. Acknowledging cognitive bias exists, but not in you personally, doesn't serve you. Instead, it may lead the jury to question your credibility on this and other statements you have made.

Have you made prior inconsistent statements? The questioner will ask about whatever you have written and testified to in the past. Aggressive cross-examining counsel will comb those written materials for inconsistency.

Does your behavior suggest insecurity? The skillful cross-examining attorney will observe you carefully. If you have your hand near your mouth or face, you may be withholding information, according to the attorney's way of thinking. If you flush or your hand trembles, you may feel insecure. If you hesitate and stammer or fumble through papers and files, you may feel a lack of confidence in your own ability. Skillful examining attorneys sense a weak, inadequately prepared, or unsure witness. When that sixth sense is activated, they will move in for the kill. Your best option is to agree—up to a point—and wait for the right moment to counteract the line of questioning:

Q: If we did a tape lift, say, on that chair, might we catch one of your hairs?
A: It's possible.
Q: Possible to catch one of the fibers on your shirt?
A: That's also possible.
Q: And if I came up and sat in that very same chair, might those—might that hair and fiber get transferred to my jacket?
A: That's possible.
Q: And then if I sat down at the counsel table, might those fibers get transferred to the chair?
A: That's also possible, yes.
Q: And the hairs?
A: Yes.
Q: And then if Mr. Clarke sat in the chair, might those fibers then get transferred to Mr. Clarke?
A: That could happen, yes.
Q: And if he walked them into his office might they travel to his office?...

The basic tenet of cross-examination for the attorney is control of the witness. This is done by crafting leading questions. This is consistent with the rules that govern cross-examination. You should expect it. You should also focus on answering the question with a yes or a no. An expert who is well prepared, did the work, documented the work, and has conclusions supported by data and science should have no fear of a series of leading questions from opposing counsel.

However, there may be times when a simple yes or no just won't do. Note: these times will be rare. If you find yourself annotating every answer, you may not be listening carefully to the questions. To the question "Mr. Expert, isn't it correct that traffic lights sequence green to yellow to red?" the easy answer is "Yes," but the better answer may be "Yes, unless there is a malfunction," if there has been a malfunction in the case at hand.

When the attorney asks a potentially damaging question, use the same air of certainty that you evidenced on direct examination. An answer like "While that may be true in a vacuum, my analysis shows…" does three things. First, you have signaled the attorney who subpoenaed you to revisit this issue on redirect. Second, you have shown your credibility in a forthright, unapologetic manner. Finally, it helps you avoid the "Yes, but" answer where an attorney may stop you after you say "Yes…" with a curt "Thank you!" By saying yes, you have linguistically satisfied the requirement for answering the question; therefore, you may not get a chance to explain your answer (the attorney may not want the jury to hear it). By saying "While that may be true…," you have not yet fully answered the question and need to continue to have your answer make sense.

Have you made sure your language is understandable and that you translate technical terms? After you have answered the question before you— stop! Do not tell everything you know about the subject. Do not annotate with little-known facts. If possible, have the attorney prepare summaries of relevant facts and documents rather than providing the documents or client statements. This ensures the attorney is familiar with the topic. Work with the attorney to identify potential areas of cross-examination. Your careful preparation will allow you to participate in cross-examination in a meaningful way. Make sure the theories on which you rely rest on a reliable foundation, are based on scientifically valid principles, and are relevant to the case.

Understand What Happens Next

After direct and cross-examination, the attorney who did the direct exam will have the opportunity to do something called "redirect." It allows the attorney who called you to testify to ask additional questions to follow up on the cross-examination. Often, experts make an effort during cross to signal the attorney who called them to "loop back" to a particular area of testimony. Experts are advised these signals are not lost on opposing counsel or the jury. For witnesses claiming independence, it signals an agenda from someone who claims to be unbiased.

Additionally, what is important to the expert may not be what is important to the attorneys. Attorneys who try cases create a theme and theory you may or may not be privy to. Do not take offense if an attorney doesn't follow up on redirect on an issue you think is important.

Conclusion

Be alert to the eight fundamental goals of cross-examination. By knowing the objectives of cross-examination, you can use the questioning process to solidify your position. Objectives of cross-examination include use of your testimony as a springboard for the cross-examiner's own expert. The cross-examination may seek to use your testimony to contradict other experts on your side or to obtain information beneficial to the cross-examiner's case. However, your preparation, credibility, and positive demeanor will blunt the challenge afforded by cross-examination.

The usual admonition for cross-examining counsel is to stop when you are ahead, use restraint, and not overplay. These same admonitions are equally true for you as the expert witness undergoing cross-examination. Do not overplay the expert role. Do not overemphasize your superior knowledge. Be accurate with the facts. Be firm without being an advocate. Maintain control of the situation.

Review Questions

1. What is a learned treatise?
2. What is one of the major opportunities that cross-examination presents for an attorney?
3. Name four ways an attorney could try to attack the factual basis of your testimony.
4. What is a "yes, but" answer?
5. What is the historic hysteric gambit?
6. How should you act toward an attorney on cross-examination?
7. Why is cross-examination even necessary, legally speaking?
8. What are the functions of cross-examination?
9. What are the best ways to prepare for a vigorous cross-examination?
10. When you finish with cross-examination, are you finished with testimony?

Discussion Questions

1. How is cross-examination like direct examination? How are they different?
2. Think about your demeanor on direct examination and then on cross-examination. What might be some ways to calm yourself if you get nervous about cross-examination?
3. Why are experts nervous about cross-examination? How could you avoid that nervousness?

Ethics

9

Key Terms

Alterations
Ethics
Normative ethics

Introduction

"Ethics" refers to the values and customs of a person or group. The topic covers the analysis and use of concepts such as right and wrong, good and evil, and personal and professional responsibility. When people speak of ethics, typically they mean normative ethics, the study of the moral standards and behaviors that help to determine what is meant by, for example, right, wrong, unethical, and immoral. People and groups articulate what good actions and behaviors they expect from others.

Four categories of ethical problems plague the use of expert witnesses in the dispute resolution process. The first has to do with unethical conduct of forensic witnesses. The second relates to admissibility of expert testimony. The third addresses negligent performance of expert service. The fourth area concerns interprofessional relations. Examination of problems and solutions provides you with guidance for future conduct, keeping in mind always that objectivity is for the expert and advocacy is for the attorney. American law schools require a course in professional responsibility covering not only ethics but matters of professionalism as they relate to practicing law. Forty-eight of the 50 states require attorneys to sit for and pass the Multistate Professional Responsibility Examination (MPRE) before they can practice law. Similarly, the topic of ethics is required in undergraduate and graduate forensic science programs accredited by the Forensic Science Educational Program Accreditation Commission (FEPAC, at www.aafs.org).

What Is Unethical Conduct?

Proportionately speaking, only rarely are expert witnesses actually found culpable for preparing fraudulent, false, or imagined scientific, technical, or professional research. Unfortunately, those cases attract a tremendous amount of attention and bring massive disfavor to an otherwise honored profession. The horror stories circulating in legal and forensic fields about experts who falsify data to support either a prosecution or defense posture in a criminal case are all too well known today. The use of false DNA, blood, alcohol, or chemical substance testing resulting in wrongful incarceration of accused defendants stands as the most reprehensible of all forensic witness abuses. However, falsification of credentials runs a close second. Finally, in some cases, a forensic witness's testimony was so inadequate as to justify exclusion at trial.

Unethical experts may tender testimony to the court based upon supposed scientific, technical, or professional findings and research when they in fact did not do the work represented by their report. Often, others have actually done the work, but not necessarily under proper supervision, and the testimony should be excluded.

The courts are sometimes faced with the problem of forged, altered, or otherwise falsified documents, data, or lab reports supporting supposed expert testimony. In those situations, when exposed, based upon the crucible of cross-examination, the resulting exclusion of expert testimony seems most appropriate. Sanctions should also be imposed by the courts on both witnesses and attorneys who were informed beforehand of the hoax. For attorneys, the presentation of evidence known to be false is a serious ethical violation. The state Board of Professional Responsibility may very well also discipline the lawyer. For the testifying expert, offering false testimony is perjury, which carries with it both criminal and civil consequences. No case is so important to be worth compromising one's integrity, not to mention risking jail or prison time.

If an expert either willfully ignores the actual facts of the case or is deprived of access to the facts by overenthusiastic counsel, the testimony of the expert should be excluded. Sometimes an expert witness will distinguish prior testimony in a similar case because it does not particularly fit facts and circumstances of the present case. Such a matter of inconsistent testimony, while totally unprofessional, is often exposed in the courtroom by aggressive cross-examination. It is hoped this kind of chicanery will be reduced in frequency from our courts and dispute resolution processes as cross-examining skills become more articulate, professional grievance practices become more stringent, and the Internet makes discovery of prior positions of the expert more accessible.

Occasionally, expert witnesses display a lack of knowledge or professional competence to render the opinions that are sought. In those circumstances, the likely result is that expert testimony will be admitted subject to searing cross-examination, and usually discounted by the fact finder because it has insufficient weight to be persuasive.

Examples of Scientist Misconduct

One expert witness who demonstrated no scientific basis for his opinions had actually sought out the plaintiff and volunteered his services as an expert.[1] Another of the plaintiff's experts had reached a conclusion as to causation before doing any testing. As one might imagine, their testimony was excluded on the grounds that it lacked probative weight or value.

In another federal court case, the U.S. District Court was presented with an unusual testimonial dilemma.[2] A plaintiff involved in a claim against the Ford Motor Company had modified a vehicle and then obtained expert testimony that the modification had not occurred. The expert witness was aware of the deception but did not disclose it. He was involved in incomplete, dishonest, and misleading reports and testimony. The federal judge handed down a severe censure, resulting in the permanent banning of the expert as a witness in the U.S. District Court.

A number of situations can be envisioned where, because of unsupported or negligent expert testimony, a particular result occurs in the judicial process. In such circumstances, the forensic expert is subject to judicial scrutiny, just like any other professional in a contested setting.[3]

A particularly extreme example of professional ethics abuse is that of Fred Zain, who worked as a forensic scientist in West Virginia and Texas. In a report of the West Virginia Court of Appeals, it was recounted that Zain had:[4]

- Overstated the strength of results and the frequency of genetic matches on individual pieces of evidence
- Misreported the frequency of genetic matches on multiple pieces of evidence
- Reported that multiple items had been tested, when only a single item had been tested; reported inconclusive results as conclusive
- Repeatedly altered laboratory records
- Grouped results to create the erroneous impression that genetic markers had been obtained from all samples tested
- Failed to report conflicting results and failed to conduct or to report conducting additional testing to resolve conflicting results

---

[1] Socha, "Excluding Plaintiff's Expert Testimony," *For the Defense*, September 1987, page 24.

[2] *Schimdt v. Ford Motor Company*, 112 F.R.D. 216 (D. Cob. 1986).

[3] See, for example, Restatement (Second) Torts, §299 A (1965); *Bruce v. Byrne-Stevens & Associates*, 51 Wash. App. 199, 752 p.2d 949 (1988), revised 776 p.2d 666 (1989), which was just such a case. The court concluded that experts are not immune from claims when they do their work in a negligent manner. The Supreme Court of Washington, in reversing the lower appellate court, based its decision on the doctrine of testimonial immunity.

[4] West Virginia Court of Appeals, No. 21973, "In the matter of an investigation of the West Virginia State Police Crime Laboratory, Serology Division," November 4, 1993.

- Implied a match with a suspect when testing supported only a match with the victim
- Reported scientifically impossible or improbable results

His lies, misrepresentations, and bad science made Zain, who died in 2002, the canonical example of an unethical forensic scientist.

Unfortunately, Fred Zain does not stand alone. A more recent example of fraudulent conduct involves the case of Annie Dookhan. Ms. Dookhan's misconduct led to a multimillion-dollar scandal in the criminal justice system. Ms. Dookhan was a chemist working at the Department of Public Health at the Jamaica Plain Hinton Laboratory in Massachusetts. According to a statement by Massachusetts Attorney General Martha Coakley, Ms. Dookhan was charged criminally with two counts of obstruction of justice and one count of falsely pretending to hold a degree from a college or university. She pled guilty to 17 counts of obstruction of justice, 8 counts of tampering with evidence, perjury, and falsely pretending to hold a degree from a college or university. Ms. Dookhan was sentenced to three to five years in prison for her conduct.

Examples of Attorney Misconduct

Unfortunately, attorneys may also attempt to influence the investigation or the opinion of the experts. Attorneys may suppress information or ask loaded or irrelevant questions; on cross-examination, quotations out of context and hedged facts may be used. The case of the Duke lacrosse team and former Durham District Attorney Mike Nifong's mishandling of that case are just such an example of prosecutorial misconduct. The case centered around charges made by an African American escort and stripper that three members of the Duke lacrosse team, all white males, had sexually assaulted her during a team party where she was performing. The woman later changed her story multiple times regarding the method of attack, the number of attackers, and who the attackers were. During the investigation and subsequently, Nifong:[5]

- Waited six months before he spoke with the alleged victim
- Made public a series of accusations that turned out to be false
- Exaggerated and intensified racial tensions
- Unduly influenced the Durham police investigation
- Tried to manipulate potential witnesses
- Refused to hear exculpatory evidence prior to indictment

[5] Neff, J., "Lacrosse Files Show Gaps in DA's Case," *The News & Observer*, August 6, 2006.

- Never spoke directly to the alleged victim about the accusations
- Crossed ethical lines by making public comments about the case, possibly prejudicing potential jurors
- Conspired with the DNA lab director to withhold potentially exculpatory DNA

As a result of his conduct, Mike Nifong was disbarred.

In 2013, for the first time in United States jurisprudence history, a prosecutor was sentenced to jail for failing to disclose evidence. Former prosecutor and then judge Ken Anderson pled guilty to a single count of criminal contempt for intentionally failing to disclose evidence in the case of *State of Texas v. Michael Morton*. Additionally, as part of the plea agreement, Judge Anderson was forced to give up his license to practice law. While the prosecutor's conduct in that case did not involve expert testimony, it does illustrate how the culture is changing.

Across the aisle, criminal defense attorneys have different questions and different obligations. Criminal defendants are guaranteed certain rights under the United States Constitution, as well as their state constitution. Forensic scientists sometimes wonder:

- Is it proper for an attorney to cross-examine for the purpose of discrediting the reliability or credibility of an adverse witness, when by all appearances, the witness is telling the truth?
- Is it proper to put an expert witness on the stand when you know he will commit perjury? Criminal defendants are constitutionally entitled to a vigorous defense. This includes challenging the witnesses. Areas of challenge for an expert witness may include the witness's truth and veracity; the witness's education, experience, and background; the witness's training; the witness's abilities in other cases; the state of the science; and the reputation of the laboratory the scientist works for, just to name a few.

However, despite the criminal defense attorney's obligation to offer a vigorous defense, this does not extend to deliberately suborning the perjured testimony of an expert witness. The rules of professional responsibility are clear to prosecutors, plaintiff's attorneys, and defense attorneys alike.

Interprofessional Relationships

The American Bar Association published Standards for Criminal Justice. That publication included prosecution and defense standards for dealing with experts. It emphasizes the expert's independence and need for impartiality. The main professional forensic organizations have codes of ethics for their memberships as well. The codes of ethics for the American Academy of Forensic Sciences, the International Association for Identification, and the American Society of Crime Laboratory Directors are provided below.

American Academy of Forensic Sciences (AAFS)

Article II. CODE OF ETHICS AND CONDUCT

SECTION 1—THE CODE OF ETHICS AND CONDUCT: As a means to promote the highest quality of professional and personal conduct of its members and affiliates, the following constitutes the Code of Ethics and Conduct which is endorsed by all members and affiliates of the American Academy of Forensic Sciences:

a. Every member and affiliate of the Academy shall refrain from exercising professional or personal conduct adverse to the best interests and objectives of the Academy. The objectives stated in the Preamble to these bylaws shall be to promote professionalism, integrity, and competency in the membership's actions and associated activities; to promote education for and research in the forensic sciences; to encourage the study, improve the practice, elevate the standards and advance the cause of the forensic sciences; to promote interdisciplinary communications; and to plan, organize and administer meetings, reports and other projects for the stimulation and advancement of these and related purposes.

b. No member or affiliate of the Academy shall materially misrepresent his or her education, training, experience, area of expertise, or membership status within the Academy.

c. No member or affiliate of the Academy shall materially misrepresent data or scientific principles upon which his or her conclusion or professional opinion is based.

d. No member or affiliate of the Academy shall issue public statements that appear to represent the position of the Academy without first obtaining specific authority from the Board of Directors.

SECTION 2—MEMBER AND AFFILIATE LIABILITY: Any member or affiliate of the Academy who has violated any of the provisions of the Code of Ethics and Conduct (Article II, Section 1) within the preceding five (5) years may be liable to formal or informal discipline, to include reprimand, censure, suspension, or expulsion by action of the Board of Directors.

SECTION 3—SANCTIONS: If the Board of Directors finds that a member or affiliate has committed a violation of the Code of Ethics and Conduct, the Board may sanction the member or affiliate based on the nature of the violation as follows:

   a. If the Board finds that a member or affiliate has committed a minor violation of the Code of Ethics and Conduct, the member or affiliate may be censured with a confidential "Letter of Reprimand" or a non-confidential "Letter of Censure."
   b. If the Board finds that a member or affiliate has committed a serious violation of the Code of Ethics and Conduct, the Board may suspend the AAFS membership of the member or affiliate for a specific period of time.
   c. If the Board finds that a member or affiliate has committed an egregious violation of the Code of Ethics and Conduct, the Board may expel the member or affiliate from the membership of AAFS.
   d. In determining whether a violation of the Code of Ethics and Conduct is "minor," "serious," or "egregious" and the appropriate level of sanction to be imposed, the Board of Directors shall consider the following non-exclusive factors:
      1. Whether the violation was an isolated incident or a pattern of misconduct;
      2. Whether the violation was knowing and intentional;
      3. Whether the violation included prevarication, fabrication, deception, or falsification;
      4. Whether the accused has acknowledged the ethical violation, taken remedial measures, and/or expressed remorse for the conduct;
      5. Whether the violation resulted in actual harm or the potential for serious harm to the justice system and/or an individual;
      6. Whether the accused has previously been sanctioned for an ethical violation;
      7. Whether the violation involved conduct adverse to the best interests and objectives of the Academy.

International Association for Identification

Code of Ethics and Standards of Professional Conduct.

The ethical and professionally responsible International Association for Identification (IAI) member or certificant:

Professionalism

1.01 Is unbiased, and objective, approaching all assignments and examinations with due diligence and an open mind.

1.02 Conducts full and fair examinations in which conclusions are based on the evidence and reference material relevant to the evidence, not on extraneous information, political pressure, or other outside influences.

1.03 Is aware of his/her limitations and only renders conclusions that are within his/her area of expertise and about matters for which he/she has given careful consideration.

1.04 Truthfully communicates with all parties (i.e., the investigator, prosecutor, defense, and other expert witnesses) about information related to his/her analyses, when communications are permitted by law and agency practice.

1.05 Maintains confidentiality of restricted information obtained in the course of professional endeavors.

1.06 Reports to appropriate officials any conflicts between his/her ethical/ professional responsibilities and applicable agency policy, law, regulation, or other legal authority.

1.07 Does not accept or participate in any case in which he/she has any personal interest or the appearance of such an interest and shall not be compensated based upon the results of the proceeding.

1.08 Conducts oneself personally and professionally within the laws of his/ her respective jurisdiction and in a manner that does not violate public trust.

1.09 Reports to the appropriate legal or administrative authorities unethical, illegal, or scientifically questionable conduct of other practitioners of which he/she has knowledge.

1.10 Does not knowingly make, promote, or tolerate false accusations of a professional or criminal nature.

1.11 Supports sound scientific techniques and practices and does not use his/ her position to pressure a practitioner to arrive at conclusions or results that are not supported by reliable scientific data.

Competency and Proficiency

2.01 Is committed to career-long learning in the forensic disciplines in which he/she practices, and stays abreast of new technology and techniques while guarding against the misuse of methods that have not been validated.

2.02 Expresses conclusions and opinions that are based on generally accepted protocols and procedures. New and novel techniques must be validated prior to implementation in case work.

2.03 Is properly trained and determined to be competent through relevant testing prior to undertaking the examination of the evidence.

2.04 Gives utmost care to the treatment of any samples or items of potential evidentiary value to avoid tampering, adulteration, loss or unnecessary consumption.

2.05 Uses controls and standards, including reviews and verifications appropriate to his/her discipline, when conducting examinations and analyses.

Clear Communications

3.01 Accurately represents his/her education, training, experience, and area of expertise.

3.02 Presents accurate and complete data in reports, testimony, publications and oral presentations.

3.03 Makes and retains full, contemporaneous, clear and accurate records of all examinations and tests conducted, and conclusions drawn, in sufficient detail to allow meaningful review and assessment of the conclusions by an independent person competent in the field.

3.04 Does not falsify or alter reports or other records, or withhold relevant information from reports for strategic or tactical litigation advantage.

3.05 Testifies to results obtained and conclusions reached only when he/she has confidence that the opinions are based on good scientific principles and methods. Opinions are to be stated so as to be clear in their meaning.

3.06 Attempts to qualify his/her responses while testifying when asked a question with the requirement that a simple "yes" or "no" answer be given, if answering "yes" or "no" would be misleading to the judge or the jury.

The ethical and professionally responsible International Association for Identification (IAI) member:

Organizational Responsibility

4.01 Does not misrepresent his/her affiliation with the IAI.

4.02 Does not issue any misleading or inaccurate statement that gives the appearance of representing the official position of the IAI.

4.03 Reports violations of this code of which he/she knows to the President of the IAI.

4.04 Cooperates fully with any official investigation by the IAI.

American Society of Crime Laboratory Directors (ASCLD)

Section 2.—Code: As members of the AMERICAN SOCIETY OF CRIME LABORATORY DIRECTORS, we will strive to foster an atmosphere within our laboratories which will actively encourage our employees to understand and follow ethical practices. Further, we shall endeavor to discharge our responsibilities toward the public, our employers, our employees and the profession of forensic science in accordance with the following ASCLD Code of Conduct.

2.1 No member of ASCLD shall engage in any conduct that is harmful to the profession of forensic science including, but not limited to, any illegal activity, any technical misrepresentation or distortion, any scholarly falsification.

2.2 No member of ASCLD shall use their position to impose undue pressure on an employee to take technical shortcuts or arrive at a conclusion that is not supported by scientific data.

2.3 No member of ASCLD shall discriminate against any current or prospective employee in his or her organization based on race, color, religion, national origin, sex, age, or disability.

2.4 No member of ASCLD shall engage in any conduct that is detrimental to the purpose of ASCLD as outlined in Article II of the Bylaws.

2.5 No member of ASCLD shall misrepresent his or her expertise or credentials in any professional capacity.

2.6 No member of ASCLD shall offer opinions or conclusions in testimony, which are untrue or are not supported by scientific data.

2.7 No member of ASCLD shall misrepresent his or her position or authority in any professional capacity.

2.8 No member of ASCLD shall make written or oral statements, which imply that the member is speaking on behalf of ASCLD or the Board of Directors without the permission of the President.

2.9 No individual may gain membership in ASCLD nor shall he/she retain membership if they have been convicted of a felony offense.

2.10 All members shall report, to the extent permitted by law, to the Board of Directors any potential ethics violation committed by another member of ASCLD.

Other professional organizations, such as the National Society of Professional Engineers, publish codes of ethics for practitioners.

How to Avoid Abuse

When the system is abused, the players within that system are also abused. Whether it is an O. J. Simpson, a Duke lacrosse team, an exoneration, or the fallout from the allegations in the Reggie Lewis death, the forensic witnesses seem to be in the "middle of the muck." The fallout from either expert witness or attorney misconduct, however, is equally damaging to the system. The remedy for such misdirection is often a matter of knowing one's rights and responsibilities or exercising the proper steps concerning substance or procedure. This section offers an overview of and remedies for abuse of and by expert witnesses. The objective of such an examination will hopefully be a more effective, fair, and just resolution of disputes when expert testimony is involved.

As an expert, each time you perform a test, prepare a report, or testify, there is an opportunity to compromise your integrity. While at times this may seem expedient in the moment, the long-term consequences can include unemployment, public disgrace, and even prison time. Employees of government agencies are encouraged to acquaint themselves with the attorney assigned to represent the agency, should they have questions about the proper procedure in a legal matter.

Primary Ethical Issues

Some of the items disclosed and discussed previously center around ethical violations by the forensic witness. However, it might be well to itemize some ethical violations that can occur in the forensic witness arena so they can be avoided.

- Outright false data
- Investigation not done
- Data altered
- False testimony
- Intentional ignoring of available data
- Recanting prior contra-positions
- Assignments beyond competence
- Accepting unauthorized attorney influence
- Conclusion reached before research
- Conflicts of interest
- Fraudulent credentials

Outright False Data

The cross-examination process is charged with the obligation of exposing falsified information, reports, records, or other basic data. This requires the most meticulous preparation by cross-examining counsel well before the time a fallacious expert takes the witness stand.

Investigation Not Performed

The approach of aggressive counsel includes reviewing the records, reports, bench notes, and protocols to establish that purported investigations were in fact not accomplished.

Data Altered

Resorting to the original documentation is the most effective way of discovering alterations; alterations are changes to data or documents not supported by analysis. Obliterations through correction fluids, erasures, or digital tampering may be exposed by original document examination. Proper corrections, for example, in the medical field and for forensic laboratory accreditation, require a single line being drawn through a record erroneously made, with the initials of the author. Anything short of that is suggestive of document tampering.

Conditional or Limited Engagement (Private Experts)

On occasion, an expert will be conditionally engaged by counsel, only to have the undertaking terminated before any work is accomplished. The scope of engagement should be revealed through the expert's file. It would be unethical for an expert to tender opinions beyond the scope of the engagement.

False Testimony

On occasion, a witness will falsely testify based upon information either erroneously provided or carelessly gathered. Rarely, false testimony arises from an intentional desire on the part of the witness to support the claim of the sponsoring party with no regard for the truth or falsity of the statement. Here, the anvil of cross-examination provides strength for the opposition.

Ignoring Data

This oversight can occur through counsel or a client who would not reveal to the expert all requisite data, or by the expert turning a professional cold shoulder to salient facts. In either case, a cross-examination may expose such blindsiding.

Recanting Prior Contra-Positions

Often, an expert has testified to or written concerning a particular proposition. The diligent cross-examiner who uncovers a prior contra-position in another related or similar case has in hand the tools to send the expert "to the showers." Be mindful of what you say on the witness stand, understanding that those statements may come back to haunt you. If you have a legitimate reason for changing your position, be sure you can document your reasons for doing so.

Assignments Beyond Competency

This area of cross-examination often goes not to the admissibility of expert testimony, but rather to the weight given to an expert's testimony. An expert clearly out of depth should be so exposed by careful cross-examination that indicates the assignment was simply beyond the witness's experience and capability.

Unauthorized Attorney Influence

Communication between expert and attorney is the best way to uncover efforts by sponsoring counsel to influence the professional's expert opinions. Normally, such correspondence is not privileged in any way except if it is pure attorney work product and was not relied on by the expert in forming a professional opinion. In the event the witness has relied in whole or in part on the attorney statement, such information is proper for production and examination.

Reaching Conclusions before Research

One of the delightful opportunities to cross-examining attorneys is to have an expert jump to a conclusion before any study or research has been done to buttress or support the conclusion. Through cross-examination and meticulous file analysis, it is often possible to uncover the fact that an expert opinion or conclusion was reached before any research was done. This likewise goes most often to weight and not admissibility. If the circumstances are sufficiently egregious, it may be that the witness's entire testimony will be stricken.

Conflict of Interest

Conflicts of interest can provide a legal basis for expert challenge and a court-ordered disqualification of an expert witness. In the event materials were made available to an expert on the other side of an assignment, prior to the current assignment, there is case law that will prohibit an expert from testifying in the current case. Aside from circumstances that justify disqualification, a conflict-of-interest situation presents a viable area of cross-examination that may go to weight of the testimony and really impinges on the expert's integrity.

Fraudulent Credentials

Here, the task is prediscovery checking of details of an expert's curriculum vitae and personal résumé. While experts are admonished to maintain a careful recitation of historic accomplishments, some tend to exaggerate their own credentials. By verifying the data contained in the résumé prior to trial, it is possible to expose the expert to outright falsehoods in the résumé. Falsehoods in the résumé obviously lead the fact finder to a conclusion there are falsehoods in the report as well.

Contingent Fee (Private Experts)

Obviously, if an expert's compensation is driven by a contingency outcome, witness credibility and weight given to such testimony are highly suspect. If an expert reveals a compensation formula that is contingent on case outcome, serious doubt can be cast on the veracity and credibility of such an expert witness.

Abuses of Experts

The following conduct represents a nonexhaustive list of conduct an attorney should not engage in:

- Inquiry into personal and individual finances (unless that inquiry could relate directly to bias or partiality).
- Threats by attorney concerning possible contempt of court or sanctions for not answering questions, unless you are being intentionally evasive.
- Refusal to allow physical setting and circumstances of the deposition room to be comfortable for you.
- Not permitting reasonable breaks in the proceedings for fatigue or physical comfort.
- Counsel continually asking repetitive, argumentative, redundant, or insignificant questions for purposes of "wearing down" the expert.
- Examining attorney engages in badgering or overly aggressive questioning techniques.
- Unreasonable time demands placed on expert for preliminary or final report.
- Seeking "expert opinion" without affording any opportunity for expert to explore data, inspect premises, do testing, or otherwise investigate the matter.
- Expert is not provided access to key underlying information.
- Witness pushed to render opinions beyond limits of engagement.

- Expert asked to opine in areas beyond the witness's expertise.
- Expert contacted by opposite party without notice to the retaining attorney.
- Expert asked to perform analysis on the stand.
- Expert expected to or instructed to make findings consistent with the attorney's theory of the case.
- Expert asked to testify without adequate deposition or pretrial preparation.
- Inquiry into private life or habits that embarrass, humiliate, intimidate, or harass the expert (drugs, alcohol, sexual practices, etc.), where the questions do not relate to competency or impeachment and have no bearing on the expert's ability or effort as an expert witness.

Abuses by Experts

- Interrogatory responses not updated and made current by experts.
- Expert did not disclose all opinions intended to be rendered as required by pretrial order.
- Expert violated some other order of the court.
- Expert withheld information.
- Destruction of evidence in testing.
- "Consulting" expert volunteers to testify against the side hiring him or her.
- Expert tenders false credentials.
- Expert renders untrue opinion or report.
- Expert tenders opinion based on "vast experience" only, without doing any real scientific, technical, or professional investigation (see Appendices C and D).
- Witness generates long, rambling preamble to every question.
- Expert takes on an assignment that will involve disclosure of confidential information received from the opposite party in an earlier matter.

Asserting Your Rights as a Witness

You have the right not to be abused as an expert testifying witness, either in trial or deposition. Abuse of an expert witness may be subtle or direct. Of course, sponsoring counsel has some obligation to keep the examination on proper course. You may ask sponsoring counsel what procedures will be followed if abusive questioning is encountered.

There are many devices available to you for self-protection. You may benefit from knowing what to do in such an emergency. An answer such as, "I really think that is an abusive question," should probably do the job to alert the attorney you think the line of questioning is becoming aggressive. However, this response should be reserved for extremely rare circumstances.

Above all, refuse to engage in shouting matches or arguments with abusive attorneys or in response to convoluted or incomprehensible questioning. Be aware of how your comments, answers, or objections might look in print. Know your rights and be ready to exercise them, but do not fire too quickly from the hip.

The attack and challenge of a forensic witness can be magnified if lack of documentation for the circumstance that is the basis of the expert's testimony can be shown. Often, the quantum of evidence gathered by the expert is inadequate to establish the particular causation for which the witness has been called to testify.

If experimental evidence is generally insufficient to support the witness's conclusion, such testimony will be elicited during cross-examination to erode the believability of the forensic witness. The prepared cross-examiner will know this inadequacy prior to taking on the expert. While there may be some support for the expert witness's testimony in scientific, technical, or professional literature, if the support is of a minimal nature or generally undocumented, or if the support comes from discredited spokespersons, all of those items go to the weight and lack of reliability that would attach to the tendered witness.

Sometimes an expert witness will testify to a conclusion and will not rule out alternative causes of the condition that may have created the circumstance. The skillful expert will eliminate each and every alternative cause. The inadequately prepared expert may not be able to know these are areas of vulnerability on cross-examination.

Aggressive cross-examination may reveal the expert did not rely on proprietary or regulatory standards of agencies to support the conclusions tendered. To the contrary, if there are relevant standards, either industry-wide or promulgated by government entities, and if the testimony does not comport with those standards, major headway is made in the cross-examination process.

Countering the Claim of Junk Science

The phrase "junk science" has been popularized by an author who may himself have been, in the opinion of some legal scholars, guilty of doing junk research to write about junk science. In any case, the phrase has triggered elements of inadequate forensic testimony that create a good checklist for cross-examiners to follow as they address a supposedly inadequate, incompetent, or unprofessional forensic witness.

Show the witness is just not knowledgeable on the subject. Expose lack of meticulous attention to detail that the expert witness failed to follow in preparation. Cross-examine as to lack of activity in the professional field, particularly with regard to absence of current education and training and lack of appropriate seminar and workshop attendance. Whenever possible, the cross-examining attorney should avoid allowing his or her expert to recognize the charlatan as an "expert." Establishing that the witness has never testified to the same effect previously is damning cross-examination. If the cross-examiner can establish the findings of the witness are not consistent with studies of others, credibility of the testifying witness is seriously eroded. If cross-examination can suggest findings of the expert often lead to erroneous results, the expert's credibility is again jeopardized.

Often, an expert will indicate that present methods are positively related to prior methodology. If that linkage and connection can be dispelled, weight of testimony and credibility of the witness are threatened. The witness should be pressed for literature that tends to support the testimony. The absence of such literature bolsters the claim of lack of competence and credibility. If tests or examinations conducted by the forensic expert have never been admitted as evidence in a court or other dispute resolution process on previous occasions, such lack of admission seriously questions the validity of the extant testimony. The aggressive cross-examiner will often show there is no government regulation or statutory support for the expert testimony, or that the expert testimony is simply not approved, either by the scientific community or any government-sponsored methodology. If the cross-examining attorney can establish the scientific, technical, or professional community does not rely on the same tests, procedures, or techniques followed by the expert, a serious erosion of the expert witness's testimony occurs. To state these issues in a positive format, the expert must:

- Be a knowledgeable professional.
- Be meticulous with detail.
- Be active in the field as well as an expert witness.
- Show you have testified to the same effect previously.
- Show your findings are consistent with studies by others.
- Show your findings seldom lead to erroneous results.
- Prove new methods are positively related to prior methods.
- Identify literature that establishes your approach.
- Show prior admission of these same tests in other cases.
- Relate your tests to the same type of tests by the opposition.
- Show approval of your methodology through published standards.
- Establish the scientific community's reliance on these same tests.

Conclusion

Statements of ethical behavior often sound preachy or strident. Ethical behavior, however, is what makes or breaks your reputation. To end on a positive note, the correlative of each of the negatives contained in this article should provide ample warning to the careful forensic witness and sponsoring attorney as to methods and procedures to be used to avoid these kinds of attack based upon fraudulent, unethical, or improper conduct by the expert.

The objective always is to improve the quality of the criminal justice system, not trap or trick the serious and dedicated forensic witness who is attempting to assist the judicial system in resolving disputes.

Review Questions

1. What are ethics?
2. What are normative ethics?
3. Name three codes of ethics from the AAFS.
4. Name three codes of ethics from the IAI.
5. Name three codes of ethics from the ASCLD.
6. Name three codes of ethics from another forensic professional organization.
7. Name three codes of ethics from one organization that do not appear in another's.
8. Name three primary ethical issues.
9. What is the best way to prevent witnesses from using fraudulent data?
10. State five ways you can be an ethical expert.

Discussion Questions

1. Why are ethics so important? Can ethics be learned later in life, or are they set through your upbringing?
2. Why do you think the ethical codes of various organizations vary? What does this say about ethics?
3. What is the best way to deal with unethical behavior, either yours or that of others? How should a laboratory deal with unethical behavior of its employees?

Appendix A: Federal Rules of Evidence 701 through 706

Evidence rules in the various states vary considerably, and these rules have themselves been interpreted by many court decisions and opinions.

Rule 701. Opinion Testimony by Lay Witnesses

If a witness is not testifying as an expert, testimony in the form of an opinion is limited to one that is:

(a) rationally based on the witness's perception;
(b) helpful to clearly understanding the witness's testimony or to determining a fact in issue; and
(c) not based on scientific, technical, or other specialized knowledge within the scope of Rule 702.

Rule 702. Testimony by Expert Witnesses

A witness who is qualified as an expert by knowledge, skill, experience, training, or education may testify in the form of an opinion or otherwise if:

(a) the expert's scientific, technical, or other specialized knowledge will help the trier of fact to understand the evidence or to determine a fact in issue;
(b) the testimony is based on sufficient facts or data;
(c) the testimony is the product of reliable principles and methods; and
(d) the expert has reliably applied the principles and methods to the facts of the case.

Rule 703. Bases of an Expert

An expert may base an opinion on facts or data in the case that the expert has been made aware of or personally observed. If experts in the particular field would reasonably rely on those kinds of facts or data in forming an opinion on the subject, they need not be admissible for the opinion to be admitted. But if the facts or data would otherwise be inadmissible, the proponent of the opinion may disclose them to the jury only if their probative value in helping the jury evaluate the opinion substantially outweighs their prejudicial effect.

Rule 704. Opinion on an Ultimate Issue

(a) **In General — Not Automatically Objectionable.** An opinion is not objectionable just because it embraces an ultimate issue.
(b) **Exception.** In a criminal case, an expert witness must not state an opinion about whether the defendant did or did not have a mental state or condition that constitutes an element of the crime charged or of a defense. Those matters are for the trier of fact alone.

Rule 705. Disclosing the Facts or Data Underlying an Expert

Unless the court orders otherwise, an expert may state an opinion — and give the reasons for it — without first testifying to the underlying facts or data. But the expert may be required to disclose those facts or data on cross-examination.

Rule 706. Court-Appointed Expert Witnesses

(a) **Appointment Process.** On a party's motion or on its own, the court may order the parties to show cause why expert witnesses should not be appointed and may ask the parties to submit nominations. The court may appoint any expert that the parties agree on and any of its own choosing. But the court may only appoint someone who consents to act.
(b) **Expert's Role.** The court must inform the expert of the expert's duties. The court may do so in writing and have a copy filed with the clerk or may do so orally at a conference in which the parties have an opportunity to participate. The expert:
  (1) must advise the parties of any findings the expert makes;
  (2) may be deposed by any party;
  (3) may be called to testify by the court or any party; and
  (4) may be cross-examined by any party, including the party that called the expert.

(c) **Compensation.** The expert is entitled to a reasonable compensation, as set by the court. The compensation is payable as follows:

   (1) in a criminal case or in a civil case involving just compensation under the Fifth Amendment, from any funds that are provided by law; and

   (2) in any other civil case, by the parties in the proportion and at the time that the court directs — and the compensation is then charged like other costs.

(d) **Disclosing the Appointment to the Jury.** The court may authorize disclosure to the jury that the court appointed the expert.

(e) **Parties' Choice of Their Own Experts.** This rule does not limit a party in calling its own experts.

Appendix B: A Proposed Code of Conduct

CAROL HENDERSON

American Academy of Forensic Sciences
Jurisprudence Section Code of Professionalism

Preamble

This Code of Professionalism was proposed by the Jurisprudence Section of the American Academy of Forensic Sciences to provide guidance to its members in the performance of their professional relationships with forensic experts.[1] The goal of the Code is to assist members in achieving the highest quality of professional conduct and to promote the cooperation between lawyers and forensic scientists which is essential to protect the legal interests of the public they serve.

In order to meet the public's need for legal services, lawyers and the quality of the service they provide must command the respect of the public as well as the other participants in the legal process. The fundamental principles set out in this Code are to provide an ethical framework for the Jurisprudence Section's members, although each lawyer must decide for himself the extent to which his conduct should rise above these minimum standards. The desire for the respect and confidence of the members of the society in which he serves and of the members of his profession should motivate him to maintain the highest possible degree of ethical conduct.

Lawyer professionalism includes accepting responsibility for one's own professional conduct as well as others in the profession and includes a desire to uphold professional standards and foster peer regulations to ensure each member is competent and public-spirited. Professionalism also includes reinforcing and communicating the ideals of professionalism among our membership and eliminating abrasive or abusive conduct with others, particularly our colleagues in the forensic sciences. Such behavior does not serve justice, but tends to delay and sometimes deny justice.

---

[1] Special thanks to Carol Henderson, Director, National Clearinghouse for Science, Technology and the Law, for this material. Copyright © 2000 by Carol Henderson. All rights reserved.

Compliance with the rules depends primarily upon voluntary compliance, secondary upon reinforcement by peer pressure and public opinion and finally, when necessary, by enforcement by the Court's inherent powers and ethics rules already in existence. The Academy, of course, may still sanction its members who are in violation of its Code of Ethics contained in the By-laws. Also, each state where the attorney is individually licensed may sanction the attorney for any violations of his state's Codes or Rules of Professional Conduct.

Terminology

1. "Belief" or "Believes" denotes that the person involved actually supposed the fact in question to be true. A person's belief may be inferred from circumstances.
2. "Expert" denotes a person who possesses special skill, training and knowledge in a vocation or occupation.
3. "Knowingly," "Known," or "Knows" denotes actual knowledge of the fact in question. A person's knowledge may be inferred from circumstances.
4. "Reasonable" or "Reasonably" when used in relation to conduct by a lawyer denotes the conduct of a reasonably prudent and competent lawyer.
5. "Reasonable belief" or "Reasonably believes" when used in reference to a lawyer denotes that the lawyer believes the matter in question and that the circumstances are such that the belief is reasonable.

Rules

1. I shall treat all expert witnesses with professional courtesy and will acknowledge their obligations to their codes of ethics or conduct, and will not ask them to breach their legitimate confidential relationships with their clients or patients.
2. I shall verify the credentials of any expert witnesses I use.
3. I shall not knowingly proffer an expert witness with fraudulent credentials.
4. I shall report fraudulent experts to the appropriate authorities.
5. I shall not pay an excessive fee for the purpose of influencing an expert's testimony or fix the amount of fee contingent upon the content of his testimony or the outcome of the case. I will communicate to the expert that he is being paid for his time and his expertise, not the nature of his opinion.
6. I shall refrain from making any material misrepresentation of the education, training, experience or expertise of the expert witness.

I shall not misrepresent nor mischaracterize an expert witness' credentials, qualifications, data, findings or opinion. I will not withhold nor suppress any relevant facts, evidence, documents or other material at my disposal that may be relevant to the expert's opinion.

7. I shall not request nor require an expert to express an opinion on matters outside his field of expertise or within his field of qualifications to which he has not given formal consideration.

8. I shall not attempt to prevent opposing counsel from communicating with my expert witness, nor will I instruct my expert witness to not communicate with opposing counsel about the subject of a lawsuit unless such contact is otherwise prohibited or regulated by law and the parties' attorneys have consented.

9. Any and all demonstrative evidence shall not be intentionally altered or distorted with a view to misleading the court or jury.

10. I shall keep all consulting and testifying experts reasonably informed of the status of the matter in which they are engaged and promptly comply with reasonable legally permissible requests for information.

11. I shall compensate the expert for the total amount of the undisputed portion of the fee agreed upon between the expert and the client or attorney representing the client.

Appendix C: An Expert's Bill of Rights

HAROLD FEDER

John Stuart Mill (1806–1973), philosopher and economist, was a constant commentator concerning the relationship of the individual to society. Among other things, he said:

> "...[E]veryone who receives the protection of society owes a return for the benefit. The fact of living in society renders it indispensable that each should be bound to observe a certain line of conduct towards the rest.... As soon as any part of a person's conduct affects prejudicially the interests of others, society has jurisdiction over it..."

That is merely another way of saying that with each right an individual possesses, there exists a commensurate responsibility which attends that circumstance, a balancing act of sorts, to keep both the individual and society in proper relationship to each other. When out-of-balance occurs, the system has certain rules to deal with the problem.

That identical paradigm exists with regard to expert witnesses who seek to understand their rights, and at the same time learn of responsibilities which the dispute resolution system imposes upon them.

The great jurist Learned Hand in 1901 stated: "The whole object of the expert is to tell the jury...general truths derived from his specialized experience."[1] From that lofty premise of almost 100 years ago, University of Texas law professor Michael Tigar, on expert witnesses, said in a recent publication: "An expert is someone who wasn't there when it happened, but who for a fee will gladly imagine what it must have been like."[2] It is obvious from a comparison of these two extremes that the expert witnessing process has traveled considerable distance in the last 94 years. However, that does not mean that we should abandon the effort to keep the process on the high road, the ethical road and the proper road, to assist triers of fact in the dispute resolution process.

The first ten amendments to the Constitution of the United States have become known as the "Bill of Rights," primarily because those provisions are

---

[1] Learned Hand, "Historical and Practical Considerations Regarding Expert Testimony," 15 *Harvard Law Review* 40 (1901): 54.
[2] *ABA Journal* 81 (1995): 39.

so fundamental to the web and fabric of this country's very existence. The list of tendered expert witness rights will bear a similar relationship to the process of forensic testimony which we have all experienced through various phases of the dispute resolution process. Before you are able to affectively assert your rights as a forensic witness, you must have a full, clear and accurate conception of exactly what entitlements you have as a forensic expert.

Throughout the dispute resolution process, abuse opportunities can occur to the expert witness. It may be in the engagement phase, created by indistinct assignment parameters. It may arise from qualification problems, investigation inadequacies, or even the mundane matter of improper, inadequate or absent payment.

Deposition and discovery phases of the dispute resolution process present new problems. Where is the deposition to be held? Has adequate preparation been afforded to the witness? And, of course, there is the ever-present problem of abusive questioning techniques. The trial setting presents a third arena for expert witness abuse. Discourtesy by counsel or the forum itself is a hazard. Lack of proper preparation by sponsoring counsel or "Rambo-ism" by opposing counsel must be anticipated. There are a few circumstances when a consulting witness may be called to testify in a dispute resolution proceeding. However, those circumstances must pass stringent tests.

With these few words of introduction, let us examine what might be crafted at some time in the future, by some agency or organization yet unknown, a document entitled "The Expert Witness Bill of Rights." As we present this itemization of rights of expert witnesses, we must be always mindful of the existence of counterbalancing responsibilities which attend each of the stated privileges. Some of the rights are cast in the form of positives. Others are cast in the form of negatives. In combination, however, they should constitute a beginning outline of what hopefully will become an established doctrine amounting to a bill of rights for protection of forensic witnesses.

The Expert Witness Bill of Rights

1. You have the right to abide by the code of ethics of your profession.
2. You have the right to fair technical review of your work product.
3. You have the right to use reliable scientific, technical or professionally based data and tests to support your conclusions and opinions.
4. You have the right to receive adequate and fair compensation for your services.
5. You have the right to assist the fact finder in reaching a just and fair determination of the matters in dispute (Rule 702, Federal Rules of Evidence).

6. You have the right to render your opinions based upon your knowledge, training and experience (Rule 702, Federal Rules of Evidence).

7. You have the right in certain cases to rely on hearsay to support your conclusions if it is usual for professionals such as you to regularly rely on such hearsay information (Rule 703, Federal Rules of Evidence).

8. You have the right to use relevant and reliable data gained from the scientific method to support your opinions and conclusions (*Daubert v. Merrell Dow Pharmaceuticals, Inc.*, 509 U.S. 113 S. Ct. 2786, L. Ed. 2d 469 (1993)).

9. You have the right to tender probative evidence if the offered material outweighs the danger of unfair prejudice to any party (Rule 403, Federal Rules of Evidence).

10. You have the right to be given all relevant data by counsel engaging your services.

11. You have the right to render unbiased professional, technical and scientific opinions based upon your investigation and examination of the relevant facts and data concerning the matter presented to you.

12. You have the right to be kept informed as to new developments and new evidence in the case which could alter your expert opinions.

13. You have the right to assume that other investigations done upon which you rely were properly accomplished.

14. You have the right to unconditional engagements, that is, engagements which are not outcome driven.

15. You have the right to have adequate time to prepare and complete the assignments presented to you.

16. You have the right to be free of threats by attorney or client concerning possible contempt of court or court sanction for not answering questions presented to you.

17. You have the right to have a deposition conducted in a comfortable and physically agreeable setting.

18. You have the right to be permitted reasonable recesses during deposition or testimony episodes to accommodate for fatigue and physical comfort.

19. You have the right to adequate notice of your endorsement as an expert witness in any proceeding in which you are so denominated.

20. You have the right to have interrogatory and other written discovery responses updated and made current by the attorney engaging your services.

21. You have the right to make reasonable destructive tests of evidence on condition that adequate notice is given to the opposing party and opposition experts are provided an opportunity to be present during those destructive tests. (Caution: Court orders may be required.)

Having stated a number of expert witness rights in the affirmative, it is now essential to examine some of the rights of forensic witnesses which are cast in a negative setting. Whether the rights are cast as an affirmative or negative statement, they should all apply with equal force to the dispute resolution process and the role of the expert witness in that process.

1. You should not be subject to any coercion by counsel or client.
2. You should not be subjected to corruption of scientific fact to reach a predetermined result.
3. You should not be required to use particular tests which are outcome-prescribed.
4. You should not be required to be an advocate for a dispute outcome; to advocate is to argue; to be enthusiastic is good teaching.
5. You should not be asked to use questionable scientific, technical or professional methods to support research or investigation.
6. You should not be denied written documentation of the test results of other experts.
7. You should not be subjected to threats of demotion or transfer for your test results.
8. You should not be subjected to any external or distorting pressure of any kind which would shade, color, alter or amend your professional, technical or scientific judgment or findings.
9. You should not be subjected to the withholding of key documents or facts from you by counsel or client.
10. You should not be subjected to having your private life inquired into in improper ways in the deposition or trial process.
11. You should not be subjected to frivolous discovery requests.
12. You should not be required to ever tender false evidence in any dispute resolution process or proceeding.
13. You should never be required to use tests of questionable scientific validity.
14. You should not be tricked or misled by engaging counsel or cross-examining counsel.
15. You should not be subjected to selective fact gathering or being "blindsided" by inadequate presentation of facts.
16. You should not be forced to recant prior inconsistent positions without ample and adequate fact or research justification.
17. You should not be pressed to assignments beyond your competence.
18. You should not be pressed to answer questions beyond the scope of your engagement.
19. You should not be subjected to testimonial situations creating conflicts of interest in completing your assignment.

20. You should not be required to ever serve as a forensic expert on a contingent fee basis.
21. You should not be the subject of inquiry into your personal finances, unless that inquiry could directly relate to your bias, prejudice or partiality.
22. You should not be subjected to repetitive, argumentative, redundant or insignificant questioning.
23. You should not be subjected to badgering or overly aggressive examinations.
24. You should not be physically threatened in any way in any dispute resolution proceeding.
25. You should not have your opinion as an expert sought without affording you the opportunity to conduct appropriate data, premises, or test investigation.
26. You should not have a specific opinion of a favorable nature be a condition of payment for your professional services.
27. You should not be forced to wait inordinate lengths of time to testify while under subpoena.
28. You should not be forced to reveal the names or other identification concerning clients when such information is protected by rules of confidentiality.
29. You should not be contacted by opposing counsel without notice to the attorney retaining your services.
30. You should not be forced to testify if you are a consulting witness (subject to very narrow, limiting exceptions).
31. You should not be asked about a case merely to disqualify you as an expert witness in that matter.
32. You should not be asked to testify without adequate deposition or trial preparation.
33. You should not be subjected to inquiry into any aspect of your personal and private life or habits which would embarrass, humiliate, intimidate or harass you where such questions do not relate to your competency as an expert witness. This includes inquiry into religion, political beliefs, sexual preference, health and finances.
34. You should not be forced to make disclosure of confidential business, commercial, industrial or other trade secret information.
35. You should not be subjected to an examination protocol which is designed to wear you down and not really discover relevant information.
36. You should not be subjected to any examination or treatment which is beyond the bounds of professional common sense and courtesy.

Asserting Your Rights as an Expert Witness

Counsel sponsoring your services as an expert witness has considerable obligation to maintain the examination either in deposition or trial on a proper course. You and sponsoring counsel should determine in advance what procedures will be followed if abusive, harassing, antagonistic or improper questioning is encountered.

Many devices are available to you for self-protection. Knowing what you may properly do to protect your expert witness role and position may mean the difference between success and failure for you as an expert in a particular case or in general.

Fully and completely understand the extent of your rights as an expert witness.

You may ask the court reporter in deposition to mark a particular question and answer for future reference in the event you believe a question is calculated to be improper for any number of reasons.

You could, in a polite and professional way, refuse to answer an objectionable question or be examined in an objectionable way. Control of your voice, emotions and the moment are essential in such a setting.

During a deposition proceeding you may ask for a recess at reasonable times for purposes of consulting with your own private attorney who you may have engaged for the purpose of assisting you in deposition or trial matters. Your personal attorney is to be distinguished from the attorney who has engaged your professional services as an expert witness. It is often necessary in grossly abusive situations to engage and have your personal attorney present during deposition or trial proceedings. You have the right to your own counsel, in or out of the deposition.

The expert should treat opposing counsel courteously, no matter how abusive or aggressive the attorney might become. Never should the expert engage in a oneupmanship discourse with opposing counsel. To show that opposing counsel does not understand the testimony or the field results in the expert appearing arrogant and adversarial. Such demeanor is certain to antagonize. After all, your expertise should shine through without it being overstated.

Understanding and asserting your rights as an expert witness requires constant attention to detail. Your maintenance of a professional, polite, calm, cool and collected demeanor will predict a better result in the event of overly aggressive examinations. Know your rights. Be ready to assert your rights, but do not fire from the hip too quickly without thinking and assessing the situation.

Understanding your rights and knowing how to preserve and protect those rights places you on the road to remedies, and eliminates problems which might be suggested by abusive, improper or inappropriate conduct.

Knowledge is power. Confucius said: "The essence of knowledge is, having it, to apply it; not having it, [is] to confess your ignorance." Use of knowledge without common sense is folly. The examination of your rights as an expert witness requires that you constantly keep in mind your obligations to the dispute resolution process each time you consider and assert those rights.

Appendix D: Frye v. United States

Frye v. United States
54 App. D.C. 46; 293 F. 1013
No. 3968
Court of Appeals of District of Columbia
Submitted November 7, 1923 Decided December 3, 1923

Before SMYTH, Chief Justice, VAN ORSDEL, Associate Justice, and MARTIN, Presiding Judge of the United States Court of Customs Appeals.

VAN ORSDEL, Associate Justice. Appellant, defendant below, was convicted of the crime of murder in the second degree, and from the judgment prosecutes this appeal.

A single assignment of error is presented for our consideration. In the course of the trial counsel for defendant offered an expert witness to testify to the result of a deception test made upon defendant. The test is described as the systolic blood pressure deception test. It is asserted that blood pressure is influenced by change in the emotions of the witness, and that the systolic blood pressure rises are brought about by nervous impulses sent to the sympathetic branch of the autonomic nervous system. Scientific experiments, it is claimed, have demonstrated that fear, rage, and pain always produce a rise of systolic blood pressure, and that conscious deception or falsehood, concealment of facts, or guilt of crime, accompanied by fear of detection when the person is under examination, raises the systolic blood pressure in a curve, which corresponds exactly to the struggle going on in the subject's mind, between fear and attempted control of that fear, as the examination touches the vital points in respect of which he is attempting to deceive the examiner.

In other words, the theory seems to be that truth is spontaneous, and comes without conscious effort, while the utterance of a falsehood requires a conscious effort, which is reflected in the blood pressure. The rise thus produced is easily detected and distinguished from the rise produced by mere fear of the examination itself. In the former instance, the pressure rises higher than in the latter, and is more pronounced as the examination proceeds, while in the latter case, if the subject is telling the truth, the pressure registers highest at the beginning of the examination, and gradually diminishes as the examination proceeds.

Prior to the trial defendant was subjected to this deception test, and counsel offered the scientist who conducted the test as an expert to testify to the results obtained. The offer was objected to by counsel for the government, and the court sustained the objection. Counsel for defendant then offered to have the proffered witness conduct a test in the presence of the jury. This also was denied.

Counsel for defendant, in their able presentation of the novel question involved, correctly state in their brief that no cases directly in point have been found. The broad ground, however, upon which they plant their case, is succinctly stated in their brief as follows:

"The rule is that the opinions of experts or skilled witnesses are admissible in evidence in those cases in which the matter of inquiry is such that inexperienced persons are unlikely to prove capable of forming a correct judgment upon it, for the reason that the subject-matter so far partakes of a science, art, or trade as to require a previous habit or experience or study in it, in order to acquire a knowledge of it. When the question involved does not lie within the range of common experience or common knowledge, but requires special experience or special knowledge, then the opinions of witnesses skilled in that particular science, art, or trade to which the question relates are admissible in evidence."

Numerous cases are cited in support of this rule. Just when a scientific principle or discovery crosses the line between the experimental and demonstrable stages is difficult to define. Somewhere in this twilight zone the evidential force of the principle must be recognized, and while courts will go a long way in admitting expert testimony deduced from a well-recognized scientific principle or discovery, the thing from which the deduction is made must be sufficiently established to have gained general acceptance in the particular field in which it belongs.

We think the systolic blood pressure deception test has not yet gained such standing and scientific recognition among physiological and psychological authorities as would justify the courts in admitting expert testimony deduced from the discovery, development, and experiments thus far made.

The judgment is affirmed.

Appendix E: Daubert v. Merrell Dow Pharmaceuticals, Inc.

Daubert v. Merrell Dow Pharmaceuticals, Inc., 509 U.S. 113 S. Ct. 2786, L. Ed. 2d 469 (1993).

NOTICE: This opinion is subject to formal revision before publication in the preliminary print of the United States Reports. Readers are requested to notify the Reporter of Decisions, Supreme Court of the United States, Washington,
D.C. 20543, of any typographical or other formal errors, in order that corrections may be made before the preliminary print goes to press.

SUPREME COURT OF THE UNITED STATES

No. 92–102

WILLIAM DAUBERT, et ux., etc., et al., PETITIONERS v. MERRELL DOW PHARMACEUTICALS, INC.
ON WRIT OF CERTIORARI TO THE UNITED STATES COURT OF APPEALS FOR THE NINTH CIRCUIT
[June 28, 1993]

Justice Blackmun delivered the opinion of the Court.

In this case we are called upon to determine the standard for admitting expert scientific testimony in a federal trial.

Petitioners Jason Daubert and Eric Schuller are minor children born with serious birth defects. They and their parents sued respondent in California state court, alleging that the birth defects had been caused by the mothers' ingestion of Bendectin, a prescription anti-nausea drug marketed by respondent. Respondent removed the suits to federal court on diversity grounds.

After extensive discovery, respondent moved for summary judgment, contending that Bendectin does not cause birth defects in humans and that petitioners would be unable to come forward with any admissible evidence that it does. In support of its motion, respondent submitted an affidavit of Steven

161

H. Lamm, physician and epidemiologist, who is a well-credentialed expert on the risks from exposure to various chemical substances.[1] Doctor Lamm stated that he had reviewed all the literature on Bendectin and human birth defects—more than 30 published studies involving over 130,000 patients. No study had found Bendectin to be a human teratogen (i.e., a substance capable of causing malformations in fetuses). On the basis of this review, Doctor Lamm concluded that maternal use of Bendectin during the first trimester of pregnancy has not been shown to be a risk factor for human birth defects.

Petitioners did not (and do not) contest this characterization of the published record regarding Bendectin. Instead, they responded to respondent's motion with the testimony of eight experts of their own, each of whom also possessed impressive credentials.[2] These experts had concluded that Bendectin can cause birth defects. Their conclusions were based upon "in vitro" (test tube) and "in vivo" (live) animal studies that found a link between Bendectin and malformations; pharmacological studies of the chemical structure of Bendectin that purported to show similarities between the structure of the drug and that of other substances known to cause birth defects; and the "reanalysis" of previously published epidemiological (human statistical) studies.

The District Court granted respondent's motion for summary judgment. The court stated that scientific evidence is admissible only if the principle upon which it is based is "'sufficiently established to have general acceptance in the field to which it belongs.'" 727 F. Supp. 570, 572 (SD Cal. 1989), quoting *United States v. Kilgus*, 571 F. 2d 508, 510 (CA9 1978). The court concluded that petitioners' evidence did not meet this standard. Given the vast body of epidemiological data concerning Bendectin, the court held, expert opinion which is not based on epidemiological evidence is not admissible to establish causation. 727 F. Supp., at 575. Thus, the animal-cell studies, live-animal studies, and chemical-structure analyses on which petitioners had relied could not raise by themselves a reasonably disputable jury issue regarding causation. Ibid. Petitioners' epidemiological analyses, based as they were

---

[1] Doctor Lamm received his master's and doctor of medicine degrees from the University of Southern California. He has served as a consultant in birth-defect epidemiology for the National Center for Health Statistics and has published numerous articles on the magnitude of risk from exposure to various chemical and biological substances. App. 34–44.

[2] For example, Shanna Helen Swan, who received a master's degree in biostatics from Columbia University and a doctorate in statistics from the University of California at Berkeley, is chief of the section of the California Department of Health and Services that determines causes of birth defects, and has served as a consultant to the World Health Organization, the Food and Drug Administration, and the National Institutes of Health. App. 113–114, 131–132. Stewart A. Newman, who received his master's and a doctorate in chemistry from Columbia University and the University of Chicago, respectively, is a professor at New York Medical College and has spent over a decade studying the effect of chemicals on limb development. App. 54–56. The credentials of the others are similarly impressive. See App. 61–66, 73–80, 148–153, 187–192, and Attachment to Petitioners' Opposition to Summary Judgment, Tabs 12, 20, 21, 26, 31, 32.

on recalculations of data in previously published studies that had found no causal link between the drug and birth defects, were ruled to be inadmissible because they had not been published or subjected to peer review. Ibid.

The United States Court of Appeals for the Ninth Circuit affirmed. 951 F.2d 1128 (1991). Citing *Frye v. United States*, 54 App. D.C. 46, 47, 293 F. 1013, 1014 (1923), the court stated that expert opinion based on a scientific technique is inadmissible unless the technique is "generally accepted" as reliable in the relevant scientific community. 951 F. 2d, at 1129–1130. The court declared that expert opinion based on a methodology that diverges "significantly from the procedures accepted by recognized authorities in the field...cannot be shown to be 'generally accepted as a reliable technique.'" Id., at 1130, quoting *United States v. Solomon*, 753 F. 2d 1522, 1526 (CA9 1985).

The court emphasized that other Courts of Appeals considering the risks of Bendectin had refused to admit reanalyses of epidemiological studies that had been neither published nor subjected to peer review. 951 F. 2d, at 1130–1131. Those courts had found unpublished reanalyses "particularly problematic in light of the massive weight of the original published studies supporting [respondent's] position, all of which had undergone full scrutiny from the scientific community." Id., at 1130. Contending that reanalysis is generally accepted by the scientific community only when it is subjected to verification and scrutiny by others in the field, the Court of Appeals rejected petitioners' reanalyses as "unpublished, not subjected to the normal peer review process and generated solely for use in litigation." Id., at 1131. The court concluded that petitioners' evidence provided an insufficient foundation to allow admission of expert testimony that Bendectin caused their injuries and, accordingly, that petitioners could not satisfy their burden of proving causation at trial.

We granted certiorari, ___ U.S. ___ (1992), in light of sharp divisions among the courts regarding the proper standard for the admission of expert testimony. Compare, e.g., *United States v. Shorter*, 257 U.S. App. D.C. 358, 363–364, 809 F. 2d 54, 59–60 (applying the "general acceptance" standard), cert. denied, 484 U.S. 817 (1987), with *DeLuca v. Merrell Dow Pharmaceuticals, Inc.*, 911 F. 2d 941, 955 (CA3 1990) (rejecting the "general acceptance" standard).

In the 70 years since its formulation in the *Frye* case, the "general acceptance" test has been the dominant standard for determining the admissibility of novel scientific evidence at trial. See E. Green & C. Nesson, Problems, Cases, and Materials on Evidence 649 (1983). Although under increasing attack of late, the rule continues to be followed by a majority of courts, including the Ninth Circuit.[3]

The *Frye* test has its origin in a short and citation-free 1923 decision concerning the admissibility of evidence derived from a systolic blood pressure

---

[3] For a catalogue of the many cases on either side of this controversy, see P. Gianelli & E. Imwinkelried, Scientific Evidence §1–5, 10–14 (1986 & Supp. 1991).

deception test, a crude precursor to the polygraph machine. In what has become a famous (perhaps infamous) passage, the then Court of Appeals for the District of Columbia described the device and its operation and declared:

> "Just when a scientific principle or discovery crosses the line between the experimental and demonstrable stages is difficult to define. Somewhere in this twilight zone the evidential force of the principle must be recognized, and while courts will go a long way in admitting expert testimony deduced from *a well-recognized scientific principle or discovery, the thing from which the deduction is made must be sufficiently established to have gained general acceptance in the particular field in which it belongs.*" 54 App. D.C., at 47, 293 F., at 1014 (emphasis added).

Because the deception test had "not yet gained such standing and scientific recognition among physiological and psychological authorities as would justify the courts in admitting expert testimony deduced from the discovery, development, and experiments thus far made," evidence of its results was ruled inadmissible. Ibid.

The merits of the *Frye* test have been much debated, and scholarship on its proper scope and application is legion.[4] Petitioners' primary attack, however, is not on the content but on the continuing authority of the rule. They contend that the *Frye* test was superseded by the adoption of the Federal Rules of Evidence.[5] We agree.

---

[4] See, e.g., Green, Expert Witnesses and Sufficiency of Evidence in Toxic Substances Litigation: The Legacy of Agent Orange and Bendectin Litigation, 86 Nw. U. L. Rev. 643 (1992) (hereinafter Green); Becker & Orenstein, The Federal Rules of Evidence After Sixteen Years—The Effect of "Plain Meaning" Jurisprudence, the Need for an Advisory Committee on the Rules of Evidence, and Suggestions for Selective Revision of the Rules, 60 Geo. Wash. L. Rev. 857, 876–885 (1992); Hanson, "James Alphonso Frye Is Sixty-Five Years Old; Should He Retire?" 16 W. St. U. L. Rev. 357 (1989); Black, A Unified Theory of Scientific Evidence, 56 Ford. L. Rev. 595 (1988); Imwinkelried, The "Bases" of Expert Testimony: The Syllogistic Structure of Scientific Testimony, 67 N.C. L. Rev. 1 (1988); Proposals for a Model Rule on the Admissibility of Scientific Evidence, 26 Jurimetrics J. 235 (1986); Gianelli, The Admissibility of Novel Scientific Evidence: *Frye v. United States*, A Half-Century Later, 80 Colum. L. Rev. 1197 (1980); The Supreme Court, 1986 Term, 101 Harv. L. Rev. 7, 119, 125–127 (1987). Indeed, the debates over *Frye* are such a well-established part of the academic landscape that a distinct term—"*Frye*-ologist"—has been advanced to describe those who take part. See Behringer, Introduction, Proposals for a Model Rule on the Admissibility of Scientific Evidence, 26 Jurimetrics J., at 239, quoting Lacey, Scientific Evidence, 24 Jurimetrics J. 254, 264 (1984).

[5] Like the question of *Frye*'s merit, the dispute over its survival has divided courts and commentators. Compare, e.g., *United States v. Williams*, 583 F. 2d 1194 (CA2 1978), cert. denied, 439 U.S. 1117 (1979) (*Frye* is superseded by the Rules of Evidence), with *Christopherson v. Allied-Signal Corp.*, 939 F. 2d 1106, 1111, 1115–1116 (CA5 1991) (en banc) (*Frye* and the Rules coexist), cert. denied, ___ U.S. ___ (1992), 3 J. Weinstein & M. Berger, Weinstein's Evidence ¶702[03], 702–36 to 702–37 (1988) (hereinafter Weinstein & Berger) (*Frye* is dead), and M. Graham, Handbook of Federal Evidence §703.2 (2d ed. 1991) (*Frye* lives). See generally P. Gianelli & E. Imwinkelried, Scientific Evidence §1–5, pp. 28–29 (1986 & Supp. 1991) (citing authorities).

We interpret the legislatively-enacted Federal Rules of Evidence as we would any statute. *Beech Aircraft Corp. v. Rainey*, 488 U.S. 153, 163 (1988). Rule 402 provides the baseline:

"All relevant evidence is admissible, except as otherwise provided by the Constitution of the United States, by Act of Congress, by these rules, or by other rules prescribed by the Supreme Court pursuant to statutory authority. Evidence which is not relevant is not admissible."

"Relevant evidence" is defined as that which has "any tendency to make the existence of any fact that is of consequence to the determination of the action more probable or less probable than it would be without the evidence." Rule 401. The Rule's basic standard of relevance thus is a liberal one.

Frye, of course, predated the Rules by half a century. In *United States v. Abel*, 469 U.S. 45 (1984), we considered the pertinence of background common law in interpreting the Rules of Evidence. We noted that the Rules occupy the field, id., at 49, but, quoting Professor Cleary, the Reporter, explained that the common law nevertheless could serve as an aid to their application:

"In principle, under the Federal Rules no common law of evidence remains. 'All relevant evidence is admissible, except as otherwise provided...' In reality, of course, the body of common law knowledge continues to exist, though in the somewhat altered form of a source of guidance in the exercise of delegated powers." Id., at 51–52.

We found the common-law precept at issue in the *Abel* case entirely consistent with Rule 402's general requirement of admissibility, and considered it unlikely that the drafters had intended to change the rule. Id., at 50–51. In *Bourjaily v. United States*, 483 U.S. 171 (1987), on the other hand, the Court was unable to find a particular common-law doctrine in the Rules, and so held it superseded.

Here there is a specific Rule that speaks to the contested issue. Rule 702, governing expert testimony, provides

"If scientific, technical, or other specialized knowledge will assist the trier of fact to understand the evidence or to determine a fact in issue, a witness qualified as an expert by knowledge, skill, experience, training, or education, may testify thereto in the form of an opinion or otherwise."

Nothing in the text of this Rule establishes "general acceptance" as an absolute prerequisite to admissibility. Nor does respondent present any clear indication that Rule 702 or the Rules as a whole were intended to incorporate a "general acceptance" standard. The drafting history makes no mention of *Frye*, and a rigid "general acceptance" requirement would be at odds with the "liberal thrust" of the Federal Rules and their "general approach of relaxing the traditional barriers to 'opinion' testimony." *Beech Aircraft Corp. v. Rainey*, 488 U.S., at 169 (citing Rules 701 to 705). See also Weinstein, Rule 702 of the Federal Rules of Evidence Is Sound; It Should Not Be Amended, 138 F.R.D. 631, 631 (1991) ("The Rules were designed to depend primarily upon lawyer-adversaries and sensible triers of fact to evaluate conflicts"). Given the Rules' permissive backdrop and their inclusion of a specific rule on expert testimony that does not mention "general acceptance," the assertion that the Rules somehow assimilated *Frye* is unconvincing. *Frye* made "general acceptance" the exclusive test for admitting expert scientific testimony. That austere standard, absent from and incompatible with the Federal Rules of Evidence, should not be applied in federal trials.[6]

That the *Frye* test was displaced by the Rules of Evidence does not mean, however, that the Rules themselves place no limits on the admissibility of purportedly scientific evidence.[7] Nor is the trial judge disabled from screening such evidence. To the contrary, under the Rules the trial judge must ensure that any and all scientific testimony or evidence admitted is not only relevant, but reliable.

The primary locus of this obligation is Rule 702, which clearly contemplates some degree of regulation of the subjects and theories about which an expert may testify. "If scientific, technical, or other specialized knowledge will assist the trier of fact to understand the evidence or to determine a fact in issue" an expert "may testify thereto." The subject of an expert's testimony must be "scientific...knowledge."[8] The adjective "scientific" implies a grounding in the methods and procedures of science. Similarly, the word "knowledge" connotes more than subjective belief or unsupported speculation. The term "applies to any body of known facts or to any body of ideas inferred from such facts or accepted as truths on good grounds." Webster's *Third New International Dictionary* 1252 (1986). Of course, it would be unreasonable to conclude that the subject of scientific testimony must be "known" to a certainty; arguably, there are no certainties in science. See, e.g., Brief for Nicolaas Bloembergen et al. as Amici Curiae 9 ("Indeed, scientists do not assert that they know what is immutably 'true'—they are committed to searching for new, temporary theories to explain, as best they can, phenomena"); Brief for American Association for the Advancement of Science and the National

---

[6] Because we hold that *Frye* has been superseded and base the discussion that follows on the content of the congressionally-enacted Federal Rules of Evidence, we do not address petitioners' argument that application of the *Frye* rule in this diversity case, as the application of a judge-made rule affecting substantive rights, would violate the doctrine of *Erie R. Co. v. Tompkins*, 304 U.S. 64 (1938).

[7] The Chief Justice "do[es] not doubt that Rule 702 confides to the judge some gatekeeping responsibility," post, at 4, but would neither say how it does so, nor explain what that role entails. We believe the better course is to note the nature and source of the duty.

[8] Rule 702 also applies to "technical, or other specialized knowledge." Our discussion is limited to the scientific context because that is the nature of the expertise offered here.

Academy of Sciences as Amici Curiae 7–8 ("Science is not an encyclopedic body of knowledge about the universe. Instead, it represents a process for proposing and refining theoretical explanations about the world that are subject to further testing and refinement") (emphasis in original). But, in order to qualify as "scientific knowledge," an inference or assertion must be derived by the scientific method. Proposed testimony must be supported by appropriate validation—i.e., "good grounds," based on what is known. In short, the requirement that an expert's testimony pertain to "scientific knowledge" establishes a standard of evidentiary reliability.[9]

Rule 702 further requires that the evidence or testimony "assist the trier of fact to understand the evidence or to determine a fact in issue." This condition goes primarily to relevance. "Expert testimony which does not relate to any issue in the case is not relevant and, ergo, non-helpful." 3 Weinstein & Berger ¶702[02], 702–18. See also *United States v. Downing*, 753 F. 2d 1224, 1242 (CA3 1985) ("An additional consideration under Rule 702—and another aspect of relevancy—is whether expert testimony proffered in the case is sufficiently tied to the facts of the case that it will aid the jury in resolving a factual dispute"). The consideration has been aptly described by Judge Becker as one of "fit." Ibid. "Fit" is not always obvious, and scientific validity for one purpose is not necessarily scientific validity for other, unrelated purposes. See Starrs, *Frye v. United States* Restructured and Revitalized: A Proposal to Amend Federal Evidence Rule 702, and 26 Jurimetrics J. 249, 258 (1986). The study of the phases of the moon, for example, may provide valid scientific "knowledge" about whether a certain night was dark, and if darkness is a fact in issue, the knowledge will assist the trier of fact. However (absent creditable grounds supporting such a link), evidence that the moon was full on a certain night will not assist the trier of fact in determining whether an individual was unusually likely to have behaved irrationally on that night. Rule 702's "helpfulness" standard requires a valid scientific connection to the pertinent inquiry as a precondition to admissibility.

---

[9] We note that scientists typically distinguish between "validity" (does the principle support what it purports to show?) and "reliability" (does application of the principle produce consistent results?). See Black, A Unified Theory of Scientific Evidence, 56 Ford. L. Rev. 595, 599 (1988). Although "the difference between accuracy, validity, and reliability may be such that each is distinct from the other by no more than a hen's kick," Starrs, *Frye v. United States* Restructured and Revitalized: A Proposal to Amend Federal Evidence Rule 702, 26 Jurimetrics J. 249, 256 (1986), our reference here is to *evidentiary* reliability—that is, trustworthiness. Cf., e.g., Advisory Committee's Notes on Fed. Rule Evid. 602 ("'[T]he rule requiring that a witness who testifies to a fact which can be perceived by the senses must have had an opportunity to observe, and must have actually observed the fact' is a 'most pervasive manifestation' of the common law insistence upon 'the most reliable sources of information.'" (citation omitted)); Advisory Committee's Notes on Art. VIII of the Rules of Evidence (hearsay exceptions will be recognized only "under circumstances supposed to furnish guarantees of trustworthiness"). In a case involving scientific evidence, *evidentiary reliability* will be based upon *scientific validity*.

That these requirements are embodied in Rule 702 is not surprising. Unlike an ordinary witness, see Rule 701, an expert is permitted wide latitude to offer opinions, including those that are not based on first-hand knowledge or observation. See Rules 702 and 703. Presumably, this relaxation of the usual requirement of firsthand knowledge—a rule which represents "a 'most pervasive manifestation' of the common law insistence upon 'the most reliable sources of information,'" Advisory Committee's Notes on Fed. Rule Evid. 602 (citation omitted)—is premised on an assumption that the expert's opinion will have a reliable basis in the knowledge and experience of his discipline.

Faced with a proffer of expert scientific testimony, then, the trial judge must determine at the outset, pursuant to Rule 104(a),[10] whether the expert is proposing to testify to (1) scientific knowledge that (2) will assist the trier of fact to understand or determine a fact in issue.[11] This entails a preliminary assessment of whether the reasoning or methodology underlying the testimony is scientifically valid and of whether that reasoning or methodology properly can be applied to the facts in issue. We are confident that federal judges possess the capacity to undertake this review. Many factors will bear on the inquiry, and we do not presume to set out a definitive checklist or test. But some general observations are appropriate.

Ordinarily, a key question to be answered in determining whether a theory or technique is scientific knowledge that will assist the trier of fact will be whether it can be (and has been) tested. "Scientific methodology today is based on generating hypotheses and testing them to see if they can be falsified; indeed, this methodology is what distinguishes science from other fields of human inquiry." Green, at 645. See also C. Hempel, Philosophy of Natural Science 49 (1966) ("[T]he statements constituting a scientific explanation must be capable of empirical test"); K. Popper, Conjectures and Refutations: The Growth of Scientific Knowledge 37 (5th ed. 1989) ("[T]he criterion of the scientific status of a theory is its falsifiability, or refutability, or testability").

Another pertinent consideration is whether the theory or technique has been subjected to peer review and publication. Publication (which is but one element of peer review) is not a sine qua non of admissibility; it does

[10] Rule 104(a) provides: "Preliminary questions concerning the qualification of a person to be a witness, the existence of a privilege, or the admissibility of evidence shall be determined by the court, subject to the provisions of subdivision (b) [pertaining to conditional admissions]. In making its determination it is not bound by the rules of evidence except those with respect to privileges." These matters should be established by a preponderance of proof. See *Bourjaily v. United States*, 483 U.S. 171, 175–176 (1987).

[11] Although the *Frye* decision itself focused exclusively on "novel" scientific techniques, we do not read the requirements of Rule 702 to apply specially or exclusively to unconventional evidence. Of course, well-established propositions are less likely to be challenged than those that are novel, and they are more handily defended. Indeed, theories that are so firmly established as to have attained the status of scientific law, such as the laws of thermodynamics, properly are subject to judicial notice under Fed. Rule Evid. 201.

not necessarily correlate with reliability, see S. Jasanoff, The Fifth Branch: Science Advisors as Policymakers 61–76 (1990), and in some instances well-grounded but innovative theories will not have been published, see Horrobin, The Philosophical Basis of Peer Review and the Suppression of Innovation, 263 J. Am. Med. Assn. 1438 (1990). Some propositions, moreover, are too particular, too new, or of too limited interest to be published. But submission to the scrutiny of the scientific community is a component of "good science," in part because it increases the likelihood that substantive flaws in methodology will be detected. See J. Ziman, Reliable Knowledge: An Exploration of the Grounds for Belief in Science 130–133 (1978); Relman and Angell, How Good Is Peer Review?, 321 New Eng. J. Med. 827 (1989). The fact of publication (or lack thereof) in a peer-reviewed journal thus will be a relevant, though not dispositive, consideration in assessing the scientific validity of a particular technique or methodology on which an opinion is premised.

Additionally, in the case of a particular scientific technique, the court ordinarily should consider the known or potential rate of error, see, e.g., *United States v. Smith*, 869 F. 2d 348, 353–354 (CA7 1989) (surveying studies of the error rate of spectrographic voice identification technique), and the existence and maintenance of standards controlling the technique's operation. See *United States v. Williams*, 583 F. 2d 1194, 1198 (CA2 1978) (noting professional organization's standard governing spectrographic analysis), cert. denied, 439 U.S. 1117 (1979).

Finally, "general acceptance" can yet have a bearing on the inquiry. A "reliability assessment does not require, although it does permit, explicit identification of a relevant scientific community and an express determination of a particular degree of acceptance within that community." *United States v. Downing*, 753 F. 2d, at 1238. See also 3 Weinstein & Berger ¶702[03], 702–41 to 702–42. Widespread acceptance can be an important factor in ruling particular evidence admissible, and "a known technique that has been able to attract only minimal support within the community," *Downing*, supra, at 1238, may properly be viewed with skepticism.

The inquiry envisioned by Rule 702 is, we emphasize, a flexible one.[12] Its overarching subject is the scientific validity—and thus the evidentiary relevance and reliability—of the principles that underlie a proposed submission. The

---

[12] A number of authorities have presented variations on the reliability approach, each with its own slightly different set of factors. See, e.g., *Downing*, 753 F. 2d 1238–1239 (on which our discussion draws in part); 3 Weinstein & Berger ¶702[03], 702–41 to 702–42 (on which the *Downing* court in turn partially relied); McCormick, Scientific Evidence: Defining a New Approach to Admissibility, 67 Iowa L. Rev. 879, 911–912 (1982); and Symposium on Science and the Rules of Evidence, 99 F.R.D. 187, 231 (1983) (statement by Margaret Berger). To the extent that they focus on the reliability of evidence as ensured by the scientific validity of its underlying principles, all these versions may well have merit, although we express no opinion regarding any of their particular details.

focus, of course, must be solely on principles and methodology, not on the conclusions that they generate.

Throughout, a judge assessing a proffer of expert scientific testimony under Rule 702 should also be mindful of other applicable rules. Rule 703 provides that expert opinions based on otherwise inadmissible hearsay are to be admitted only if the facts or data are "of a type reasonably relied upon by experts in the particular field in forming opinions or inferences upon the subject." Rule 706 allows the court at its discretion to procure the assistance of an expert of its own choosing. Finally, Rule 403 permits the exclusion of relevant evidence "if its probative value is substantially outweighed by the danger of unfair prejudice, confusion of the issues, or misleading the jury...." Judge Weinstein has explained: "Expert evidence can be both powerful and quite misleading because of the difficulty in evaluating it. Because of this risk, the judge in weighing possible prejudice against probative force under Rule 403 of the present rules exercises more control over experts than over lay witnesses." Weinstein, 138 F.R.D., at 632.

We conclude by briefly addressing what appear to be two underlying concerns of the parties and amici in this case. Respondent expresses apprehension that abandonment of "general acceptance" as the exclusive requirement for admission will result in a "free-for-all" in which befuddled juries are confounded by absurd and irrational pseudoscientific assertions. In this regard respondent seems to us to be overly pessimistic about the capabilities of the jury, and of the adversary system generally. Vigorous cross-examination, presentation of contrary evidence, and careful instruction on the burden of proof are the traditional and appropriate means of attacking shaky but admissible evidence. See *Rock v. Arkansas*, 483 U.S. 44, 61 (1987). Additionally, in the event the trial court concludes that the scintilla of evidence presented supporting a position is insufficient to allow a reasonable juror to conclude that the position more likely than not is true, the court remains free to direct a judgment, Fed. Rule Civ. Proc. 50 (a), and likewise to grant summary judgment, Fed. Rule Civ. Proc. 56. Cf., e.g., *Turpin v. Merrell Dow Pharmaceuticals, Inc.*, 959 F. 2d 1349 (CA6) (holding that scientific evidence that provided foundation for expert testimony, viewed in the light most favorable to plaintiffs, was not sufficient to allow a jury to find it more probable than not that defendant caused plaintiff's injury), cert. denied, 506 U.S. ___ (1992); *Brock v. Merrell Dow Pharmaceuticals, Inc.*, 874 F. 2d 307 (CA5 1989) (reversing judgment entered on jury verdict for plaintiffs because evidence regarding causation was insufficient), modified, 884 F. 2d 166 (CA5 1989), cert. denied, 494 U.S. 1046 (1990); Green 680–681. These conventional devices, rather than wholesale exclusion under an uncompromising "general acceptance" test, are the appropriate safeguards where the basis of scientific testimony meets the standards of Rule 702.

Petitioners and, to a greater extent, their amici exhibit a different concern. They suggest that recognition of a screening role for the judge that allows for the exclusion of "invalid" evidence will sanction a stifling and repressive scientific orthodoxy and will be inimical to the search for truth. See, e.g., Brief for Ronald Bayer et al. as Amici Curiae. It is true that open debate is an essential part of both legal and scientific analyses. Yet there are important differences between the quest for truth in the courtroom and the quest for truth in the laboratory. Scientific conclusions are subject to perpetual revision. Law, on the other hand, must resolve disputes finally and quickly. The scientific project is advanced by broad and wide-ranging consideration of a multitude of hypotheses, for those that are incorrect will eventually be shown to be so, and that in itself is an advance. Conjectures that are probably wrong are of little use, however, in the project of reaching a quick, final, and binding legal judgment—often of great consequence—about a particular set of events in the past. We recognize that in practice, a gatekeeping role for the judge, no matter how flexible, inevitably on occasion will prevent the jury from learning of authentic insights and innovations. That, nevertheless, is the balance that is struck by Rules of Evidence designed not for the exhaustive search for cosmic understanding but for the particularized resolution of legal disputes.[13]

To summarize: "general acceptance" is not a necessary precondition to the admissibility of scientific evidence under the Federal Rules of Evidence, but the Rules of Evidence—especially Rule 702—do assign to the trial judge the task of ensuring that an expert's testimony both rests on a reliable foundation and is relevant to the task at hand. Pertinent evidence based on scientifically valid principles will satisfy those demands.

The inquiries of the District Court and the Court of Appeals focused almost exclusively on "general acceptance," as gauged by publication and the decisions of other courts. Accordingly, the judgment of the Court of Appeals is vacated and the case is remanded for further proceedings consistent with this opinion.

It is so ordered.

---

[13]This is not to say that judicial interpretation, as opposed to adjudicative factfinding, does not share basic characteristics of the scientific endeavor: "The work of a judge is in one sense enduring and in another ephemeral.... In the endless process of testing and retesting, there is a constant rejection of the dross and a constant retention of whatever is pure and sound and fine." B. Cardozo, The Nature of the Judicial Process 178, 179 (1921).

Appendix F: Kumho Tire v. Carmichael

119 S. Ct. 1167 (1999)

SUPREME COURT OF THE UNITED STATES

No. 97–1709

KUMHO TIRE COMPANY, LTD., et al., PETITIONERS
v. PATRICK CARMICHAEL, etc., et al.
ON WRIT OF CERTIORARI TO THE UNITED STATES COURT OF APPEALS FOR THE ELEVENTH CIRCUIT
[March 23, 1999]

Justice Breyer delivered the opinion of the Court.

In *Daubert v. Merrell Dow Pharmaceuticals, Inc.*, 509 U.S. 579 (1993), this Court focused upon the admissibility of scientific expert testimony. It pointed out that such testimony is admissible only if it is both relevant and reliable. And it held that the Federal Rules of Evidence "assign to the trial judge the task of ensuring that an expert's testimony both rests on a reliable foundation and is relevant to the task at hand." *Id.*, at 597. The Court also discussed certain more specific factors, such as testing, peer review, error rates, and "acceptability" in the relevant scientific community, some or all of which might prove helpful in determining the reliability of a particular scientific "theory or technique." *Id.*, at 593–594.

This case requires us to decide how *Daubert* applies to the testimony of engineers and other experts who are not scientists. We conclude that *Daubert*'s general holding—setting forth the trial judge's general "gatekeeping" obligation—applies not only to testimony based on "scientific" knowledge, but also to testimony based on "technical" and "other specialized" knowledge. See Fed. Rule Evid. 702. We also conclude that a trial court *may* consider one or more of the more specific factors that *Daubert* mentioned when doing so will help determine that testimony's reliability. But, as the Court stated in *Daubert*, the test of reliability is "flexible," and *Daubert's* list of specific factors neither necessarily nor exclusively applies to all experts or in every case. Rather, the law grants a district court the same broad latitude when it decides *how* to determine reliability as it enjoys in respect to its ultimate reliability determination. See *General Electric Co. v. Joiner*, 522 U.S. 136, 143 (1997) (courts of appeals are to apply "abuse of discretion" standard when reviewing district court's reliability determination). Applying these standards, we determine that the District Court's decision in this case—not to admit certain expert testimony—was within its discretion and therefore lawful.

I

On July 6, 1993, the right rear tire of a minivan driven by Patrick Carmichael blew out. In the accident that followed, one of the passengers died, and others were severely injured. In October 1993, the Carmichaels brought this diversity suit against the tire's maker and its distributor, whom we refer to collectively as Kumho Tire, claiming that the tire was defective. The plaintiffs rested their case in significant part upon deposition testimony provided by an expert in tire failure analysis, Dennis Carlson, Jr., who intended to testify in support of their conclusion.

Carlson's depositions relied upon certain features of tire technology that are not in dispute. A steel-belted radial tire like the Carmichaels' is made up of a "carcass" containing many layers of flexible cords, called "plies," along which (between the cords and the outer tread) are laid steel strips called "belts." Steel wire loops, called "beads," hold the cords together at the plies' bottom edges. An outer layer, called the "tread," encases the carcass, and the entire tire is bound together in rubber, through the application of heat and various chemicals. See generally, e.g., J. Dixon, Tires, Suspension and Handling 68–72 (2d ed. 1996). The bead of the tire sits upon a "bead seat," which is part of the wheel assembly. That assembly contains a "rim flange," which extends over the bead and rests against the side of the tire. See M. Mavrigian, Performance Wheels & Tires 81, 83 (1998) (illustrations). A. Markovich, How To Buy and Care For Tires 4 (1994).

Carlson's testimony also accepted certain background facts about the tire in question. He assumed that before the blowout the tire had traveled far. (The tire was made in 1988 and had been installed some time before the Carmichaels bought the used minivan in March 1993; the Carmichaels had driven the van approximately 7,000 additional miles in the two months they had owned it.) Carlson noted that the tire's tread depth, which was 11/32 of an inch when new, App. 242, had been worn down to depths that ranged from 3/32 of an inch along some parts of the tire, to nothing at all along others. *Id.*, at 287. He conceded that the tire tread had at least two punctures which had been inadequately repaired. *Id.*, at 258–261, 322.

Despite the tire's age and history, Carlson concluded that a defect in its manufacture or design caused the blowout. He rested this conclusion in part upon three premises which, for present purposes, we must assume are not in dispute: First, a tire's carcass should stay bound to the inner side of the tread for a significant period of time after its tread depth has worn away. *Id.*, at 208–209. Second, the tread of the tire at issue had separated from its inner steel-belted carcass prior to the accident. *Id.*, at 336. Third, this "separation" caused the blowout. Ibid.

Carlson's conclusion that a defect caused the separation, however, rested upon certain other propositions, several of which the defendants strongly dispute. First, Carlson said that if a separation is *not* caused by a certain kind of tire misuse called "overdeflection" (which consists of underinflating the tire or causing it to carry too much weight, thereby generating heat that can undo the chemical tread/carcass bond), then, ordinarily, its cause is a tire defect. *Id.*, at 193–195, 277–278. Second, he said that if a tire has been subject to sufficient overdeflection to cause a separation, it should reveal certain physical symptoms. These symptoms include (a) tread wear on the tire's shoulder that is greater than the tread wear along the tire's center, *id.*, at 211; (b) signs of a "bead groove," where the beads have been pushed too hard against the bead seat on the inside of the tire's rim, *id.*, at 196–197; (c) sidewalls of the tire with physical signs of deterioration, such as discoloration, *id.*, at 212; and/ or (d) marks on the tire's rim flange, *id.*, at 219–220. Third, Carlson said that where he does not find *at least two* of the four physical signs just mentioned (and presumably where there is no reason to suspect a less common cause of separation), he concludes that a manufacturing or design defect caused the separation. *Id.*, at 223–224.

Carlson added that he had inspected the tire in question. He conceded that the tire to a limited degree showed greater wear on the shoulder than in the center, some signs of "bead groove," some discoloration, a few marks on the rim flange, and inadequately filled puncture holes (which can also cause heat that might lead to separation). *Id.*, at 256–257, 258–261, 277, 303–304, 308. But, in each instance, he testified that the symptoms were not significant, and he explained why he believed that they did not reveal overdeflection. For example, the extra shoulder wear, he said, appeared primarily on one shoulder, whereas an overdeflected tire would reveal equally abnormal wear on both shoulders. *Id.*, at 277. Carlson concluded that the tire did not bear at least two of the four overdeflection symptoms, nor was there any less obvious cause of separation; and since neither overdeflection nor the punctures caused the blowout, a defect must have done so.

Kumho Tire moved the District Court to exclude Carlson's testimony on the ground that his methodology failed Rule 702's reliability requirement. The court agreed with Kumho that it should act as a *Daubert*-type reliability "gatekeeper," even though one might consider Carlson's testimony as "technical," rather than "scientific." See *Carmichael v. Samyang Tires, Inc.*, 923 F. Supp. 1514, 1521–1522 (SD Ala. 1996). The court then examined Carlson's methodology in light of the reliability-related factors that *Daubert* mentioned, such as a theory's testability, whether it "has been a subject of peer review or publication," the "known or potential rate of error," and the "degree of acceptance…within the relevant scientific community." 923 F. Supp., at 1520 (citing *Daubert*, 509 U.S., at 592–594). The District Court found that all those factors argued against the reliability of Carlson's methods, and it granted the motion to exclude the testimony (as well as the defendants' accompanying motion for summary judgment).

The plaintiffs, arguing that the court's application of the *Daubert* factors was too "inflexible," asked for reconsideration. And the Court granted that motion. *Carmichael v. Samyang Tires, Inc.*, Civ. Action No. 93–0860–CB–S (SD Ala., June 5, 1996), App. to Pet. for Cert. 1c. After reconsidering the matter, the court agreed with the plaintiffs that *Daubert* should be applied flexibly, that its four factors were simply illustrative, and that other factors could argue in favor of admissibility. It conceded that there may be widespread acceptance of a "visualinspection method" for some relevant purposes. But the court found insufficient indications of the reliability of

> "the component of Carlson's tire failure analysis which most concerned the Court, namely, the methodology employed by the expert in analyzing the data obtained in the visual inspection, and the scientific basis, if any, for such an analysis." *Id.*, at 6c.

It consequently affirmed its earlier order declaring Carlson's testimony inadmissible and granting the defendants' motion for summary judgment.

The Eleventh Circuit reversed. See *Carmichael v. Samyang Tire, Inc.*, 131 F.3d 1433 (1997). It "review[ed]…*de novo*" the "district court's legal decision to apply *Daubert*." *Id.*, at 1435. It noted that "the Supreme Court in *Daubert* explicitly limited its holding to cover only the 'scientific context,'" adding that "a *Daubert* analysis" applies only where an expert relies "on the application of scientific principles," rather than "on skillor experience-based observation." *Id.*, at 1435–1436. It concluded that Carlson's testimony, which it viewed as relying on experience, "falls outside the scope of *Daubert*," that "the district court erred as a matter of law by applying *Daubert* in this case," and that the case must be remanded for further (non-*Daubert*type) consideration under Rule 702. *Id.*, at 1436.

Kumho Tire petitioned for certiorari, asking us to determine whether a trial court "may" consider *Daubert*'s specific "factors" when determining the "admissibility of an engineering expert's testimony." Pet. for Cert. i. We granted certiorari in light of uncertainty among the lower courts about whether, or how, *Daubert* applies to expert testimony that might be characterized as based not upon "scientific" knowledge, but rather upon "technical" or "other specialized" knowledge. Fed. Rule Evid. 702; compare, e.g., *Watkins v. Telsmith, Inc.*, 121 F.3d 984, 990–991 (CA5 1997), with, e.g., *Compton v. Subaru of America, Inc.*, 82 F.3d 1513, 1518–1519 (CA10), cert. denied, 519 U.S. 1042 (1996).

II

A

In *Daubert*, this Court held that Federal Rule of Evidence 702 imposes a special obligation upon a trial judge to "ensure that any and all scientific testimony…is not only relevant, but reliable." 509 U.S., at 589. The initial question before us is whether this basic gatekeeping obligation applies only to "scientific" testimony or to all expert testimony. We, like the parties, believe that it applies to all expert testimony. See Brief for Petitioners 19; Brief for Respondents 17.

For one thing, Rule 702 itself says:

> "If scientific, technical, or other specialized knowledge will assist the trier of fact to understand the evidence or to determine a fact in issue, a witness qualified as an expert by knowledge, skill, experience, training, or education, may testify thereto in the form of an opinion or otherwise."

This language makes no relevant distinction between "scientific" knowledge and "technical" or "other specialized" knowledge. It makes clear that any such knowledge might become the subject of expert testimony. In *Daubert*, the Court specified that it is the Rule's word "knowledge," not the words (like "scientific") that modify that word, that "establishes a standard of evidentiary reliability." 509 U.S., at 589–590. Hence, as a matter of language, the Rule applies its reliability standard to all "scientific," "technical," or "other specialized" matters within its scope. We concede that the Court in *Daubert* referred only to "scientific" knowledge. But as the Court there said, it referred to "scientific" testimony "because that [wa]s the nature of the expertise" at issue. *Id.*, at 590, n. 8.

Neither is the evidentiary rationale that underlay the Court's basic *Daubert* "gatekeeping" determination limited to "scientific" knowledge. *Daubert* pointed out that Federal Rules 702 and 703 grant expert witnesses testimonial latitude unavailable to other witnesses on the "assumption that the expert's opinion will have a reliable basis in the knowledge and experience of his discipline." *Id.*, at 592 (pointing out that experts may testify to opinions, including those that are not based on firsthand knowledge or observation). The Rules grant that latitude to all experts, not just to "scientific" ones.

Finally, it would prove difficult, if not impossible, for judges to administer evidentiary rules under which a gatekeeping obligation depended upon a distinction between "scientific" knowledge and "technical" or "other specialized" knowledge. There is no clear line that divides the one from the others. Disciplines such as engineering rest upon scientific knowledge. Pure scientific theory itself may depend for its development upon observation and properly engineered machinery. And conceptual efforts to distinguish the two are unlikely to produce clear legal lines capable of application in particular cases. Cf. Brief for National Academy of Engineering as *Amicus Curiae* 9 (scientist seeks to understand nature while the engineer seeks nature's modification); Brief for Rubber Manufacturers Association as *Amicus Curiae* 14–16 (engineering, as an "applied science," relies on "scientific reasoning and methodology"); Brief for John Allen et al. as *Amici Curiae* 6 (engineering relies upon "scientific knowledge and methods").

Neither is there a convincing need to make such distinctions. Experts of all kinds tie observations to conclusions through the use of what Judge Learned Hand called "general truths derived from…specialized experience." Hand, Historical and Practical Considerations Regarding Expert Testimony, 15 Harv. L. Rev. 40, 54 (1901). And whether the specific expert testimony focuses upon specialized observations, the specialized translation of those observations into theory, a specialized theory itself, or the application of such a theory in a particular case, the expert's testimony often will rest "upon an experience confessedly foreign in kind to [the jury's] own." *Ibid.* The trial judge's effort to assure that the specialized testimony is reliable and relevant can help the jury evaluate that foreign experience, whether the testimony reflects scientific, technical, or other specialized knowledge.

We conclude that *Daubert*'s general principles apply to the expert matters described in Rule 702. The Rule, in respect to all such matters, "establishes a standard of evidentiary reliability." 509 U.S., at 590. It "requires a valid… connection to the pertinent inquiry as a precondition to admissibility." *Id.*, at 592. And where such testimony's factual basis, data, principles, methods, or their application are called sufficiently into question, see Part III, *infra*, the trial judge must determine whether the testimony has "a reliable basis in the knowledge and experience of [the relevant] discipline." 509 U.S., at 592.

B

The petitioners ask more specifically whether a trial judge determining the "admissibility of an engineering expert's testimony" *may* consider several more specific factors that *Daubert* said might "bear on" a judge's gatekeeping determination. These factors include:

—Whether a "theory or technique...can be (and has been) tested";
—Whether it "has been subjected to peer review and publication";
—Whether, in respect to a particular technique, there is a high "known or potential rate of error" and whether there are "standards controlling the technique's operation"; and
—Whether the theory or technique enjoys "general acceptance" within a "relevant scientific community." 509 U.S., at 592–594.

Emphasizing the word "may" in the question, we answer that question yes.

Engineering testimony rests upon scientific foundations, the reliability of which will be at issue in some cases. See, e.g., Brief for Stephen Bobo et al. as *Amici Curiae* 23 (stressing the scientific bases of engineering disciplines). In other cases, the relevant reliability concerns may focus upon personal knowledge or experience. As the Solicitor General points out, there are many different kinds of experts, and many different kinds of expertise. See Brief for United States as *Amicus Curiae* 18–19, and n. 5 (citing cases involving experts in drug terms, handwriting analysis, criminal *modus operandi*, land valuation, agricultural practices, railroad procedures, attorney's fee valuation, and others). Our emphasis on the word "may" thus reflects *Daubert*'s description of the Rule 702 inquiry as "a flexible one." 509 U.S., at 594. *Daubert* makes clear that the factors it mentions do *not* constitute a "definitive checklist or test." *Id.*, at 593. And *Daubert* adds that the gatekeeping inquiry must be "'tied to the facts'" of a particular "case." *Id.*, at 591 (quoting *United States v. Downing*, 753 F.2d 1224, 1242 (CA3 1985)). We agree with the Solicitor General that "[t]he factors identified in *Daubert* may or may not be pertinent in assessing reliability, depending on the nature of the issue, the expert's particular expertise, and the subject of his testimony." Brief for United States as *Amicus Curiae* 19. The conclusion, in our view, is that we can neither rule out, nor rule in, for all cases and for all time the applicability of the factors mentioned in *Daubert*, nor can we now do so for subsets of cases categorized by category of expert or by kind of evidence. Too much depends upon the particular circumstances of the particular case at issue.

Daubert itself is not to the contrary. It made clear that its list of factors was meant to be helpful, not definitive. Indeed, those factors do not all necessarily apply even in every instance in which the reliability of scientific testimony is challenged. It might not be surprising in a particular case, for example, that a claim made by a scientific witness has never been the subject of peer review, for the particular application at issue may never previously have interested any scientist. Nor, on the other hand, does the presence of *Daubert*'s general acceptance factor help show that an expert's testimony is reliable where the discipline itself lacks reliability, as, for example, do theories grounded in any so-called generally accepted principles of astrology or necromancy.

At the same time, and contrary to the Court of Appeals' view, some of *Daubert*'s questions can help to evaluate the reliability even of experience-based testimony. In certain cases, it will be appropriate for the trial judge to ask, for example, how often an engineering expert's experience-based methodology has produced erroneous results, or whether such a method is generally accepted in the relevant engineering community. Likewise, it will at times be useful to ask even of a witness whose expertise is based purely on experience, say, a perfume tester able to distinguish among 140 odors at a sniff, whether his preparation is of a kind that others in the field would recognize as acceptable.

We must therefore disagree with the Eleventh Circuit's holding that a trial judge may ask questions of the sort *Daubert* mentioned only where an expert "relies on the application of scientific principles," but not where an expert relies "on skillor experience-based observation." 131 F.3d, at 1435. We do not believe that Rule 702 creates a schematism that segregates expertise by type while mapping certain kinds of questions to certain kinds of experts. Life and the legal cases that it generates are too complex to warrant so definitive a match.

To say this is not to deny the importance of *Daubert*'s gatekeeping requirement. The objective of that requirement is to ensure the reliability and relevancy of expert testimony. It is to make certain that an expert, whether basing testimony upon professional studies or personal experience, employs in the courtroom the same level of intellectual rigor that characterizes the practice of an expert in the relevant field. Nor do we deny that, as stated in *Daubert*, the particular questions that it mentioned will often be appropriate for use in determining the reliability of challenged expert testimony. Rather, we conclude that the trial judge must have considerable leeway in deciding in a particular case how to go about determining whether particular expert testimony is reliable. That is to say, a trial court should consider the specific factors identified in *Daubert* where they are reasonable measures of the reliability of expert testimony.

C

The trial court must have the same kind of latitude in deciding *how* to test an expert's reliability, and to decide whether or when special briefing or other proceedings are needed to investigate reliability, as it enjoys when it decides *whether* that expert's relevant testimony is reliable. Our opinion in *Joiner* makes clear that a court of appeals is to apply an abuse-of-discretion standard when it "review[s] a trial court's decision to admit or exclude expert testimony." 522 U.S., at 138–139. That standard applies as much to the trial court's decisions about how to determine reliability as to its ultimate conclusion. Otherwise, the trial judge would lack the discretionary authority needed both to avoid unnecessary "reliability" proceedings in ordinary cases where the reliability of an expert's methods is properly taken for granted, and to require appropriate proceedings in the less usual or more complex cases where cause for questioning the expert's reliability arises. Indeed, the Rules seek to avoid "unjustifiable expense and delay" as part of their search for "truth" and the "jus[t] determin[ation]" of proceedings. Fed. Rule Evid. 102. Thus, whether *Daubert*'s specific factors are, or are not, reasonable measures of reliability in a particular case is a matter that the law grants the trial judge broad latitude to determine. See *Joiner, supra,* at 143. And the Eleventh Circuit erred insofar as it held to the contrary.

III

We further explain the way in which a trial judge "may" consider *Daubert*'s factors by applying these considerations to the case at hand, a matter that has been briefed exhaustively by the parties and their 19 *amici*. The District Court did not doubt Carlson's qualifications, which included a master's degree in mechanical engineering, 10 years' work at Michelin America, Inc., and testimony as a tire failure consultant in other tort cases. Rather, it excluded the testimony because, despite those qualifications, it initially doubted, and then found unreliable, "the methodology employed by the expert in analyzing the data obtained in the visual inspection, and the scientific basis, if any, for such an analysis." Civ. Action No. 93–0860–CB–S (SD Ala., June 5, 1996), App. to Pet. for Cert. 6c. After examining the transcript in "some detail," 923 F. Supp., at 1518–519, n. 4, and after considering respondents' defense of Carlson's methodology, the District Court determined that Carlson's testimony was not reliable. It fell outside the range where experts might reasonably differ, and where the jury must decide among the conflicting views of different experts, even though the evidence is "shaky." *Daubert*, 509 U.S., at 596. In our view, the doubts that triggered the District Court's initial inquiry here were reasonable, as was the court's ultimate conclusion. For one thing, and contrary to respondents' suggestion, the specific issue before the court was not the reasonableness *in general* of a tire expert's use of a visual and tactile inspection to determine whether overdeflection had caused the tire's tread to separate from its steel-belted carcass. Rather, it was the reasonableness of using such an approach, along with Carlson's particular method of analyzing the data thereby obtained, to draw a conclusion regarding *the particular matter to which the expert testimony was directly relevant.* That matter concerned the likelihood that a defect in the tire at issue caused its tread to separate from its carcass. The tire in question, the expert conceded, had traveled far enough so that some of the tread had been worn bald; it should have been taken out of service; it had been repaired (inadequately) for punctures; and it bore some of the very marks that the expert said indicated, not a defect, but abuse through overdeflection. See *supra*, at 3–5; App. 293–294. The relevant issue was whether the expert could reliably determine the cause of *this* tire's separation.

Nor was the basis for Carlson's conclusion simply the general theory that, in the absence of evidence of abuse, a defect will normally have caused a tire's separation. Rather, the expert employed a more specific theory to establish the existence (or absence) of such abuse. Carlson testified precisely that in the absence of *at least two* of four signs of abuse (proportionately greater tread wear on the shoulder; signs of grooves caused by the beads; discolored sidewalls; marks on the rim flange) he concludes that a defect caused the separation. And his analysis depended upon acceptance of a further implicit proposition, namely, that his visual and tactile inspection could determine that the tire before him had not been abused despite some evidence of the presence of the very signs for which he looked (and two punctures).

For another thing, the transcripts of Carlson's depositions support both the trial court's initial uncertainty and its final conclusion. Those transcripts cast considerable doubt upon the reliability of both the explicit theory (about the need for two signs of abuse) and the implicit proposition (about the significance of visual inspection in this case). Among other things, the expert could not say whether the tire had traveled more than 10, or 20, or 30, or 40, or 50 thousand miles, adding that 6,000 miles was "about how far" he could "say with any certainty." *Id.*, at 265. The court could reasonably have wondered about the reliability of a method of visual and tactile inspection sufficiently precise to ascertain with some certainty the abuse-related significance of minute shoulder/center relative tread wear differences, but insufficiently precise to tell "with any certainty" from the tread wear whether a tire had traveled less than 10,000 or more than 50,000 miles. And these concerns might have been augmented by Carlson's repeated reliance on the "subjective[ness]" of his mode of analysis in response to questions seeking specific information regarding how he could differentiate between a tire that actually had been overdeflected and a tire that merely looked as though it had been. *Id.*, at 222, 224–225, 285–286. They would have been further augmented by the fact that Carlson said he had inspected the tire itself for the first time the morning of his first deposition, and then only for a few hours. (His initial conclusions were based on photographs.) *Id.*, at 180.

Moreover, prior to his first deposition, Carlson had issued a signed report in which he concluded that the tire had "not been…overloaded or underinflated," not because of the absence of "two of four" signs of abuse, but simply because "the rim flange impressions…were normal." *Id.*, at 335–336. That report also said that the "tread depth remaining was 3/32 inch," *id.*, at 336, though the opposing expert's (apparently undisputed) measurements indicate that the tread depth taken at various positions around the tire actually ranged from .5/32 of an inch to 4/32 of an inch, with the tire apparently showing greater wear along *both* shoulders than along the center, *id.*, at 432–433.

Further, in respect to one sign of abuse, bead grooving, the expert seemed to deny the sufficiency of his own simple visual-inspection methodology. He testified that most tires have some bead groove pattern, that where there is reason to suspect an abnormal bead groove he would ideally "look at a lot of [similar] tires" to know the grooving's significance, and that he had not looked at many tires similar to the one at issue. *Id.*, at 212–213, 214, 217.

Finally, the court, after looking for a defense of Carlson's methodology as applied in these circumstances, found no convincing defense. Rather, it found (1) that "none" of the *Daubert* factors, including that of "general acceptance" in the relevant expert community, indicated that Carlson's testimony was reliable, 923 F. Supp., at 1521; (2) that its own analysis "revealed no countervailing factors operating in favor of admissibility which could outweigh those identified in *Daubert*," App. to Pet. for Cert. 4c; and (3) that the "parties identified no such factors in their briefs," *ibid.* For these three reasons *taken together*, it concluded that Carlson's testimony was unreliable.

Respondents now argue to us, as they did to the District Court, that a method of tire failure analysis that employs a visual/tactile inspection is a reliable method, and they point both to its use by other experts and to Carlson's long experience working for Michelin as sufficient indication that that is so. But no one denies that an expert might draw a conclusion from a set of observations based on extensive and specialized experience. Nor does anyone deny that, as a general matter, tire abuse may often be identified by qualified experts through visual or tactile inspection of the tire. See Affidavit of H. R. Baumgardner 1–2, cited in Brief for National Academy of Forensic Engineers as *Amici Curiae* 16 (Tire engineers rely on visual examination and process of elimination to analyze experimental test tires). As we said before, *supra*, at 14, the question before the trial court was specific, not general. The trial court had to decide whether this particular expert had sufficient specialized knowledge to assist the jurors "in deciding the particular issues in the case." 4 J. McLaughlin, Weinstein's Federal Evidence ¶702.05[1], 702–33 (2d ed. 1998); see also Advisory Committee's Note on Proposed Fed. Rule Evid. 702, Preliminary Draft of Proposed Amendments to the Federal Rules of Civil Procedure and Evidence: Request for Comment 126 (1998) (stressing that district courts must "scrutinize" whether the "principles and methods" employed by an expert "have been properly applied to the facts of the case").

The particular issue in this case concerned the use of Carlson's two-factor test and his related use of visual/tactile inspection to draw conclusions on the basis of what seemed small observational differences. We have found no indication in the record that other experts in the industry use Carlson's two-factor test or that tire experts such as Carlson normally make the very fine distinctions about, say, the symmetry of comparatively greater shoulder tread wear that were necessary, on Carlson's own theory, to support his conclusions. Nor, despite the prevalence of tire testing, does anyone refer to any articles or papers that validate Carlson's approach. Compare Bobo, Tire Flaws and Separations, in Mechanics of Pneumatic Tires 636–637 (S. Clark ed. 1981); C. Schnuth et al., Compression Grooving and Rim Flange Abrasion as Indicators of Over-Deflected Operating Conditions in Tires, presented to Rubber Division of the American Chemical Society, Oct. 21–24, 1997; J. Walter & R. Kiminecz, Bead Contact Pressure Measurements at the Tire-Rim Interface, presented to Society of Automotive Engineers, Feb. 24–28, 1975. Indeed, no one has argued that Carlson himself, were he still working for Michelin, would have concluded in a report to his employer that a similar tire was similarly defective on grounds identical to those upon which he rested his conclusion here. Of course, Carlson himself claimed that his method was accurate, but, as we pointed out in *Joiner*, "nothing in either *Daubert* or the Federal Rules of Evidence requires a district court to admit opinion evidence that is connected to existing data only by the *ipse dixit* of the expert." 522 U.S., at 146.

Respondents additionally argue that the District Court too rigidly applied *Daubert*'s criteria. They read its opinion to hold that a failure to satisfy any one of those criteria automatically renders expert testimony inadmissible. The District Court's initial opinion might have been vulnerable to a form of this argument. There, the court, after rejecting respondents' claim that Carlson's testimony was "exempted from *Daubert*-style scrutiny" because it was "technical analysis" rather than "scientific evidence," simply added that "none of the four admissibility criteria outlined by the *Daubert* court are satisfied." 923 F. Supp., at 1522. Subsequently, however, the court granted respondents' motion for reconsideration. It then explicitly recognized that the relevant reliability inquiry "should be 'flexible,'" that its "'overarching subject [should be]...validity' and reliability," and that "*Daubert* was intended neither to be exhaustive nor to apply in every case." App. to Pet. for Cert. 4c (quoting *Daubert*, 509 U.S., at 594–595). And the court ultimately based its decision upon Carlson's failure to satisfy either *Daubert*'s factors *or any other* set of reasonable reliability criteria. In light of the record as developed by the parties, that conclusion was within the District Court's lawful discretion.

In sum, Rule 702 grants the district judge the discretionary authority, reviewable for its abuse, to determine reliability in light of the particular facts and circumstances of the particular case. The District Court did not abuse its discretionary authority in this case. Hence, the judgment of the Court of Appeals is *Reversed*.

Appendix G: General Electric Company v. Joiner

118 S. Ct. 512 (1997)

NOTICE: This opinion is subject to formal revision before publication in the preliminary print of the United States Reports. Readers are requested to notify the Reporter of Decisions, Supreme Court of the United States, Washington, D.C. 20543, of any typographical or other formal errors, in order that corrections may be made before the preliminary print goes to press.

SUPREME COURT OF THE UNITED STATES

No. 96–188

GENERAL ELECTRIC COMPANY, et al., PETITIONERS v. ROBERT K. JOINER et ux.
ON WRIT OF CERTIORARI TO THE UNITED STATES COURT OF APPEALS FOR THE ELEVENTH CIRCUIT
[December 15, 1997]

Chief Justice Rehnquist delivered the opinion of the Court.

We granted certiorari in this case to determine what standard an appellate court should apply in reviewing a trial court's decision to admit or exclude expert testimony under *Daubert v. Merrell Dow Pharmaceuticals, Inc.*, 509 U.S. 579 (1993). We hold that abuse of discretion is the appropriate standard. We apply this standard and conclude that the District Court in this case did not abuse its discretion when it excluded certain proffered expert testimony.

I

Respondent Robert Joiner began work as an electrician in the Water & Light Department of Thomasville, Georgia (City) in 1973. This job required him to work with and around the City's electrical transformers, which used a mineral-based dielectric fluid as a coolant. Joiner often had to stick his hands and arms into the fluid to make repairs. The fluid would sometimes splash onto him, occasionally getting into his eyes and mouth. In 1983 the City discovered that the fluid in some of the transformers was contaminated with polychlorinated biphenyls (PCBs). PCBs are widely considered to be hazardous to human health. Congress, with limited exceptions, banned the production and sale of PCBs in 1978. See 90 Stat. 2020, 15 U.S.C.§ 2605(e)(2)(A).

Joiner was diagnosed with small cell lung cancer in 1991. He[1] sued petitioners in Georgia state court the following year. Petitioner Monsanto manufactured PCBs from 1935 to 1977; petitioners General Electric and Westinghouse Electric manufactured transformers and dielectric fluid. In his complaint Joiner linked his development of cancer to his exposure to PCBs and their derivatives, polychlorinated dibenzofurans (furans) and polychlorinated dibenzodioxins (dioxins). Joiner had been a smoker for approximately eight years, his parents had both been smokers, and there was a history of lung cancer in his family. He was thus perhaps already at a heightened risk of developing lung cancer eventually. The suit alleged that his exposure to PCBs "promoted" his cancer; had it not been for his exposure to these substances, his cancer would not have developed for many years, if at all.

Petitioners removed the case to federal court. Once there, they moved for summary judgment. They contended that (1) there was no evidence that Joiner suffered significant exposure to PCBs, furans, or dioxins, and (2) there was no admissible scientific evidence that PCBs promoted Joiner's cancer. Joiner responded that there were numerous disputed factual issues that required resolution by a jury. He relied largely on the testimony of expert witnesses. In depositions, his experts had testified that PCBs alone can promote cancer and that furans and dioxins can also promote cancer. They opined that since Joiner had been exposed to PCBs, furans, and dioxins, such exposure was likely responsible for Joiner's cancer.

The District Court ruled that there was a genuine issue of material fact as to whether Joiner had been exposed to PCBs. But it nevertheless granted summary judgment for petitioners because (1) there was no genuine issue as to whether Joiner had been exposed to furans and dioxins, and (2) the testimony of Joiner's experts had failed to show that there was a link between exposure to PCBs and small cell lung cancer. The court believed that the testimony of respondent's experts to the contrary did not rise above "subjective belief or unsupported speculation." 864 F. Supp. 1310, 1329 (ND Ga. 1994). Their testimony was therefore inadmissible.

The Court of Appeals for the Eleventh Circuit reversed. 78 F.3d 524 (1996). It held that "[b]ecause the Federal Rules of Evidence governing expert

---

[1] Joiner's wife was also a plaintiff in the suit and is a respondent here. For convenience, we refer to respondent in the singular.

testimony display a preference for admissibility, we apply a particularly stringent standard of review to the trial judge's exclusion of expert testimony." *Id.* at 529. Applying that standard, the Court of Appeals held that the District Court had erred in excluding the testimony of Joiner's expert witnesses. The District Court had made two fundamental errors. First, it excluded the experts' testimony because it "drew different conclusions from the research than did each of the experts." The Court of Appeals opined that a district court should limit its role to determining the "legal reliability of proffered expert testimony, leaving the jury to decide the correctness of competing expert opinions." *Id.* at 533. Second, the District Court had held that there was no genuine issue of material fact as to whether Joiner had been exposed to furans and dioxins. This was also incorrect, said the Court of Appeals, because testimony in the record supported the proposition that there had been such exposure.

We granted petitioners' petition for a writ of certiorari, 520 U.S. _____ (1997), and we now reverse.

II

Petitioners challenge the standard applied by the Court of Appeals in reviewing the District Court's decision to exclude respondent's experts' proffered testimony. They argue that that court should have applied traditional "abuse of discretion" review. Respondent agrees that abuse of discretion is the correct standard of review. He contends, however, that the Court of Appeals applied an abuse of discretion standard in this case. As he reads it, the phrase "particularly stringent" announced no new standard of review. It was simply an acknowledgement that an appellate court can and will devote more resources to analyzing district court decisions that are dispositive of the entire litigation. All evidentiary decisions are reviewed under an abuse of discretion standard. He argues, however, that it is perfectly reasonable for appellate courts to give particular attention to those decisions that are outcome-determinative.

We have held that abuse of discretion is the proper standard of review of a district court's evidentiary rulings. *Old Chief v. United States*, 519 U.S. ____, ____ n. 1 (1997) (slip op., at 1–2, n.1), *United States v. Abel*, 469 U.S. 45, 54 (1984). Indeed, our cases on the subject go back as far as *Spring Co. v. Edgar*, 99 U.S. 645, 658 (1879) where we said that "cases arise where it is very much a matter of discretion with the court whether to receive or exclude the evidence; but the appellate court will not reverse in such a case, unless the ruling is manifestly erroneous." The Court of Appeals suggested that *Daubert* somehow altered this general rule in the context of a district court's decision to exclude scientific evidence. But *Daubert* did not address the standard of appellate review for evidentiary rulings at all. It did hold that the "austere" *Frye* standard of "general acceptance" had not been carried over into the Federal Rules of Evidence. But the opinion also said:

> "That the *Frye* test was displaced by the Rules of Evidence does not mean, however, that the Rules themselves place no limits on the admissibility of purportedly scientific evidence. Nor is the trial judge disabled from screening such evidence. To the contrary, under the Rules the trial judge must ensure that any and all scientific testimony or evidence admitted is not only relevant, but reliable." 509 U.S., at 589 (footnote omitted).

Thus, while the Federal Rules of Evidence allow district courts to admit a somewhat broader range of scientific testimony than would have been admissible under *Frye*, they leave in place the "gatekeeper" role of the trial judge in screening such evidence. A court of appeals applying "abuse of discretion" review to such rulings may not categorically distinguish between rulings allowing expert testimony and rulings which disallow it. Compare *Beech Aircraft Corp v. Rainey*, 488 U.S. 153, 172 (1988) (applying abuse of discretion review to a lower court's decision to exclude evidence) with *United States v. Abel, supra* at 54 (applying abuse of discretion review to a lower court's decision to admit evidence). We likewise reject respondent's argument that because the granting of summary judgment in this case was "outcome determinative," it should have been subjected to a more searching standard of review. On a motion for summary judgment, disputed issues of fact are resolved against the moving party—here, petitioners. But the question of admissibility of expert testimony is not such an issue of fact, and is reviewable under the abuse of discretion standard.

We hold that the Court of Appeals erred in its review of the exclusion of Joiner's experts' testimony. In applying an overly "stringent" review to that ruling, it failed to give the trial court the deference that is the hallmark of abuse of discretion review. See, e.g., *Koon v. United States*, 518 U.S. ____, ____ (1996) (slip op., at 14–15).

III

We believe that a proper application of the correct standard of review here indicates that the District Court did not abuse its discretion. Joiner's theory of liability was that his exposure to PCBs and their derivatives "promoted" his development of small cell lung cancer. In support of that theory he proffered the deposition testimony of expert witnesses. Dr. Arnold Schecter testified that he believed it "more likely than not that Mr. Joiner's lung cancer was causally linked to cigarette smoking and PCB exposure." App. at 107.

Dr. Daniel Teitelbaum testified that Joiner's "lung cancer was caused by or contributed to in a significant degree by the materials with which he worked." *Id.* at 140.

Petitioners contended that the statements of Joiner's experts regarding causation were nothing more than speculation. Petitioners criticized the testimony of the experts in that it was "not supported by epidemiological studies…[and was] based exclusively on isolated studies of laboratory animals." Joiner responded by claiming that his experts had identified "relevant animal studies which support their opinions." He also directed the court's attention to four epidemiological studies[2] on which his experts had relied.

The District Court agreed with petitioners that the animal studies on which respondent's experts relied did not support his contention that exposure to PCBs had contributed to his cancer. The studies involved infant mice that had developed cancer after being exposed to PCBs. The infant mice in the studies had had massive doses of PCBs injected directly into their peritoneums[3] or stomachs. Joiner was an adult human being whose alleged exposure to PCBs was far less than the exposure in the animal studies. The PCBs were injected into the mice in a highly concentrated form. The fluid with which Joiner had come into contact generally had a much smaller PCB concentration of between 0–500 parts per million. The cancer that these mice developed was alveologenic adenomas; Joiner had developed small-cell carcinomas. No study demonstrated that adult mice developed cancer after being exposed to PCBs. One of the experts admitted that no study had demonstrated that PCBs lead to cancer in any other species.

Respondent failed to reply to this criticism. Rather than explaining how and why the experts could have extrapolated their opinions from these seemingly far-removed animal studies, respondent chose "to proceed as if the only issue [was] whether animal studies can ever be a proper foundation for an expert's opinion." *Joiner*, 864 F. Supp. at 1324. Of course, whether animal studies can ever be a proper foundation for an expert's opinion was not the issue. The issue was whether *these* experts' opinions were sufficiently supported by the animal studies on which they purported to rely. The studies were so dissimilar to the facts presented in this litigation that it was not an abuse of discretion for the District Court to have rejected the experts' reliance on them.

The District Court also concluded that the four epidemiological studies on which respondent relied were not a sufficient basis for the experts' opinions. The first such study involved workers at an Italian capacitor[4] plant who had been exposed to PCBs. Bertazzi, Riboldi, Pesatori, Radice, & Zocchetti,

---

[2] Epidemiological studies examine the pattern of disease in human populations.
[3] The peritoneum is the lining of the abdominal cavity.
[4] A capacitor is an electrical component that stores an electric charge.

Cancer Mortality of Capacitor Manufacturing Workers, 11 American Journal of Industrial Medicine 165 (1987). The authors noted that lung cancer deaths among ex-employees at the plant were higher than might have been expected, but concluded that "there were apparently no grounds for associating lung cancer deaths (although increased above expectations) and exposure in the plant." *Id.* at 172. Given that Bertazzi et al. were unwilling to say that PCB exposure had caused cancer among the workers they examined, their study did not support the experts' conclusion that Joiner's exposure to PCBs caused his cancer.

The second study followed employees who had worked at Monsanto's PCB production plant. J. Zack & D. Munsch, Mortality of PCB Workers at the Monsanto Plant in Sauget, Illinois (Dec. 14, 1979) (unpublished report), 3 Rec., Doc. No. 11. The authors of this study found that the incidence of lung cancer deaths among these workers was somewhat higher than would ordinarily be expected. The increase, however, was not statistically significant and the authors of the study did not suggest a link between the increase in lung cancer deaths and the exposure to PCBs.

The third and fourth studies were likewise of no help. The third involved workers at a Norwegian cable manufacturing company who had been exposed to mineral oil. Ronneberg, Andersen, Skyberg, Mortality and Incidence of Cancer Among Oil-Exposed Workers in a Norwegian Cable Manufacturing Company, 45 British Journal of Industrial Medicine 595 (1988). A statistically significant increase in lung cancer deaths had been observed in these workers. The study, however, (1) made no mention of PCBs and (2) was expressly limited to the type of mineral oil involved in that study, and thus did not support these experts' opinions. The fourth and final study involved a PCB-exposed group in Japan that had seen a statistically significant increase in lung cancer deaths. Kuratsune, Nakamura, Ikeda, & Hirohata, Analysis of Deaths Seen Among Patients with Yusho—A Preliminary Report, 16 Chemosphere, Nos. 8/9, 2085 (1987). The subjects of this study, however, had been exposed to numerous potential carcinogens, including toxic rice oil that they had ingested. Respondent points to *Daubert*'s language that the "focus, of course, must be solely on principles and methodology, not on the conclusions that they generate." 509 U.S., at 595. He claims that because the District Court's disagreement was with the conclusion that the experts drew from the studies, the District Court committed legal error and was properly reversed by the Court of Appeals. But conclusions and methodology are not entirely distinct from one another. Trained experts commonly extrapolate from existing data. But nothing in either *Daubert* or the Federal Rules of Evidence requires a district court to admit opinion evidence which is connected to existing data only by the *ipse dixit* of the expert. A court may conclude that there is simply too great an analytical gap between the data and the opinion proffered. See *Turpin v. Merrell Dow Pharmaceuticals, Inc.*, 959 F.2d 1349, 1360 (CA 6), cert.

denied, 506 U.S. 826 (1992). That is what the District Court did here, and we hold that it did not abuse its discretion in so doing.

We hold, therefore, that abuse of discretion is the proper standard by which to review a district court's decision to admit or exclude scientific evidence. We further hold that, because it was within the District Court's discretion to conclude that the studies upon which the experts relied were not sufficient, whether individually or in combination, to support their conclusions that Joiner's exposure to PCBs contributed to his cancer, the District Court did not abuse its discretion in excluding their testimony. These conclusions, however, do not dispose of this entire case.

Respondent's original contention was that his exposure to PCBs, furans, and dioxins contributed to his cancer. The District Court ruled that there was a genuine issue of material fact as to whether Joiner had been exposed to PCBs, but concluded that there was no genuine issue as to whether he had been exposed to furans and dioxins. The District Court accordingly never explicitly considered if there was admissible evidence on the question whether Joiner's alleged exposure to furans and dioxins contributed to his cancer. The Court of Appeals reversed the District Court's conclusion that there had been no exposure to furans and dioxins. Petitioners did not challenge this determination in their petition to this Court. Whether Joiner was exposed to furans and dioxins, and whether if there was such exposure, the opinions of Joiner's experts would then be admissible, remain open questions. We accordingly reverse the judgment of the Court of Appeals and remand this case for proceedings consistent with this opinion.

Appendix H: *Expert Testimony in the Wake of* Daubert, Joiner, *and* Kumho Tire

SIDNEY W. JACKSON III

Very special thanks to Sidney W. Jackson III and Jackson, Foster and Graham, L.L.C., Mobile, Alabama, for generously contributing this article. Mr. Jackson's areas of specialty include personal injury/wrongful death, insurance fraud, admiralty injury, and class action litigation. Mr. Jackson is a lecturer at the Cumberland School of Law, and he was counsel for the respondents in the U.S. Supreme Court case *Kumho Tire Co. v. Carmichael*. This material is used with permission.

These three cases, especially *Daubert*, refine the way that judges address expert testimony. In federal court and state courts that have adopted *Daubert*, there has been a sea change in the admissibility of expert testimony. While the Court's ruling in *Kumho* was intended to create a system where a rational decision-making process will be implemented in gauging expert testimony, the exact opposite has occurred. Modern jurists have, for the most part, turned *Daubert* on its ear and elevated the role of a judge from that of being an umpire calling balls and strikes and keeping a level playing field to that of a "gate keeper." The "gate keeper" concept has usurped the role and function of cross-examination resulting in the wholesale exclusion of valid expert testimony.

Cases that have been dismissed based on a "*Daubert* hearing" are legion. More product liability cases are disposed of at/or following a "*Daubert* hearing" than they are by jury verdict. Such hearings can last days and even weeks and the cost of the litigation is exorbitant. It is critical for the expert to understand the *Daubert* criteria and its background.

In studying the background of Federal Rule of Evidence 702, the *Frye* case of 1923 and the trilogy of *Daubert, Joiner,* and *Kumho Tire*, it is academically frustrating to discover that a rule statutorily designed to liberate the introduction of expert evidence and testimony is being rigidly applied to areas of soft science, forensics, and knowledge-based testimony.

Frye v. United States

54 APP. D.C. 46; 293 F. 1013 (1923)

The rule given in *Frye* states: "Just when a scientific principle or discovery crosses the line between the experimental and the demonstrable stages is difficult to define. Somewhere in this twilight zone the evidential force of the principle must be recognized, and while courts go a long way in admitting expert testimony deduced from well-recognized scientific principle or discover, *the thing from which the deduction is made must be sufficiently established to have gained general acceptance in the particular field in which it belongs*" (emphasis added).

The "General Acceptance" Rule of *Frye*

Most states adopted *Frye*'s general acceptance requirement in the fifty years following the decision, e.g., *People v. Morse*, 325 Mich. 270; 38 N.W.2d 322 (1949) (the Harger drunkometer); *Kiminski v. State*, 63 So.2d 339 (Fla. 1952); *Henderson v. State*, 151 Neb. 268, 37 N.W.2d 593 (1949); *State v. Helmer*, 278 N.W.2d 808 (S.D. 1979).

Other states have subsequently rejected *Frye* as the basis for admission of scientific evidence, e.g., *State v. Catanese*, 368 So.2d 975 (La. 1979) (general acceptance standard "is an unjustifiable obstacle to the admission of polygraph test results," but results still inadmissible under a balancing test); *State v. Williams*, 4 Ohio St. 2d 53, 446 N.E. 444 (1983) ("scientific nose-counting" not required for spectrogram to be admissible); *Phillips v. Jackson*, 615 P.2d 1288 (Utah 1980) ("sufficient proof of a reliability and an adequate explanation of the pertinent variables and potential inaccuracies" of HLA test for paternity not established in the record); *Barmeyer v. Montana Pwr. Co.*, 202 Mont. 185, 657 P.2d 594 (1983) (general acceptance rule not in conformity with spirit of new rules of evidence).

Frye Overruled: *Daubert v. Merrell Dow Pharmaceuticals, Inc.*

509 U.S. 579; 113 S. CT. 2786 (1993)

In *Daubert*, the court held that *Frye* is superseded by the Federal Rules of Evidence, particularly Rule 702.

Scientific evidence is admissible if it is "relevant" and "reliable." To determine relevancy, the court must first determine under Rule 104(a) whether the scientific theory is sufficiently tied to the facts of the case so that it will aid the jury in resolving a factual dispute. For scientific evidence to be "reliable," the inference or assertion must derive from the scientific *method*.

The court noted an important distinction between "scientific reliability" and "evidentiary reliability." "Scientific reliability" implies general acceptance, which is rejected as the sole criterion for admissibility in this case. "Evidentiary reliability," on the other hand, means that the evidence is "scientifically valid." Evidence is scientifically valid if (a) it is grounded in the methods and procedures of science; and (b) the evidence is grounded on reliability information or theories, i.e., either known facts or ideas inferred from such known facts. To evaluate scientific validity, the court suggested four factors:

1. Whether the principle has been tested;
2. Whether the principle has been published in a peer reviewed publication;
3. The error rate associated with the principle;
4. Whether the principle has achieved "general acceptance."

Post-*Daubert: General Electric Co. v. Joiner*

118 S. CT. 512 (1997)

In *General Electric Co. v. Joiner*, the Supreme Court did not specifically rely on the "general observations" offered in this earlier decision in *Daubert*, but instead underscored the necessity that an expert explains how and why he or she applied their methodology to reach their opinion. In other words, the Court was not concerned so much with whether the expert's testimony met the four tests as set forth in *Daubert*, but rather, whether the expert's opinions were "connected" closely enough to the underlying methodology in reaching those opinions.

In this case, the Eleventh Circuit reversed the trial court's exclusion upon the plaintiff. In so doing the Eleventh Circuit applied what it described as "a particularly stringent standard of review to the trial court's exclusion of expert testimony."

General Electric sought *certiorari*, which was granted by the Supreme Court. In its decision, the Supreme Court reaffirmed that the traditional "abuse of discretion" standard applies in reviewing a trial court's decision to exclude expert testimony. It further discussed the implication of *Daubert* and how an expert's opinion must be in some way logically connected to the proffer made, noting that merely because an expert says it was closely related may not be enough in order to meet the required burden or threshold of admissibility. In so holding, the Supreme Court reversed the Eleventh Circuit's opinion.

Kumho Tire Co. v. Carmichael

119 S. CT. 1167 (1999)

In this case, several members of the Plaintiff's family were injured and/or killed as the result of a tire blow-out. The Plaintiffs brought suit in federal court alleging that the tire was defectively designed and/or manufactured. In order to support their burden under the AEMLD (Alabama Extended Manufacturer's Liability Doctrine), the Plaintiff offered the testimony of one tire failure analysis expert, Dennis Carlson, who offered testimony that the tire was defectively manufactured and/or designed.

The Defendant filed a motion *in limine* and motion to strike the testimony of Dennis Carlson, claiming that said testimony was not admissible under the mandates of *Daubert v. Merrell Dow.* After briefs in the matter, the trial court excluded the testimony of Dennis Carlson, claiming that because he was unable to meet any of the four factors set forth in *Daubert*, the testimony was inadmissible. The Plaintiffs were unable to present any other evidence of defect, and hence, the trial court granted Defendant's motion for summary judgment.

On appeal, the Eleventh Circuit reversed, claiming that the trial court had erred in characterizing Carlson's testimony as "scientific." Since the testimony was not scientific, the court concluded that the four factors as set forth in *Daubert* were inapplicable to judge the reliability and admissibility of Carlson's testimony. In so holding, the appellate court in essence concluded that the four factors were not exclusive, and remanded the case back down to the trial court for further proceedings, which would include a determination by the trial court as to whether or not Carlson's testimony was reliable based upon the record evidence that was submitted initially.

The Defendant Kumho filed a petition for *certiorari* which was granted by the United States Supreme Court. The issue as phrased by Petitioners was:

> Whether a trial judge may consider the factors set forth by this Court in *Daubert v. Merrell Dow*, in a Federal Rule of Evidence 702 analysis of the admissibility of an engineering expert's testimony.

On certiorari, the Plaintiffs argued that the four factors were irrelevant and inadmissible in addressing the issue of whether or not Dennis Carlson's testimony met the threshold requirement of admissibility under Rule 702. To the contrary, Plaintiff suggested to the Court that it should look to other factors which would bear on reliability of the expert's testimony. Generally, it was Plaintiff's position that the trial court must first look to the discipline at issue and determine whether or not the methodology used in that particular expertise was a method that was generally accepted within the field of discipline.

In this case, it was Plaintiff's position that tire failure analysis experts generally look at the tire for tell-tale signs of certain indicia of overdeflection. Upon recognizing certain factors, the experts could then rule out whether or not the tire failed due to abuse or whether it failed due to defect. In this particular case, Plaintiff's expert was able to rule out abuse as a possible cause of its failure, and thus, the only other possible cause was defect. In fact, in the trial court's opinion, the court specifically found that this "process of elimination methodology" was acceptable, as long as the underlying methodology was supported and was in fact reliable.

On the other hand, Defendant argued that because Plaintiff's expert was unable to meet within the four strict criteria set forth in *Daubert,* the evidence was inadmissible per se. Both parties agreed that this method of ruling out abuse had never been tested, was not subject to peer review, had no error rate, and was used by a handful of tire expert analysts that testify in courts across the country. Based on these arguments, it was Defendant's position that the *Daubert* factors were not met, and thus, Plaintiff had failed to meet its initial burden and threshold of admissibility.

To counter this argument, Plaintiff made clear to the court that these factors were irrelevant, and thus, bore no relationship to determining whether or not the testimony was in fact reliable. Further, Plaintiff was able to show through record evidence that "Carlson's methodology" was the same methodology as used by Defendant's expert in the case, namely, ruling out abuse as a means of determining whether a defect occurred. In fact, on appeal to the Eleventh Circuit, the Court there noted that both experts used similar methodologies in coming up with their opinions. The experts merely disagreed as to what the physical evidence reflected.

The Supreme Court held that the basic "gatekeeping" obligation of the trial judge applies not only to "scientific" testimony, but to *all* expert testimony. The Court based its finding on the plain language of Rule 702:

> "If scientific, technical, or other specialized knowledge will assist the trier of fact to understand the evidence or to determine a fact in issue, a witness qualified as an expert by knowledge, skill, experience, training, or education, may testify thereto in the form of an opinion or otherwise."

The Supreme Court noted that the rule makes no relevant distinction between "scientific" knowledge and "technical" or "other specialized" knowledge, and that the rule makes clear that such knowledge might become the subject of expert testimony. The Court noted that it is the Rule's word "knowledge," not the words (like "scientific") that modify that word, that establishes a standard of evidentiary reliability.

The Court also noted that it would prove difficult, if not impossible, for judges to administer evidentiary rules under which a gatekeeping obligation depended upon a distinction between "scientific" knowledge and "technical" or "other specialized" knowledge.

The Supreme Court held that a trial court *may* consider one or more of the four factors set out in *Daubert* to aid in determining whether expert testimony is reliable, but stressed that Court's determination that the test of reliability is "flexible," the factors do not constitute a "definitive checklist or test," and the four factors neither necessarily nor exclusively apply to all experts or in every case. The gatekeeping inquiry must be tied to the particular facts. Those factors may or may not be pertinent in assessing reliability, depending on the nature of the issue, the expert's particular expertise, and the subject of his testimony.

The Supreme Court, in finding that those factors may be helpful in evaluating the reliability even of experience-based expert testimony, held that the Court of Appeals erred insofar as it ruled those factors out in such cases. In determining whether particular testimony is reliable, the trial court should consider the four factors set out in *Daubert* when they are reasonable measures of the reliability of expert testimony. The trial court is *not*, however, required to apply the four factors to the expert testimony if they are not helpful in the particular case at hand, and the law grants the trial judge broad latitude whether the *Daubert* factors should be used.

The Court in *Kumho* upheld the District Court's determination that the expert testimony was inadmissible. The trial court based its decision upon the expert's failure to satisfy either *Daubert*'s factors or *any other set of reasonably reliable criteria*. The Court, in citing Rule 702, found that the trial court did not abuse its discretionary authority and, therefore, reversed the judgment of the Court of Appeals.

Of course, the trial court's decision to exclude or admit the testimony will always be reviewed on appeal on an abuse of discretion standard which has been the law for over 100 years. Hence, it is important to present evidence at the trial court level to show that the experts' methodology is sound and has a logical basis in fact and in theory. As the Supreme Court held in *Kumho*, the law grants a district court the same broad latitude when it decides *how* to determine reliability as it enjoys in respect to its ultimate reliability determination. This means that the first and final determination of whether expert testimony will be admitted will often be made by the trial judge. This does not mean, however, that a trial court will not be reviewed when the judge has abused his discretion.

How Courts are Implementing *Daubert,* *Joiner,* and *Kumho Tire*

In *Black v. Food Lion, Inc.*, 1999 WL 173001 (5th Cir.(TX)), the United States Court of Appeals addressed the "may" language used by the Supreme Court in *Kumho Tire* in stating that a trial court may consider one or more of the four *Daubert* factors:

> "'[M]ay' should not be misunderstood to grant open season on the admission of expert testimony by permitting courts discretionarily to disavow the *Daubert* factors. On the contrary, the Supreme Court simply recognized the obvious facts that there are many kinds of experts and expertise, that the *Daubert* inquiry is always fact-specific, and that the *Daubert* factors may not all apply even to the admissibility of pure scientific testimony. The Supreme Court in *Kumho Tire* stressed that the *Daubert* factors may be relevant to the reliability of experience-based testimony. The overarching goal of *Daubert*'s gatekeeping requirement is to ensure the reliability and relevancy of expert testimony. It is to make certain that an expert, whether basing testimony upon professional studies or personal experience, employs in the courtroom the same level of intellectual rigor that characterizes the practice of an expert in the relevant field."

In *Black v. Food Lion*, Mrs. Black slipped and fell in a Food Lion establishment. Dr. Mary Reyna hypothesized that the fall caused physical trauma to Mrs. Black, which caused "hormonal changes," which Food Lion argued that Dr. Reyna's testimony could not causally link the fall at Food Lion with Mrs. Black's present medical condition with any degree of medical certainty. The trial court rejected Food Lion's arguments and allowed Dr. Reyna to testify. Judgment was entered for Mrs. Black.

The Court of Appeals held Dr. Reyna's testimony inadmissible. The Court found Dr. Reyna's testimony to be "unsupported by a scientific methodology that could be relied upon in this case and contradicted by the general level of current medical knowledge." The Court, therefore, held that the trial court abused its discretion by allowing the doctor's testimony and remanded the case for recalculation of damages consistent with its holding.

Recent Federal Decisions

McClain v. Metabolife Int'l, Inc. 401 F.3d. 1233 (11th Circuit 2005). User of herbal weight loss supplement containing ephedrine and caffeine sued supplement manufacturer alleging that manufacturer marketed and sold an unreasonably dangerous diet drug, resulting in strokes in three of the uses and a heart attack in the other. The court allowed expert pharmacological testimony and the Plaintiff won a jury verdict. ADMISSIBILITY REVERSED. The court held that neither experts utilized by Plaintiff based their testimony on a reliable methodology to prove the use of Metabolife 356 actually causes strokes or heart attacks. The medical literature does not support such opinions and Plaintiff's expert took leaps of faith and substituted their own *ipse dixit* for scientific proof on the central points. The experts did not employ the same level of intellectual rigor that characterizes the practice of an expert testifying about causation in a toxic tort case. Their opinions were not based on sufficient data and were not the product of reliable methods. The lower court abused its discretion by abdicating its gatekeeper responsibilities by admitting the expert testimony.

U.S. v. Brown 415 F.3d 1257 (11th Circuit, Alabama, 2005). Two brothers were convicted of selling a GHB copy cat drug on the basis that the drug sold was close enough to GHB to invoke federal criminal jurisdiction. The brothers defended saying the chemical structure of their drug was substantially different from GHB. Not surprisingly, the 11th Circuit (Carns) affirmed the two government chemist experts, but excluded the Defendants' expert. The government witnesses testified that their opinions were based on a "gut level thing" or "intuition," but later explained that the judgment was based on 30 years of learning and experience as a chemist. The 11th Circuit affirmed the exclusion of the defense witness on the basis that his methodology was suspect and that he was "not aware of the methods of other chemists" and could not adequately explain the basis for his opinion.

Rink v. Cheminova, Inc. 400 F.3d 1286 (11th Circuit, Florida, 2005). Putative class representatives brought products liability and toxic trespass claims against a pesticide manufacturer, alleging they became seriously ill as a result of their exposure to the pesticide. The district court excluded the Plaintiffs expert testimony on causation. EXCLUSION AFFIRMED. The 11th Circuit affirmed the district court's faulting of the expert for his facile transposition of temperature data from one site to another. Under this procedure, temperature data from a Texas storage site was applied to Georgia and Florida sites even though the expert did not personally conduct inspections or take measurements. Transposition of data based on such conjecture and rough approximation lacked the "intellectual rigor" required by *Daubert*.

Nelson v. Freightliner, LLC 2005 WL 2981959 (11th Circuit, Florida, 2005). Widow brought suit against Freightliner for carbon monoxide poisoning of her husband cause by defective Freightliner truck. The Plaintiff offered evidence in the form of laboratory reports performed in Kentucky. ADMISSIBILITY AFFIRMED. The 11th Circuit lambasted the magistrate's ruling that the methodology and peer review of the Kentucky lab report was reliable. However, the court held that the admission of the lab report was not an abuse of discretion by the district court: "The alleged flaws in [the Kentucky methodology] are of a character that impugned the accuracy of the results, not the general scientific validity of the methods. The identification of such flaws in generally reliable scientific evidence is precisely the role of cross-examination."

Hall v. United Insurance Company of America 367 F.3d. 1255 (11th Circuit Alabama, 2004). Summary judgment in favor of insurance company relative to signature which expert opined was that of a mentally incompetent person. EXCLUSION OF EVIDENCE AFFIRMED. The court held that the Plaintiff's expert did not cite to any scientific methodology or literature supporting his conclusion that the individual was mentally incompetent. The court engaged in a "limited" review of the District Court's decision to strike the expert's affidavit and could not say the District Court abused its discretion.

Conclusion

The admissibility of expert testimony is up to the trial judge, and rarely will the trial judge be reversed since the standard is "abuse of discretion."

Some thoughts on experts having their testimony admitted are as follows:

If the nature of the testimony is such that the opposing experts employ the same methodology, then the testimony should be admitted. An example of this would be two opposing physicians using a differential diagnosis to relate trauma to soft tissue injury. One expert may say he has excluded all other causes and therefore concludes that the trauma caused the soft tissue injury. The opposing physician may say that because of existent scoliosis, previous surgeries years ago, etc., then there was a pre-existing condition. Regardless of the ultimate conclusion, both experts used the same method.

The expert should apprise the lawyer that the area of testimony may be subject to a *Daubert*-type hearing. Before *Kumho*, hearings were limited to strictly "scientific" experts. If a *Daubert* hearing is going to be held, then the most prevalent question is "has the theory been tested." If not, you may want to have another expert test the theory, provide peer review, search for supporting literature or testify that it is generally accepted. The more information and data backing up the expert's methodology, the better.

Courts will be very suspect when the area of testimony was created just for the litigation. The area of testimony needs to be used outside of the courtroom as well as inside the courtroom.

A review of post-*Kumho* cases suggests there is simply no rhyme or reason for the conclusions reached by the various courts. Prosecution expert witnesses in criminal cases seem to gain admissibility much easier than plaintiff expert witnesses in tort cases. This again emphasizes the gatekeeper function of the trial judge.

An excellent resource for this topic is www.daubertontheweb.com. The site refers to dozens of areas of expertise and case law discussing same.

Appendix I: Resources for Private Experts

Author's Note: The previous editions of *Succeeding as an Expert Witness* were geared to private experts, rather than the public forensic scientists who work in governmental laboratories. Much of the material has been integrated into this new edition, but some of it pertains solely to private experts. Those topics and resources that will benefit the new or inexperienced expert witness appear in this appendix.

Sample Interrogatories and Request for Production to Expert Witnesses

Sample of Interrogatories and Request for Production to a Party Concerning Expert Witness

By counsel of record, submits the following Interrogatories to _____ to be answered concerning that party's expert witness, pursuant to Rule 26(b) (4) and 34, of the Federal Rules of Civil Procedure, which are to be answered separately and fully in writing, under oath, within thirty (30) days after service. Answers must be updated as additional responses become available.

1. Identify each person assisting in answering this discovery and denote which questions are answered by which person.
2. State the names, addresses, and occupations of such person.
3. State all areas of specialization of the expert's occupation or profession.
4. Describe all professional or social relationships the experts have with _____ at the present and at any time in the past.
5. State when the experts were hired and by whom. Attach copies of all correspondence or notes of telephone conversations between experts and the hiring party or counsel.
6. What relationships of a social or professional nature do the experts have with counsel? Have the experts ever been engaged as an expert or testified for _____'s counsel previously? If so, provide all details of each testimonial or forensic engagement.

7. What is the expert's formal education and employment experience in detail? Attach a current curriculum vitae or detailed resume.

8. What is the expert's agreement for compensation with the hiring party? Include all amounts paid or to be paid and attach copies of the engagement agreements, billing, and timekeeping sheets.

9. State the exact manner in which the expert became familiar with the facts of this case. Detail each and every one of the expert's efforts and include the time devoted to each step.

10. What was the expert's specific assignment? Describe each and every action taken in completing such assignment.

11. What is the subject matter of the expert's prospective testimony in the case? How was that assignment given? Produce all documentation of that assignment. Produce all of the expert's files with regard to assignments as they now exist, in original form, without addition or subtraction, and in the original file folders. If material is in computer storage, print it out and produce the printout.

12. Provide copies of all documents obtained or generated in the course of employment as an expert in this case including, but not limited to: (following should be 1, 2, 3, ..., 7)

    a. All notes made of conversations with other witnesses, parties, other experts, or attorneys for the hiring party;

    b. All reports or writings examined in arriving at the expert's opinion;

    c. All correspondence with the hiring party and their counsel;

    d. Any other documentation generated in arriving at conclusions;

    e. All investigative reports obtained prepared by others, or generated by the expert;

    f. Any photographs, recordings, drawings of calculations prepared as part of the expert's study; and

    g. Any documents which the expert located, specifying the source of such documents.

13. How much time has the expert spent on this project? Allocate such time to each particular task performed.

14. Give the name, address, and telephone number of any attorney, witness, party or other expert with whom the expert has conferred about this assignment. Detail the response or information obtained from any such person.

15. State what experience the expert has had with similar or comparable projects. What prior expert testimony or reports has the expert ever prepared or given concerning a project similar to that of this case.

16. State whether any field investigation was performed. Give the name, address, and telephone number of any person with whom the expert met during such field investigation. Detail the time devoted to such effort.

17. Provide a bibliography of all documents, books, publications, treatises, or any other written material upon which the expert relied in forming opinions. Be page specific.

18. Provide a bibliography of all documents, books, publications, treatises, or any other written material considered by the expert to be authoritative on the subject matter of projected testimony.

19. State the facts, opinions, and conclusions to which the expert intends to testify at trial or hearing in this case.

20. What other additional specific opinions and conclusions did the expert reach concerning this project?

21. Give a summary of the technical, factual, professional, or scientific basis and ground for each opinion reached by the expert to support each conclusion or opinion.

22. State the expert's reasoning by which each conclusion or opinion (in paragraphs 19 and 20) is supported or reached, based on the information in paragraph 21 above, or otherwise.

23. What additional assignments has the expert been given which have not yet been completed?

24. What additional work do you believe will be necessary for the expert to complete prior to trial or hearing?

25. When is the expert expected to complete such assignments?

These are continuing interrogatories and requests for production. You must supplement your responses in a prompt and timely fashion.

Cross-Examination of Expert Witnesses

Harold A. Feder

Some Typical Questions and Answers

1. Isn't it true that scientific tests on this subject may have not conclusively established A, B and C?
   First answer: Yes, that is true.
   Better answer: Yes, that is true, but we've come a long way in understanding A, B and C.
2. Isn't it correct that traffic lights cycle green, yellow to red?
   First answer: Yes.
   Better answer: Yes, that's true, unless the light switch is malfunctioning.
3. Isn't it true, doctor, that your hourly rate of $400 is being charged for your examination and testimony time?
   First answer: Yes, that is true.
   Better answer: Your question implies that my opinions are for sale. Counselor, my integrity has no price.
4. Mr. Witness, isn't it correct that you have testified on numerous occasions for Attorney Jones, who represents the defendant in this case?
   First answer: Yes, that is true.
   Better answer: The attorney who calls upon my services has no bearing on my professional opinions.
5. Isn't it true that scientific journals have established the inaccuracy of these tests?
   First answer: Yes, there are some journals that so state.
   Better answer: Yes, but those journals have helped us understand a great deal more about the disease process.
6. Do you recognize that your tests and evaluations must meet a particular degree of burden of proof?
   First answer: I'm not sure what the legal requirements are.
   Better answer: My studies are based upon scientific standards and not courtroom rules. My conclusions are scientific and not legal. The legal system can do with my answers what it wishes.
7. Isn't it true, professor, that all of your experience has been concentrated in the classroom rather than in the laboratory?
   First answer: I guess that's true.
   Better answer: The theoretical concepts which I have been teaching are applied in the laboratory every day.
8. Isn't it correct that you have appraised this property in a community in which you have never resided?

First answer: Yes, that is true.

Better answer: Real estate values are not tied to the community of residence of the appraiser. The value is not dependent on my residence, but on the market conditions in this community.

9. Isn't it true that your experience in this area is limited to one case in 30 years?

First answer: That is clearly true.

Better answer: While I've only dealt with one case, my study of the literature plus my teaching and practical experience give me sufficient insight to deal with the present situation.

10. Isn't it true, Mr. Williams, that your opinion has changed based upon the material I have shown you in cross-examination in this case.

First answer: Yes, that seems to be true.

Better answer: I have answered your questions honestly and accurately. My fundamental opinions and conclusions have not changed and your selective questions don't serve to change my opinion. Based upon my study in this case, despite all of your questioning, my opinion remains unchanged.

11. Isn't it true that witnesses such as this often tend to lie?

First answer: That is often the case.

Better answer: While that is often the case, the facts of this witness's testimony are supported by 11 critical checkpoints.

12. In the field of subjective psychological testing, isn't is possible for you to be fooled by a patient?

First answer: Yes, that is always possible.

Better answer: Of course it is possible to be fooled, but in every clinical examination we are alert to that possibility and we test and cross test to eliminate that hazard. There are a number of ways to detect a faking examination.

13. Isn't it correct that the frequency of criminal activity in this neighborhood is higher than that found in other parts of the city?

First answer: Yes, that is correct.

Better answer: While that is correct, our study indicates that the disproportionate criminal activity in this case is due primarily to the activities of defendants.

14. Describe the theoretical and scientific foundations that allow you to reach the conclusion that the defendant was intoxicated.

First answer: His blood alcohol was .15.

Better answer: The blood alcohol was .15, speech was slurred, the eyes were bleary, the breath smelled of alcohol and his clothing was in disarray.

Sample Engagement Letter (For Private Experts)

(On letterhead)

(Date)

(Insert client's name/mailing address)

Re: (Insert subject name/matter)

This letter will set forth my understanding that I am to serve as an expert witness in the above-noted matter, as a consultant only at this time, on your behalf with regard to the pending litigation and specifically with regard to this proposition:

1. I am to determine whether there is probable cause under the professional negligence statute of the State of Colorado to file the Amended Complaint in this case.
2. I am to examine the theories of liability and determine whether they are legally supported based upon the allegations in the Complaint and such other preliminary investigation as we may feel necessary to reach that conclusion.
3. I am to determine whether there is a legal and factual basis for the allegations of negligence, breach of fiduciary duty, negligent misrepresentation, fraud, breach of contract and negligent supervision in accordance with the law and the facts and particular reference to the Code of Professional Responsibility and the Colorado statute on professional negligence claims.
4. I am to render opinions as requested from time to time regarding damage theories which are supportable in law and fact in this case.

If I have misstated the assignment in any way, please correct that statement of my assignment on acceptance of the terms of this engagement.

It should be clearly understood that nothing your attorneys have said to me thus far and none of the information they have given to me will in any way determine or predetermine my opinions in this matter. Your attorneys have made it very clear to me that they are interested in obtaining an impartial, unbiased, expert opinion based upon a factual and legal analysis as to the issues in question, and nothing they have said or shown to me is to in any way be taken so as to influence or shape my opinion in this matter.

I appreciate the forthright approach of your attorneys in this case, and I will endeavor to do the legal and factual research within the parameters of the assignment as soon as I have been formally engaged.

I believe a retainer in the $5,000 range would be appropriate. I expect that the sum necessary to render a preliminary opinion in this matter will range between $4,000 and $5,000 of time at my hourly rate of $250.00 per hour.

We will, of course, bill for any additional and incidental expenses in this assignment, such as legal research, copying costs and the like, but I expect those expenses to be minimal.

If this engagement is in line with our understanding, kindly forward your retainer check of $5,000 and execute the agreement in the space provided below, and forward a copy to my office.

I must say I am honored to be of service to you in this matter.

(Insert your firm name)

(Your signature)

(Your name)

Enclosures

CONTENTS NOTED AND APPROVED:

(Insert client name)

By _____
   (Client signature)

   _____
   (Date)

Mediation and the Expert Witness

Harold A. Feder

Introduction

The entire spectrum of Arbitration and Dispute Resolution (ADR) is clearly upon us. The public, and obviously legislators, politicians, judges, lawyers and litigants, are frankly fed up with the inefficiencies, cost, delays and apparent injustices of the present adversary dispute resolution process. For these reasons, mediation, arbitration, special masters and private dispute resolution organizations are gaining ground at an exponential rate.

To blend current skills, techniques and resources with this new wave of dispute resolution devices, it becomes highly relevant to explore how forensic experts can materially assist the parties and attorneys involved in ADR processes, particularly the mediation device.

There is real concern in forensic circles that mediation will "cut experts out of the loop" and that their services will no longer be required in mediation setting. On the other hand, there is genuine danger the expert will overdo the preparation beyond that which is necessary for effective mediation purposes, keeping in mind that cost control is one objective and benefit of the alternative dispute resolution device of mediation.

The objective here is to see how the mediation dispute resolution process can effectively benefit from and use the professional services of forensic witnesses. We will explore some of the steps and techniques of the mediation process as it draws on and effectively uses forensic expert witness input.

Step 1

Once there has been a determination to mediate, the consulting or testifying expert needs to be contacted. The matrix of areas for consideration by the expert must be developed by the client, counsel and expert witness.

It is essential to cover each and every issue involved in the case. In other words, make sure that everything that needs to be addressed is in fact adequately addressed in the preparation phase. That means a careful analysis of all fact and legal issues must be made, taking care that no essential elements are left out.

As in dispute resolution matters, there are three basic rules which must be followed: Prepare, prepare, *prepare*! The primary difference between trial and mediation preparation is the degree of depth, but not the fundamental elements of the preparation. The degree is less inclusive because proof is not as vital as persuasion, and the entire effort is to minimize costs to the participant-client. Notwithstanding those factors, it is of critical import that the laundry list of issues to be carried to the mediation session include all elements that will need to be discussed for a complete and fair resolution of the contested dispute.

Step 2

Preparation of the client for the session should encompass all the usual elements of deposition/trial witness training. This includes the situation particularly where the client goes to the session without counsel—as is often the case. A multitude of checklists and formats are available for this briefing.

The expert and client, with the aid of counsel, should meet to prepare an issue identification list. As to each, the expert should brief the client to the import of the item. The attorney can input for the client the legal effect of various "if-then" scenarios.

This stage of preparation will not include the need for full investigation by the expert, and preparation of a detailed report will not be required. The client should be encouraged to prepare "crib sheets" which list the issues and, if necessary, the hoped-for result as to each. If counsel is to be present at the mediation session, the attorney and client can work together to prepare these worksheets and notes.

Step 3

The client, attorney and expert should work through the two checklists which are incorporated here. The first is a generic analysis of the basics of negotiation technique, and is excellent self-training for all who participate in the actual mediation process.

Negotiating Techniques

Give consideration to the format of the negotiating session. It should be in comfortable surroundings. A stated atmosphere of cooperativeness should permeate the meeting.

I. Positive qualities which should be evidenced by you as a negotiator include the following:
   Analytical approach
   Perceptive of the case subtleties
   Realistic
   Convincing
   Rational
   Self-controlled

Experienced
Trustworthy
Ethical

II. Other factors of good negotiation qualities should include the following:
Your degree of preparedness
Honesty
Intelligence
Knowledge of your case
Reasonableness
Effectiveness in oral skills
Sensitive to cues

III. Among the negative qualities you should avoid are
Rudeness
Recklessness
Temerity
Complaining attitude
Hostility
Rebelliousness
Sarcasm
Intolerance
Spinelessness

IV. Things to think about in negotiating session include
Style of the opposition
Is the timing right?
What things physically have to be present?
Where should the meeting take place?
Listen carefully to what your opponent is saying
Set your goals for the conference, general or limited
What are the terms of a possible compromise?
Are there other collateral considerations which should be of concern to you?

The second is very case-specific. It requires an analysis of the dispute from both aspects, yours and that of the other side, with candid and introspective appraisal of each aspect of the process to be undertaken.

Settlement Plan Checklist

1. Your general strategy.
2. Your prediction of your opponent's strategy.
3. Information you are willing to reveal.
4. Information you must scrupulously avoid disclosing.

5. Information to learn during negotiation.
6. Your strong leverage points.
7. The weakness of your case.
8. Your opponent's strengths.
9. Your opponent's weaknesses.
10. Estimate the best you might expect to recover.
11. Set your minimum settlement point.
12. Your estimate of opponent's minimum settlement.
13. Your estimate of a realistic settlement.

Step 4

A mock mediation could be undertaken as the final step in preparation. This opportunity, which might be put on videotape for further training benefit, will give clients a sense of confidence in their own ability to deal with what may be a new process and experience.

The client should be able to demonstrate understanding of the negotiating techniques and settlement plan checklist from Step. 3. Practice application of the specific steps and techniques from Step 3.

If the expert or attorney is not present during the trial session, the client should be schooled to be able to ask for a brief adjournment so the attorney or expert can be contacted for further guidance. Such assistance should be encouraged by trained mediators who are anxious to reach fair solutions.

Report Writing for Federal Rules of Civil Procedure Rules 16 and 26

Harold A. Feder

Rule 26—Federal Rules of Civil Procedure—Rule 26(B)(2) A, B, C

1. The report must be prepared by the witness.
2. It must be signed by the witness.
3. It must contain a complete statement of all opinions to be expressed.
4. The basis and reasoning must be included.
5. The data or other significant information considered by the expert in forming the opinion must be included. (This presumptively includes data considered and discarded.)
6. Any exhibits to be used as a summary or as support are to be included.
7. All publications authored by the witness within the last ten years, regardless of relevance, must be listed.
8. The compensation to be paid for the expert's time and study must be included.
9. A list of other cases where this expert gave deposition or trial testimony within the last four years must be submitted with this report, without regard to relevance or relationship to the subject matter and issue.

Rule 16(A)(1)A (1)E and (B)(1)C of the Federal Rules of Criminal Procedure

1. On request of defendant, the government must provide opinions, qualifications, basis and reasoning of the government's expert.
2. However, if defendant asks for this information from the government witnesses, that opens the door to the government requesting and obtaining the same information from the defense as to its experts by name, their opinions, their qualifications, the basis for their opinion and the reasoning supporting their opinion.

Glossary and Important Terms

Accident reconstruction. The engineering and scientific process by which the dynamics of accidents are established.

Accreditation. The process in which certification of competency, authority, or credibility is presented and documented.

Action plan. An organized approach to accomplishing complicated tasks.

Administrative board. Nonjudicial tribunal for determining controversies, essentially involving administrative agencies at any level of government.

Administrative hearing. Judicial or legislative proceedings conducted by an administrative agency at any level of government.

Administrative law. The so-called fourth branch of government, most closely allied with the executive branch, including boards, tribunals, and officers of various federal, state, and local bureaus.

American Board of Criminalistics (ABC). A group of regional and national organizations that certify forensic practitioners through a voluntary process of peer review and testing. The ABC offers certification in criminalistics, forensic biology, drug chemistry, fire debris analysis, and trace evidence.

American Society of Crime Laboratory Directors Laboratory Accreditation Board (ASCLD-LAB). An accrediting organization for forensic science laboratories.

Anscombe's quartet. A data set that demonstrates the need for displaying quantitative information graphically.

Answer. A paper (pleading) that recites a civil defendant's response to claims of plaintiff and which may include defenses and claims on behalf of defendant against plaintiff.

Appellate court. A court that hears cases in which a lower court—either a trial court or a lower-level appellate court—has already made a decision, but in which at least one party to the action wants to challenge this ruling.

Arbitration. An organized process outside of a courtroom for resolving disputes between persons or entities.

ASTM, International. One of the largest voluntary, consensus-based standards development organizations in the world. Started in 1898, ASTM, International has over 30,000 members in 120 countries representing nearly all aspects of science, consumers, government, and academia.

Attorney work product. The thought processes of an attorney preparing a case for trial, including books, papers, writings, notes, and other tangible things that evidence the attorney's effort. These items are generally privileged and cannot be obtained during discovery.

Bench. The location in a courtroom where the judge sits, hence the judge. Also, a reference to the judiciary.

Bench trial. In the United States, a trial that has a single judge who decides issues of both law and fact.

Burden of proof. The prosecution must prove beyond a reasonable doubt that the defendant is guilty of the crime charged.

Case decision. Determinations by courts that provide guidance to attorneys and experts on the legal requirements of evidence, testimony, and substantive law.

Certified reference material (CRM). A reference material that has been tested extensively by many methods. CRMs come with certificates issued by authorized bodies guaranteeing their purity or quality.

Chain of custody. A documentary method for keeping track of physical and tangible items of evidence during the dispute resolution process.

Chartjunk. Unnecessary or confusing visual elements in graphics that detract from the data, such as grids, data labels, and artwork.

Chewbacca defense. A legal defense or speech consisting of nonsensical arguments meant to confuse a jury. The term originates from an episode of the show *South Park* parodying Johnnie Cochran's defense of O. J. Simpson in his criminal trial.

Circuit court. Also known as the U.S. courts of appeals, these are the intermediate appellate courts and are required to hear all appeals from the district courts within their federal judicial circuit.

Civil law. Civil actions are disputes between two parties that are not of significant public concern. Civil law covers the rules of dealing with these actions. Civil law also is used to describe all law outside of the criminal law context.

Competence. The demonstrated ability to do something at the expected level of performance.

Complainant. The person who feels he or she is aggrieved by some action and has filed a complaint; if a complainant files a case in civil court, he or she becomes a plaintiff (see later).

Complaint. A paper pleading that sets forth a civil plaintiff's claims.

Conflict of interest. Any situation that, because of prior relationships or known information, creates a division of loyalties making independent representation impossible.

Contempt of court. Any misconduct that takes place in the courtroom that a judge punishes with a fine or imprisonment.

Credibility. The believability of a witness.

Criminal justice process. The criminal justice process begins with an alleged crime. An accusation is made that is investigated by law enforcement officers, acting as representatives of the government. A formal complaint, also called an indictment, is presented to a group of citizens, who determine if enough evidence exists for a criminal trial. If so, the indictment is filed with a court in the appropriate jurisdiction. The trial proceeds to a verdict by the jury and eventual sentencing by a judge or a jury.

Criminal law. The body of statutory and common law that deals with crime and the legal punishment of criminal offenses.

Cross-examination. The phase of the dispute resolution process in which opposing counsel asks questions of witnesses in order to test the truth, accuracy, or thoroughness of direct testimony.

Curriculum vitae. A complete listing of a professional's career activities, including work history, publications, committees, and presentations.

Data ink. The nonerasable portion of the graphic without which the data would cease to be represented.

Defendant. A person or entity against whom a civil or criminal action has been brought.

Demonstrative evidence. Charts, graphs, drawings, computer graphics, models, audio and video presentations, or any other device used to demonstrate, characterize, or explain verbal testimony.

Deposition. Testimony given outside the presence of the trier of fact in the presence of a court reporter, counsel, and the parties, for the purpose of finding out what you know, determining what sort of witness you will be, and locking you into a position.

Destructive testing. A process by which tangible items are actually disposed of during an examination.

Direct examination. That procedure during a trial or hearing that first presents a witness's testimony to the trier of fact.

Discovery. Those processes used before a trial in order to uncover the facts of the case.

Dispute resolution process. Trials, hearings, arbitration, mediation, or other ways in which disputes between individuals and entities are resolved.

Engagement letter. A contract of employment used by expert witnesses when engaged for forensic investigation, consultation, and testimony purposes.

Enthymemes. Arguments that have unstated assumptions.

Ethics. The study of the values and customs of a person or group. The topic covers the analysis and use of concepts such as right and wrong, good and evil, and responsibility.

Exclusion of witnesses. A rule whereby a hearing officer or trial judge may bar from the court parties who will testify except during the time of their actual testimony.

Expert. An individual who, by knowledge, skill experience, training, or education, may testify in the form of an opinion or otherwise to scientific, technical, or other specialized knowledge.

Expert opinion. A major exception to the general rule of evidence that otherwise requires testimony be based upon personal knowledge. Because of their knowledge, training, and experience, experts are allowed to render opinions about what happened rather than merely recite what their senses recorded.

Expert testimony. Presentation of verbal or written evidence in the dispute resolution process in a scientific, professional, technical, or specialized field, usually beyond the knowledge of laymen.

Expert witness. A person who by reason of education, training, or experience has special knowledge not held by the general public.

Expertise. Special skill or knowledge in a particular field.

Fact witness. A person who testifies in a dispute resolution process about information gained from the senses (touch, sight, smell, sound), whose task it is to accurately report those observations.

Falsifiability. Detailed by Karl Popper, the idea that a statement must be able to be proven false if it is to be considered scientific.

Federal Rules of Civil Procedure. Those organized processes that govern trials and preliminary matters in the United States courts.

Federal Rules of Criminal Procedure. Those organized processes that govern trials and preliminary matters in the U.S. courts involving criminal proceedings.

Federal Rules of Evidence. The rules that govern the admissibility of evidence in the U.S. federal court system.

Foundation. The factual, technical, or scientific basis that supports testimony, specifically expert opinion and conclusion.

Frye **rule.** A law of court that provides that in order for an expert witness to testify concerning scientific, technical, professional, or specialized matters, the opinion testimony must be based upon a reasonable degree of acceptance within the scientific, technical, professional, or specialized field of the processes utilized by the witness to reach the conclusions tendered.

Grand jury. A group of citizens who determine if enough evidence exists for a criminal trial. If so, the indictment is filed with a court in the appropriate jurisdiction. Grand juries do not exist outside the United States and are not universal within the country (Connecticut, Pennsylvania, and the District of Columbia do not use grand jury indictments); each state that uses them has its own set of grand jury procedures.

Graphic. Information that is drawn, printed, or engraved.

Hearing. An organized process by which the contesting parties present their evidence and testimony.

Hearsay. A statement of conduct made by a witness outside of the presence of the trier of fact with no opportunity for cross-examination by the opposition. There are certain exceptions to the hearsay exclusion that are based on indicators of reliability attending such declarations or conduct and which make them admissible.

Hersay rule. A legal rule that prevents testimony by people who heard someone else say something; the person who heard the statement cannot be cross examined on the substance of what they heard but only that they heard it.

Historic hysteric gambit. A tactic used by some attorneys to make a discipline look silly or make modern ideas seem as threadbare as old discarded ones, such as phlogiston or a flat earth.

Hypothesis. A rational configuration of assumed facts subject to establishment by specific proof.

Hypothetical question. A question posed to an expert based on assumed theories of factual events. For example, "If A, B, and C exist, what is your opinion as to D?"

Impeachment. An attack on a witness that questions credibility, believability, or opportunity for testing or observation.

Indictment. A paper by which a grand jury brings criminal charges against an individual or entity.

Information. A paper by which a district attorney brings criminal charges against a person or entity, without the grand jury process.

International Organization for Standardization (ISO, from the French *Organisation internationale de normalisation*). An international standard-setting body composed of representatives from various national standards organizations. Founded in 1947, the organization promulgates worldwide industrial and commercial standards.

Interrogatories. Written questions proposed to a party to which specific written responses under oath are required.

Jargon. Terminology that relates to a specific activity, profession, or group that acts like a shorthand slang. Jargon is to be avoided when communicating to people outside the activity, profession, or group from which it originates.

Judge. An official who presides over a court.

Judgment. A decision by a trial or appellate court.

Juror. One who serves on a jury.

Jury. A sworn body of persons convened to render a verdict and a finding of fact on a legal question officially submitted to them or to set a penalty or judgment on a convicted person or persons.

Jury education. The process by which an expert explains his profession and its activities to a jury to assist them in weighing any evidence he presents to them.

Jury trial. A legal proceeding where the verdict is determined by a jury.

Justices of the peace. Judicial officers with limited authority, who preside over misdemeanors, traffic violations, and other lesser violations.

Lawyer. An attorney, counselor, or advocate serving as representative of a party in the dispute resolution process.

Lay witness. A fact witness; a nonexpert witness.

Learned treatise. A book, publication, journal, or any other professional, scientific, technical, or specialized writing that is considered authoritative in a particular field.

Mistrial. The cancellation of a trial prior to a verdict.

Motion in limine. A motion to limit testimony or evidence in a contested proceeding.

Narratives. A strong narrative is a factual, carefully managed narrative based upon circumstantial evidence that endeavors to prove something more encompassing than personal, direct examination.

National Institute of Standards and Technology (NIST). A nonregulatory agency of the U.S. Department of Commerce whose mission is to promote U.S. innovation and industrial competitiveness by advancing measurement science, standards, and technology in ways that enhance economic security and improve quality of life.

Negligence. Failure to exercise that degree of care which a reasonably prudent person would have exercised under usual circumstances and conditions; conduct marked by carelessness or neglect.

Normal science. The relatively routine works of scientists experimenting within a paradigm, slowly accumulating detail in accord with established broad theory. A concept originated by Thomas Kuhn, who also characterized normal science as "puzzle solving."

Normative ethics. The study of the moral standards and behaviors that help to determine what is meant by, for example, right, wrong, unethical, and immoral.

Opinion. A person's ideas and thoughts on something; it is an assessment, judgment, or evaluation of something.

Opinion witness. A forensic or expert witness who is entitled to render opinions, as opposed to testifying about factual matters based upon the senses.

Paradigm. A consensual understanding of how the world works. Within a given paradigm, scientists add information, ideas, and methods that steadily accumulate and reinforce their understanding of the world.

Paradigm shift. A change in the basic assumptions within the ruling theory of science.

Petite jury. An archaic term for a trial jury of six or twelve jurors.

Plaintiff. A person or entity that brings a civil action.

Pleading. A paper prepared by an attorney that is filed with a court that contains a factual or legal position for a litigant, usually with copies provided to all other parties to a case.

Presumption. A rule of law that states that if certain facts exist, then other conclusions, as a matter of law, are deemed to exist. For example, "If A and B are true, then C, as a matter of law, must also be true."

Privileged. Those communications, written or verbal, between certain classes of persons that cannot be reached by the opposition in the dispute resolution process.

Professional negligence. Failure of a professional person to perform or conduct themselves in accordance with the standards of care and attention usually displayed by persons in that field in the same or similar circumstances.

Prosecutor. The attorney who represents the people (the prosecution) in a criminal case.

Protocol. A series of steps, processes, or procedures usually followed in a scientific, technical, professional, or specialized area.

Public defender. An attorney who works for a government assigned to defend an accused person in a criminal trial.

Request for production. A written request to a party to produce documents and other tangible things for copying or inspection.

Resume. A summary of a person's background, training, education, and experience.

Rhetoric. The art or technique of persuasion through the use of oral or written language.

Rules of evidence. Rules that determine what is and is not admissible in various dispute resolution processes. They may be enacted by the legislative bodies, determined by appellate decision, or controlled by court order.

Scientific revolution. The deconstruction of a dominant paradigm in science and its replacement by a new, signficantly different paradigm. The shift from Newtonian to Einsteinian physics is a good example of a scientific revolution.

Sixth Amendment of the Constitution of the United States. This amendment gives citizens the right to a speedy and public trial, in both state and federal courts, by an impartial jury of the state and district wherein the crime was committed; the right to be informed of the nature and cause of the accusation; the right to be confronted with the witnesses against the defendant; the right of the compulsory process for obtaining witnesses in his favor; and the right of the assistance of counsel for his defense.

Small claims court. Courts that hear private disputes where smaller amounts of money, not more than $3000 to $5000, depending on the jurisdiction, are at stake.

Statute. An enactment by a legislative body that constitutes the law of a particular state or country.

Supreme Court of the United States. The highest judicial body in the United States and the only part of the judical branch made explicit in the U.S. Constitution.

Syllogism. An argument in which one proposition is inferred from the previous two. For example. All men are mortal. Socrates is a man. Therefore, Socrates is mortal.

Technique. A standard method that can be taught.

Testimony. The process of conveying information from a witness to a judge, jury, arbitration, or other hearing panel.

Testing. A means of analysis, examination, or diagnosis.

Tort. A wrongful act involving injury or damage to persons or property for which a civil action may exist.

Toxic tort. An act or event by which a contaminant or pollutant is introduced into the environment, causing injury or damage to persons or property.

Transcript. A written version of verbal statements.

Trial. The method by which disputes are resolved in the court system, with either a jury or judge as the trier of fact.

Trial chart. The name typically given to visual representations used by forensic witnesses.

Trier of fact. The judge, jury, administrative body, board, or arbitration panel that determines the fact issues of the controversy in the dispute resolution process.

U.S. courts of appeals. Also known as circuit courts, these are the intermediate appellate courts of the U.S. federal court system. A court of appeals decides appeals from the district courts within its federal judicial circuit.

U.S. district court. The general trial courts of the U.S. federal court system. Both civil and criminal cases are fielded in the district court.

Verdict. A trial decision by a jury in a criminal or civil case.

Voir dire. The examination by which attorneys or the court are allowed to question jurors as to their fitness to serve as impartial triers of fact. Also, the examination conducted by an attorney or the court in a trial or hearing by which a witness or a document is tested for reliability. Expert witnesses are sometimes subjected to voir dire examination before being allowed to render opinions. The phrase comes from the Middle French for "speak the truth."

"Yes, but" answer. Yes-or-no questions may require explanation. If the answer starts with "Yes, but…" or "No…," the linguistic requirements for answering the question have been satisfied; therefore, an explanation for the answer may not be possible if the attorney cuts off the expert's answer. An answer that helps ensure a complete answer breaks up the response, such as, "While that may be true…" or "Although it may appear to be that way.…"

Bibliography

Adelson, Lester. "The Pathology of Homicide." Chap. XVI in *The Pathologist as Witness*. Springfield, IL: Charles C. Thomas Publisher, 1974.

Anderson, Patrick R., and Winfree, Jr., L. Thomas, eds. *Expert Witnesses: Criminologists in the Courtroom*, 208. Albany NY: State University of New York Press, 1987.

The Art of Advocacy: Expert Witnesses [A video series]. Notre Dame, IN: N.I.T.A., Notre Dame Law School, 1988.

Blau, Theodore H. *The Psychologist as Expert Witness*. New York: Wiley Law Publications, 1984.

Broecker, Howard W., and Kleeman, Jr., Robert E. "The Use of Financial Experts in Marital Litigation: The Attorney's Viewpoint and the Expert's Viewpoint." *American Journal of Family Law* 1 (1987): 277.

Brown, Louis M., and Tachna, Ruth C. "Dealing with the Lawyer as Expert Witness." *The Practical Lawyer*, October 1985, p. 11.

Byard, Roger, Corey, Tracy, Henderson, Carol, and Jason-Pay, James, eds. *Encyclopedia of Forensic and Legal Medicine*. New York: Academic Press, 2005.

Clifford, Robert C. *Qualifying and Attacking Expert Witnesses*. Costa Mesa, CA: James Publishing, 1989.

Commercial Arbitration Rules. American Arbitration Association, as amended and in effect April 1, 1985.

Dombroff, Mark A. *Expert Witnesses in Civil Trials*. San Francisco, CA: Bancroft Whitney Co., 1989.

Dunbar, Jack F., and Colón-Pagán, Francisco J. "Excluding, Limiting or Mitigating the Opinion of the 'Professional Testifier' in a Products Case." *For the Defense*, April 1993, p. 12.

A Guide to Forensic Engineering Expert and Service as an Expert Witness. Silver Springs, MD: Association of Soil and Foundation Engineers, 1985.

Halligan, R. Mark. "Cross Examination of an Expert Witness." *For the Defense*, September 1990.

Handbook of Forensic Science. U.S. Department of Justice, Federal Bureau of Investigation, revised March 1984.

Henderson, Carol, Moenssens, Andre, and Portwood, Sharon. *Scientific Evidence in Civil and Criminal Cases*. Mincola, NY: Foundation Press, 2007.

Herman, Russ. "Going by the Book: Direct and Cross-Examination of Medical Experts." *Trial Magazine*, August 1991.

Herrmann, Richard K., and Luczak, Daniel W. *The Proper Care and Feeding of Your Forensic Engineer: A Practical Guide for Using Engineering Expert Services*. Annapolis, MD: Forensic Technologies International Corporation, 1986.

Hersley, Jack. *Testifying in Court: The Advanced Course*. Oradell, NJ: Medical Economics, 1972.

Hollander, Nancy, and Baldwin, Lauren M. "Winning with Experts." *Trial Magazine*, March 1993, p. 16.

Hough, James E. "The Engineer as Expert Witness." *Civil Engineering*, December 1981, pp. 56–58.

Huber, Peter W. *Galileo's Revenge: Junk Science in the Courtroom*. New York: Basicbooks, 1991.

Imwinkelried, Edward J. "The Admissibility of Expert Testimony in Christophersen vs. Allied-Signal Corp.: The Neglected Issue of the Validity of Nonscientific Reasoning by Scientific Witnesses." *Denver University Law Review* 70 (1993): 473.

Jeans, J. W. *Trial Advocacy*. St. Paul, MN: West Publishing, 1975.

Levin, Edwin, and Grody, Donald. *Witnesses in Arbitration*. Bureau of National Affairs, 1987.

Lustberg, Arch *Testifying with Impact*. Rev. ed. Washington, DC: Association Department, U.S. Chamber of Commerce, 1983.

Kuzmack, N. T. *In Forensic Science Handbook, Legal Aspects of Forensic Science*, ed. R. Saferstein. Englewood Cliffs, NJ: Prentice-Hall, 1982.

Mulligan, William G. *Expert Witnesses: Direct and Cross-Examination*. New York: Wiley Law Publications, 1987.

Pagan, Alfred R. *Ten Commandments (More or Less) for the Expert Witness*. 2nd ed. Rosemont, IL: Better Roads, 1987.

Philo, Harry. *Lawyers Desk Reference*. San Francisco, CA: Bancroft Whitney and Co., 1987.

Rankin, Jr., Terry. *How to Be an Effective Expert Witness*. Office of Continuing Education and Extension, College of Engineering, University of Kentucky, April 1985.

Rules for Admissibility of Scientific Evidence. St. Paul, MN: West Publishing, 1987.

Jasanoff, Sheila. "Science in the Courts: Advice for a Troubled Marriage." In *Natural Resources & Environment*, vol. 2. 1986.

The Scientist and Engineer in Court. Washington, DC: American Geophysical Union, 1983.

Shepard's Expert and Scientific Evidence Quarterly. Colorado Springs, CO: Shepard's McGraw-Hill, Inc.

Siegel, Jay, and Pirko, Sikka, eds. *Encyclopedia of Forensic Sciences*. New York: Academic Press, 2002.

Smith, Jr., Wallstein. *Is the Appraisal Witness Qualified?* Chicago, IL: Society of Real Estate Appraisers, 1979.

Sunar, D. G. *Expert Witness Handbook: A Guide for Engineers*. San Carlos, CA: Professional Publications, Inc., 1985.

Tealy, Alfred. *Handbook for the Executive as a Witness*. New York: United States Trademark Association, 1983.

Wawro, Mark L. D. "Effective Presentation of Experts." *Litigation* 19 (1993): 31.

Wecht, Cyril H., ed. *Forensic Sciences*. Matthew Bender, 1989.

Weinstein, J. B., and Berger, M. A. *Weinstein's Evidence: Commentary on the Rules of Evidence for the United States' Courts and State Courts*. 3 vols. New York: Matthew Bender, 1981.

Wrightsman, L., Willis, C., and Kassin, S. *On the Witness Stand*. Beverly Hills, CA: Sage Publications, 1987.

Index

A

AAFS, *see* American Academy of Forensic Sciences
ABC, *see* American Board of Criminalistics
Accident reconstruction, 215
Accreditation, 16, 136, 215
Action plan, 215
ADDIE model, 89–90
Administrative board, 215
Administrative hearing, 215
Administrative law, 215
Alterations, ethics and, 136
American Academy of Forensic Sciences (AAFS), 130–131
American Academy of Forensic Sciences Jurisprudence Section Code of Professionalism, 147–149
  preamble, 147–148
  rules, 148–149
  terminology, 148
American Board of Criminalistics (ABC), 16, 215
American Society for Testing and Materials, International (ASTM, International), 16, 20, 215
American Society of Crime Laboratory Directors (ASCLD), 133–134
American Society of Crime Laboratory Directors Laboratory Accreditation Board (ASCLD-LAB), 15, 215
American Society of Forensic Questioned Document Examiners, 16
Anscombe's quartet, 96, 215
Answer, 215
Appellate court, 8–9, 29, 127, 215
Arbitration, 215
ASCLD, *see* American Society of Crime Laboratory Directors
ASCLD-LAB, *see* American Society of Crime Laboratory Directors Laboratory Accreditation Board

ASTM, International, *see* American Society for Testing and Materials, International
Attorneys misconduct, examples of, 128–129
Attorney's role, in U.S. justice system, 26–28
Attorney work product, 216

B

Bacon's theory, 17
Bailiff, 82
Bench, 216
Bench trials, 31, 216
Body language, 110
Burden of proof, 8, 206, 216

C

Case decision, 216
Certification, 16
Certified reference material (CRM), 17, 216
Chain of custody, 216
Chartjunk, 99–101, 216
Chewbacca defense, 106, 216
Circuit courts, 29
Civil law, 7, 216
Code of conduct, proposed, 147–149
Common-law rule of evidence, 83
Competence, 38, 216
Complainant, 7, 216
Complaint, 216
Compound questions, 83–84
Conflicts of interest, 216
Contempt of court, 31, 216
Court of last resort, 29
Courts, 28–30
Credibility, 77, 216
Criminal justice process, 7–9, 217
Criminal law, 217
  definition of, 7
  discovery components in, 42
Criminal offenses, 7
CRM, *see* certified reference material

Cross-examination, 36, 78–79, 109–123, 217
    attorney's goals, 112–118
    discussion questions, 123
    friend or foe, 110–111
    historic hysteric gambit, 118
    hypothetical questions, 119
    learned treatise, 117
    redirect, 121–122
    reducing vulnerability, 119–121
    review questions, 122
    testing of entire field, 118–119
    "yes, but" answer, 121
Curriculum vitae, 217

D

Data graphics, 97–101
Data-ink, 99, 217
Daubert v. Merrell Dow Pharmaceuticals,
    Inc., 161–171
Daubert v. Merrell Dow Pharmaceuticals,
    Inc., expert testimony in wake of,
    193–201
Defendant, 217
Demonstrations, 105–107
Demonstrative evidence, 217
Deposition, 217
    challenge of, 56
    definition of, 9
    dispute resolution process, 152
    information sought by, 10
    opportunity of, 56
    preparation, 49–56
    preparation checklist, 50
Destructive testing, 217
Direct examination, 79–80, 217
    TOM I. PASTA, 91
Direct examination of experts, 77–93
    ADDIE model, 89–90
    bailiff, 82
    compound questions, 83–84
    credibility, 77
    definition, 79–80
    discussion questions, 93
    enhancement elements, 88–89
    hearsay rule, 84
    hostile witness, 86
    leading question, 86
    objection, 82
    past recollection recorded, 85
    review questions, 92–93
    and strong narratives, 79–91

be teacher, 89
    enhancement elements, 88–89
    instructional materials creation for,
        89–91
    points to remember, 81–88
    redirect examination, 88
Discovery, 35–49, 217
    components, 44–46
    in criminal cases, 42
    definition of, 9, 41
    dispute resolution process, 152
    fundamental rule in, 50
    limits of, 9
    process, expert and, 46–49
    talking too much in, 50
Dispute resolution process, 152, 217

E

Engagement letters, 217
Enthymemes, 105, 217
Erythrocyte test, 35
Ethics, 125–142, 217
    alterations, 136
    attorneys misconduct, examples of,
        128–129
    avoiding abuse, 134–135
    discussion questions, 142
    interprofessional relationships and,
        129–134
    normative, 125, 220
    primary ethical issues, 135–141
        abuses by experts, 139
        abuses of experts, 138–139
        asserting your rights as witness,
            139–140
        assignments beyond
            competency, 137
        conditional or limited engagement
            (private experts), 136
        conflicts of interest, 137
        contingent fee (private experts), 138
        countering claim of junk science,
            140–141
        data altered, 136
        false testimony, 136
        fraudulent credentials, 138
        ignoring data, 136
        investigation not performed, 136
        outright false data, 135
        reaching conclusions before
            research, 137

recanting prior contra-positions,
        136–137
    unauthorized attorney influence, 137
    review questions, 142
    scientist misconduct, examples of, 127–128
    unethical conduct, 125–126
Examination in chief, *see* direct
        examination
Exclusion of witnesses, 217
Expertise, 218
Expert opinions, 218
Expert(s), 218
    abuses by, 138–139
    bill of rights, 151–157
        asserting your rights as an expert
                witness for, 156–157
        itemization of rights of expert
                witnesses, 152
        Rambo-ism, 152
        work product, 152
    definition of, 2–3
    discovery process and, 46–49
    private, resources for, 203–214
        cross-examination of expert
                witnesses, 206–207
        engagement letter, sample of, 208–209
        interrogatories, sample of, 203–205
        mediation, 210–213
        negotiating techniques, 211–212
        report writing, 214
        settlement plan checklist, 212–213
    role of, 32–33
Expert testimony, 218
    FRE rules regarding, 58–59
    objective of, 77
    requirements, 63–64
Expert witnesses, 1–13, 218
    appellate court, 8–9
    burden of proof, 8
    civil and criminal cases, 7
    civil law, 7
    complainant, 7
    criminal justice process, 7–9
    criminal law, 7
    deposition, 9–11
    discovery, 9–11
    discussion questions, 13
    experts, 2–3
    Federal Rules of Evidence, 2, 7
    grand jury, 7
    history of experts in trials, 4–7
    indictment, 7

jargon, 3
jury of peers, 8
key terms, 1
lay witness, 2
    opinions, 2, 4, 9
Perry Mason moments, 9
petit jury, 7
preparation for trial, 11
public defenders, 8
review questions, 13
Sixth Amendment of Constitution of
        United States, 8
technique, 3
trial, 11–12
work product, 9

F

Fact witness, 218
Falsifiability, 17, 18, 218
Federal Rules of Civil Procedure, 42, 43,
        214, 218
Federal Rules of Criminal Procedure, 214, 218
Federal Rules of Evidence (FRE), 2, 7, 41,
        56–57, 218
    expert testimony, rules regarding, 58–59
    opinion testimony, rules regarding, 58–59
    Rule 701, Opinion Testimony by Lay
            Witnesses, 2, 143
    Rule 702, Testimony by Experts, 2, 7,
            59–60, 143
    Rule 703, Bases of Opinion Testimony by
            Experts, 60, 143
    Rule 704, Opinion on Ultimate Issue,
            143–144
    Rule 705, Disclosure of Facts or Data
            Underlying Expert Opinion, 144
    Rule 706, Court Appointed Experts,
            144–145
    Rule 803(18) of, 117
    witness testimony, general rules
            regarding, 57–58
FEPAC, *see* Forensic Science Educational
        Program Accreditation
        Commission
Fifth Amendment to the Constitution, 44
Forensic Science Educational Program
        Accreditation Commission
        (FEPAC), 125
Foundation, 218
FRE, *see* Federal Rules of Evidence
Frye rule, 218

Frye v. United States, 159–160
   general acceptance rule, 194
   overruled, 194–195

G

GBS, *see* Guillain-Barré syndrome
General acceptance rule, 194
General Electric Company v. Joiner, 185–191
General Electric Company v. Joiner, expert
     testimony in wake of, 193–201
Glossary, 215–223
Grand jury, 7, 8, 218
Grand jury transcripts, 44, 45
Graphics, 101–105, 218
Graphs, 101–105
Guillain-Barré syndrome (GBS), 48

H

Hearing, 219
Hearsay, 219
Hearsay rule, 84, 219
Historic hysteric gambit, 118, 219
Hostile witness, 86
Hypotheses, 18–19, 219
Hypothetical questions, 119, 219

I

IAI, *see* International Association for
     Identification
Impeachment, 219
Inconsistent testimony, 12
Indictment, 7, 219
Information, 219
Instructional materials creation
   complex data presentation, 91–92
   for strong narratives, 89–91
International Association for Identification
     (IAI), 131–133
International Association of Identification, 16
International Organization for
     Standardization (ISO), 20, 219
Interprofessional relationships, 129–142
Interrogatories, 54, 219
ISO, *see* International Organization for
     Standardization

J

Jargon, 3, 66, 219
Judges, 30–31

Judgment, 219
Junk science, 140
Juries, 31–32, 219
   education, 74, 220
   of peers, 8
   petite, 221
   trial, 32, 220
Jurors, 26, 31, 32, 37, 38, 219
Justices of the peace, 30, 220

K

Kumho Tire v. Carmichael, 173–184
Kumho Tire v. Carmichael, expert testimony
   in wake of, 193–201

L

Lawyer, 220
Laypersons, 2
Lay witness, 2, 143, 220
Leading question, 86
Learned treatise, 117, 220
Legal context, 41–61
   deposition/trial testimony, 49–56
     challenge of, 56
     opportunity of, 56
     preparation, 49–56
     preparation checklist, 50
   discovery, 35–44
     components, 44–46
     in criminal cases, 42
     definition of, 41
     fundamental rule in, 50
     process, expert and, 46–49
     talking too much in, 50
   discussion questions, 61
   expert and discovery process, 46–49
     civil case, 47–49
     criminal case, 46–47
   Federal Rules of Civil Procedure, 42, 43
   Federal Rules of Evidence, 56–57
     expert testimony, rules regarding,
       58–59
     opinion testimony, rules regarding,
       58–59
     Rule 702, 59–60
     Rule 703, 60
     witness testimony, general rules
       regarding, 57–58
   interrogatories, 54
   preparing for deposition, 49–56

privileged, 41
review questions, 60

M

Magna Carta, 32
Methods, testing, and science, 15–23
    accreditation, 15
    American Board of Criminalistics, 16
    American Society of Crime Laboratory
        Directors Laboratory
        Accreditation Board, 15
    American Society of Forensic Questioned
        Document Examiners, 16
    ASTM, International, 15
    certification, 15
    certified reference material, 17
    discussion questions, 23
    falsifiability, 17, 18
    formulation of working hypothesis, 19–20
    hypotheses, 18–19
    International Association of
        Identification, 16
    National Institute of Standards and
        Technology (NIST), 17
    normal science, 18
    Organization of Scientific Area
        Committee for Forensic Science
        (OSAC), 16
    paradigms, 18
    published methods, 20–21
    review questions, 22–23
    science, definition of, 17–19
    scientific revolution, 18
    Society of Forensic Toxicologists, 16
    standardization, 15–16
    standard protocol, use of, 20
    toward admissibility, 21–22
Mill, John Stuart, 151
Misconceptions, 32
Mistrial, 32, 220
Motion in limine, 220
MPRE, *see* Multistate Professional
    Responsibility Examination
Multistate Professional Responsibility
    Examination (MPRE), 125

N

Narratives, 26, 27, 220
National Institute of Standards and
    Technology (NIST), 17, 220

Negligence, 220
NIST, *see* National Institute of Standards
    and Technology
Normal science, 18, 220
Normative ethics, 125, 220
Novum Organum, 17

O

Objection, 82
Objective physical evidence, 27
Opinions, 2, 4, 9, 220
    changed, 206
    government witness, 200
    preliminary, 209
    reasoning supporting, 214
    witness, 220
Opinion testimony, FRE rules regarding,
    58–59
Organization of Scientific Area Committee
    for Forensic Science (OSAC), 16
OSAC, *see* Organization of Scientific Area
    Committee for Forensic Science

P

Paradigms, 18, 220
Paradigm shift, 35, 220
Participants, 25–40
    attorney's role, 26–28
    bench trials, 31
    circuit courts, 29
    competence, 38
    contempt of court, 31
    court of last resort, 29
    courts, 28–30
    discussion questions, 40
    expert's role, 32–33
    expert's role in court, 37
        ability to persuade, 38–39
        ability to teach, 37–38
        believability, 38
        competence, 38
        enthusiasm, 39
        thorough analysis, 37
    judge's role, 30–31
    juries, 31–32
    jurors, 26, 31, 32, 37, 38
    jury's role, 31–32
    jury trial, 32
    justices of the peace, 30
    mistrial, 32

Participants (*Continued*)
   narratives, 26, 27
   paradigm shift, 35
   prosecutors, 28
   public defender, 28
   review questions, 39–40
   rhetoric, 27
   scientist, role of, 33–36
   small claims court, 30–31
   Supreme Court of the United States, 28, 29
   U.S. circuit courts, 29
   U.S. courts of appeals, 28–29
   U.S. district courts, 28, 29
   U.S. federal courts, 29
   voir dire, 32
Past recollection recorded, 85
Perry Mason moments, 9
Persuasion, technique of, 27
Petite jury, 7, 221
Physical evidence, objective, 27
Plaintiff, 221
Pleading, 221
Presumption, 221
Privileged, 41, 221
Professional negligence, 221
Prosecutors, 28, 221
Protection from self-incrimination, 44
Protocol, 221
Proxy data, 80
Public defenders, 8, 28, 221

Q

Quantitative information, visually
   displaying of, 96–99

R

Rambo-ism, 152
Redirect examination, 88
Reference materials, 17
Relevance, 9
Request for production, 221
Resume, 221
Rhetoric, 27, 221
Rules of evidence, 2, 7, 41, 56–57, 218, 221

S

Scientific literature, 20–21
Scientific prostitution, 35
Scientific revolution, 18, 221
Scientist, role of, 33–36

Scientist misconduct, examples of, 127–128
Serological test, 35
Settlement plan checklist, 212–213
Sixth Amendment of Constitution of
   United States, 8, 28, 221
Small claims court, 30–31, 222
Society of Forensic Toxicologists, 16
Standard, 16
Standardization, 16–17
Standard protocol, use of, 20
State of Texas v. Michael Morton, 129
Statute, 222
Strong representation, 26
Supreme Court of the United States, 28,
   29, 222
Suspects, 67
Syllogism, 106, 222
Synchronicity, 15

T

Technique, 222
   definition of, 3
   direct examination, 79–80
   negotiating, 211–212
   persuasion, 27
Testimony, 63–76, 222
   demeanor, dress, and deportment, 71–72
   discussion questions, 76
   inconsistent, 74
   jargon, 66
   jury education, 74
   preparation and communicating with
      attorneys, 66–69
   preparation and communicating
      without attorneys, 70–71
   report, 64–66
   review questions, 75–76
   suspects, 67
   at trial, 73–75
Testing, 222
TOM I. PASTA, 91
Tort, 222
Toxic tort, 222
Transcript, 222
Trial chart, 222
Trial(s), 222
   bench, 31
   chart, 101
   jury, 32
   preparation for, 69
Trier of fact, 222

U

Unethical conduct, 125–126
U.S. circuit courts, 29, 222
U.S. courts of appeals, 28–29, 222
U.S. district courts, 28, 29, 127, 222
U.S. federal courts, 29

V

Verdict, 222
Visual display of information, 95–108
    Anscombe's quartet, 96
    chartjunk, 99–101
    Chewbacca defense, 106
    data-ink, 99
    demonstrations, 105–107
    discussion questions, 107–108
    enthymemes, 105
    graphs, graphics, and comparisons in
        court, 101–105
    quantitative information, 96–99

    review questions, 107
    syllogism, 106
    trial chart, 101
Voir dire, 32, 222

W

Wall graph, 98
Witness(es); *see also* expert witnesses
    asserting your rights as, 139–140
    expert, 1–13, 218
    fact, 218
    hostile, 86
    lay witness, 2
Witness testimony, FRE general rules
        regarding, 57–58
Work product, 9, 41, 137, 152, 216

Y

"Yes, but" answer, 121, 223

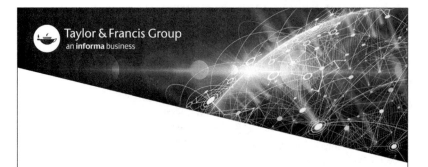